The French Revolution

BLOOMSBURY SOURCEBOOKS

Bloomsbury Sourcebooks offers students diverse source collections on key subjects in modern history. Each sourcebook provides a comprehensive general introduction to the topic in question, followed by a selection of both classic and lesser-known primary sources and making use of both written and visual sources. These selections introduce students to the main subject themes from a variety of perspectives, including but not limited to, class, gender, race and nationality. The sourcebooks also include useful features, such as timelines and thematic bibliographies, to further assist students with their learning.

New and forthcoming:

The French Revolution: A History in Documents, Micah Alpaugh (ed.)
Nineteenth-Century Germany: A History in Documents, George S. Williamson (ed.)

The French Revolution

A History in Documents

Edited by
Micah Alpaugh

BLOOMSBURY ACADEMIC
LONDON • NEW YORK • OXFORD • NEW DELHI • SYDNEY

BLOOMSBURY ACADEMIC
Bloomsbury Publishing Plc
50 Bedford Square, London, WC1B 3DP, UK
1385 Broadway, New York, NY 10018, USA
29 Earlsfort Terrace, Dublin 2, Ireland

BLOOMSBURY, BLOOMSBURY ACADEMIC and the Diana logo are trademarks of Bloomsbury Publishing Plc

First published in Great Britain 2021

Series design by Ben Anslow
Cover image: Jean Baptiste Lesueur (1749-1826) Motion in the Gardens of the Palais Royal, 'Long live the Nation'. Paris, musee Carnavalet. (Photo by: Christophel Fine Art / Universal Images Group / Getty Images)

A catalogue record for this book is available from the British Library.

Library of Congress Cataloging-in-Publication Data

Names: Alpaugh, Micah, editor.
Title: The French Revolution: a history in documents / edited by Micah Alpaugh.
Description: London; New York, NY: Bloomsbury Academic, 2020. | Series: Bloomsbury sourcebooks | Includes bibliographical references and index.
Identifiers: LCCN 2020036911 (print) | LCCN 2020036912 (ebook) | ISBN 9781350065307 (hardback) | ISBN 9781350065291 (paperback) | ISBN 9781350065314 (ebook) | ISBN 9781350065321 (epub)
Subjects: LCSH: France–History–Revolution, 1789–1799–Sources.
Classification: LCC DC141 .F74 2020 (print) | LCC DC141 (ebook) | DDC 944.04–dc23
LC record available at https://lccn.loc.gov/2020036911
LC ebook record available at https://lccn.loc.gov/2020036912

ISBN: HB: 978-1-3500-6530-7
PB: 978-1-3500-6529-1
ePDF: 978-1-3500-6531-4
eBook: 978-1-3500-6532-1

Typeset by Deanta Global Publishing Services, Chennai, India

To find out more about our authors and books visit www.bloomsbury.com and sign up for our newsletters.

CONTENTS

ILLUSTRATIONS

ACKNOWLEDGMENTS

My thanks to Robert Blackman, Alexandre Dubé Jessica Fripp, Philip Hazard, Joseph Krudler, Julie Landweber, Kate Marsden, Judith A. Miller, Michael Mulvey, Andrew Ross, Noah Shusterman, and Erika Vause, as well as the anonymous readers at Bloomsbury Press, for their recommendations on documents and approaches. I am grateful to Rhodri Mogford for proposing this project to me and Laura Reeves, James Tupper, and Mohammed Raffi for helping to shepherd it to completion.

More broadly, this work has been inspired in countless ways by my longtime adviser and friend, Timothy Tackett, who taught me to love studying the French Revolution and its diverse archives. This book is dedicated to him.

*

Every effort has been made to contact copyright holders of material reproduced in these volumes. If any copyright holders have not been properly acknowledged, please contact the publisher, who will be happy to rectify the omission in future editions.

Special thanks must go to the following institutions for granting us the kind permission to reproduce certain documents: Princeton University Press for allowing us to reproduce Marquis de Lafayette and Thomas Jefferson's, "Letters and Documents Concerning the Drafting of the Declaration of the Rights of Man and Citizen," January–July 1789; the Cantonal and University Library of Lausanne and the Jean-Pierre Fund Tissot for granting us the permission to reproduce Jean-Marie Goujon and Pierre-François Tissot's, "Account of Federation Festival," July 14, 1790.

TIMELINE

1787

February 22: Assembly of Notables begins
April 8: Louis XVI fires Minister Charles-Alexandre de Calonne
May 25: Assembly of Notables ends

1788

April 27: First French state budget established
July 5: Louis XVI agrees to summon an Estates General
August 25: Jacques Necker made finance minister
November 6: Second Assembly of Notables begins
December 12: Second Assembly of Notables ends
December 27: Necker announces doubling of Third Estate representatives

1789

May 5: The Estates General begins
June 17: Legislators form a National Assembly
June 19: The First Estate collectively votes to join the National Assembly
June 20: Tennis Court Oath
June 23: Third Estate defies king's orders to deliberate separately
June 27: Louis XVI reverses his opinion, orders Clergy and Nobility to join the National Assembly
July 12: Parisian uprising after Jacques Necker's dismissal
July 13: Bourgeois militia of Paris takes control of city
July 14: Parisian insurgents capture the Bastille
July 16: Louis XVI recalls Jacques Necker
July 17: Louis XVI visits Paris, confirms capital's municipal revolution
August 4: National Assembly decrees Abolition of Feudalism
August 26: National Assembly decrees the Declaration of the Rights of Man and Citizen
October 5: Parisian market women march on Versailles
October 6: King and Royal Family return with protesters to live in Paris
December 21: National Assembly approves issuing *Assignat* paper money

1790

February 26: National Assembly administratively reorganizes France into 83 departments
May 22: National Assembly adopts "Declaration of Peace to the World," renouncing wars of conquest
July 12: Legislators pass Civil Constitution of the Clergy, demanding loyalty oath
July 14: Federation Festival in Paris and throughout provinces
September 8: Louis XVI fires Necker to popular indifference
November: Edmond Burke publishes *Reflections on the Revolution in France*

1791

January 3: French priests required by National Assembly to swear oath to Civil Constitution of the Clergy
March 11: Pope Pius VI denounces Civil Constitution of the Clergy
June 20: King escapes Paris, begins flight to Varennes
June 21: King captured in Varennes
July 16: The Jacobin Club splits, with more moderate members becoming the Feuillants
July 17: Massacre of the Champ de Mars against republican protesters in Paris
August 14: Slave uprising that becomes Haitian Revolution begins
August 27: Declaration of Pilnitz, allying Austria and Prussia against the revolution
September 3: National Assembly finishes French Constitution of 1791
September 13: Louis XVI ratifies the new Constitution
October 1: New Legislative Assembly takes office

1792

January 23: Food riots over sugar and coffee shortages in Paris
April 20: French National Assembly declares war on Austria
April 25: *The Marseillaise* is sung publicly for the first time in Strasbourg
June 20: Parisian protesters march through royal palace to confront King
July 30: Soldiers from Marseille arrive to defend Paris from invasion
August 3: Brunswick Manifesto made public
August 10: Monarchy overthrown
September 2: French army at Verdun capitulates to Austro-Prussian troops
September 2–7: September Massacres in Paris
September 20: French defeat Prussians at Battle of Valmy
September 20: National Convention begins, formally declares France a republic
December 10: Trial of Louis XVI begins

1793

January 21: Louis XVI executed by guillotine
February 1: Convention declares war against England and Dutch Republic
March 3: "Mass Levy" of 300,000 conscripts attempted
March 7: Vendée uprising begins
March 10: First Revolutionary Tribunal created
April 5: General Charles Dumouriez defects to the Austrians
April 6: Committees of Public Safety and General Security established
April 8: Ambassador Edmond-Charles Genet lands in Charleston, South Carolina
May 4: "Maximum" price controls enacted on wheat and flour
May 30: Federalist revolt begins in Lyon
June 2: Parisian protesters force Girondin deputies' resignation
June 6: Federalist revolts in Bordeaux, Toulouse, and Marseille begin
June 24: Constitution of 1793 ratified by Convention
July 13: Jean-Paul Marat assassinated
September 5: Parisian protesters call for terror to be "made the order of the day"
September 17: National Convention passes Law of Suspects
October 16 (25 Vendémiaire): Marie Antoinette guillotined
November 3 (13 Brumaire): Olympe de Gouges guillotined
November 10 (20 Brumaire): Notre-Dame Cathedral in Paris rededicated as a Temple of Reason
December 14 (24 Frimaire): Frimaire Decree centralizing government power under Committee of Public Safety

1794

February 4 (16 Pluviôse): Convention abolishes slavery throughout French colonies
February 5 (17 Pluviôse): Robespierre delivers "Virtue and Terror" speech
March 24 (4 Germinal): Jacques Hébert guillotined
March 30 (10 Germinal): Georges Danton and Camille Desmoulins guillotined
June 8 (20 Prairial): Festival of the Supreme Being
June 10 (22 Prairial): Prairial Laws passed, accelerating judicial process and executions
June 26 (8 Messidor): French forces win Battle of Fleurus, ending Germanic invasion threat
June 29 (11 Messidor): After argument in Committee of Public Safety, Robespierre does not return until July 23
July 27 (9 Thermidor): Convention rebels against Robespierre
July 28 (10 Thermidor): Robespierre and close collaborators guillotined
December 3 (13 Frimaire): Convention appoints sixteen-member committee to revise Constitution of 1793
December 24 (4 Nivôse): Convention repeals food price controls

1795

April 1–2 (12–13 Germinal): Failed Parisian protests for bread and democracy; suppression of *sans-culotte* movement accelerates

May 20 (1 Prairial): Parisian uprising leads to killing of Convention legislator

August 22 (5 Fructidor): National Convention adopts Constitution of the Year III

October 5 (13 Vendémiaire): Napoleon Bonaparte leads suppression of Parisian protests over constitution

1796

May 10 (21 Floréal): Bonaparte wins Battle of Lodi over Austrians, consolidates control over northern Italy

December 24–5 (4–5 Nivôse): Storms off Irish coast prevent French military landing

1797

May 27 (8 Prairial): François-Noel Babeuf executed after leading Conspiracy of Equals

September 4 (18 Fructidor): Coup against suspected royalists in legislature

October 17 (26 Vendémiaire): French and Austrians sign Treaty of Campo Formio, ending War of the First Coalition

1798

May 11 (22 Floréal): Election of 106 neo-Jacobin legislators invalidated

May 19 (30 Floréal): Bonaparte and army sail for Egypt

May 23 (4 Prairial): United Irish uprising against British rule

July 21 (3 Thermidor): Bonaparte's forces win Battle of the Pyramids

August 1 (14 Thermidor): Lord Nelson and British Navy destroy French fleet in Battle of the Nile

1799

August 23 (6 Fructidor): Bonaparte sails for France

October 9 (17 Vendémiaire): Bonaparte lands at Saint-Raphael, in southern France

November 9 (18 Brumaire): Sieyès and Bonaparte lead coup against Directory

December 24 (3 Nivôse): Constitution of the Year VIII approved with Bonaparte as First Consul

Introduction

The French Revolution and the Possible

Though four years into a series of shocking events, the Festival of Reason still managed to astound many in France's revolutionary capital. On 20 Brumaire Year II, or November 10, 1793, as the Gregorian calendar counted time, having overthrown Catholicism as they had their king, revolutionaries concocted an imposing ceremony in Notre-Dame de Paris, ex-cathedral of the old faith. After smashing many of the exterior decorations earlier that fall, publicly decapitating the kings of David that lined the facade, revolutionaries gave the interior of the thirteenth-century Gothic behemoth a makeover. In place of the altar, a mountain (symbol of the radical Jacobins) rose above the choir. Those assembled worshipped the Goddess of Reason—personified by a hired actress, whispered to be a prostitute. The grand church, which revolutionaries had come to see as a breeding ground of superstition, dogmatic thinking, and despotism, was reconsecrated a Temple of Philosophy. Nature and reason could now be worshipped in their purity, as revolutionaries refused compromises with the Old Regime.

Whereas radicals in the Paris Commune (the city's municipal government) had planned the Festival of Reason, powerful legislator Maximillien Robespierre spearheaded the organizing of a national Festival of the Supreme Being for 20 Prairial Year II—June 8, 1794, by the old Christian calendar. The central Paris celebration, designed by renowned neoclassical artist turned Jacobin legislator and propagandist Jacques-Louis David, began in the National (Tuileries) Garden with the burning of a statue of "Hideous Atheism"—revolutionaries still wanted the mysteries of nature to be worshipped—to reveal a figure of "Wisdom" underneath. The assembled then marched over a mile westward to the giant parade grounds at the Champ de Mars, where Robespierre climbed atop a papier-mâché mountain to address his congregants. Asserting that "divinity can no longer be disfigured by superstition," the Incorruptible proclaimed, "nature will hereby retake all its power, and wisdom it's Empire! The Supreme Being cannot be annihilated." Mass adorations of knowledge, nature, and divine power occurred at the same hour across France's provinces. As the revolution forced its enemies onto the defensive on many fronts, a new order seemed to arrive for France—and perhaps the world.

The French Revolution may best be considered a revolution in the history of the possible. The power vacuum created by royal absolutism's collapse fueled successive radical ruptures in political culture that divorced the Revolutionary world from the Old Regime, opening vast new possibilities for reorganizing government, society, and even citizens' views of themselves. In virtually all fields of human endeavor, the impossible now seemed achievable. This document collection highlights the extent to which the French Revolution expanded what seemed attainable—leaving old European notions of deference and tradition behind, to build a dynamic new regime centered on liberty and reason. Through daring experimentation, revolutionaries struck bold new modern courses that have shaped our contemporary world. This collection will attempt to capture the drama, idealism, and ramifications of the unexpected and unprecedented events that drove history into the modern era.

Origins

The French Revolution was enabled by the Enlightenment era preceding it, yet unplanned and unanticipated. Thinkers integrated ideas and examples from across the globe while developing strikingly new theories—yet few made concrete plans to apply them in absolutist France before the revolutionary crisis unfolded. The origins of the French Revolution have received perhaps as much scholarly attention as the events of the Revolution themselves, bringing historians to grapple with questions of causation: most agree that good history should help us understand that events are unpredictable, sometimes leading to outcomes that people beforehand would have considered unintended or even unimaginable. Nevertheless, three elements are typically emphasized in the genesis: the ferment of Enlightenment-era ideas, unprecedented economic development, and a mismanaged financial crisis that combined to enable the most radical revolution the world had yet seen.

From the mid-seventeenth to late eighteenth century, the Enlightenment movement gathered force across Europe and the Americas, bringing new optimism and hopes for enduring changes. Behind the rising scientific revolution and belief in the power of reason, progress and change increasingly seemed possible. As the laws of nature (through advancements in physics, chemistry, biology, and other sciences) became better known, hopes grew that the laws of society could be set upon more rational bases as well. Though many eighteenth-century philosophers favored enlightened

Absolutism (at least for the time being), a growing number became interested in democratization and the establishment of human rights. Increasingly interrogating and rejecting the dogmas of the past led many to desire broader freedoms of action in their place.

Along with the enlightened love of reason came suspicion of "superstition" and dislike for brutality. As natural science became better understood, the sphere of the supernatural—God's wrath having previously been the most convincing explanation for many natural disasters—shrunk. Many mocked religion's inability to back many of its parables with scientific proofs, citing Isaac Newton's insistence on universal natural laws. Some Enlightenment leaders ceased believing in a God that supernaturally intervened in human affairs—making Deism popular (the belief that God had abandoned the world after its creation, leaving it to run on scientific natural laws), and leading a few to help invent atheism. As awe of religion decreased, so too did veneration for kings: the trappings of monarchs increasingly appeared ridiculous, their courts corrupted, and their reliance upon violence to rule heinous. War's role in society became newly questioned (some daring to dream of perpetual peace once aristocratic rivalries were settled), while humanitarians spoke out against the slave trade, use of torture, and barbaric punishments. An age of reason, many hoped, could help develop a more peaceful society—in which people would cooperate out of enlightened self-interest, rather than because of coercion or fear of damnation.

Further complicating the intellectual picture, the second half of the eighteenth century gave rise to a fashion for sentimentalism. The age of reason partially ceded to an age of passion: readers, writers, theatergoers, and the public openly empathized with protagonists (and sometimes nations and peoples) as never before. Audiences broke out weeping when misfortune befell beloved characters. Tragedies led readers to depression or occasionally suicide. Boredom with cold classicism and rationality led many writers—most famously, Jean-Jacques Rousseau—to highlight the importance of emotion, and the irrational bases of love, desire, and much other human decision-making. Most leading Enlightenment writers passed away by the 1780s. In 1778, Dr. Franz Mesmer introduced hypnosis to Paris, leading to new speculations about the mysteries of the unconscious mind. A revolutionary cocktail of reason and unreason mixed for an unprecedented explosion.

Intellectual ferment combined with economic and ensuing social change to further destabilize the Old Regime's foundations. Some scientists identify the late eighteenth century as the dawn of the Anthropocene, as aggressive European colonialism and consumerism led human beings to become the biggest agents of change for the planet. Wealthy French commoners (the historical bourgeoisie) and some liberal nobles increasingly invested in French overseas colonies in the Caribbean, Indian Ocean, and elsewhere, developing brutal, extractive slave economies for sugar, coffee, and other profitable goods. The Enlightenment, which considered itself a practical and popularizing movement, also introduced productive reforms into many older industries, reducing costs and bolstering sales. Factories opened as French investors sought to imitate recent British advances. As French wealth became more broadly dispersed—giving investors and merchants as much or more liquid cash as old noble families who lived off their land rents—the exclusive social order of the Old Regime appeared more absurd. Commercial cities disproportionately purchased Enlightenment-inspired literature and participated in salon-style discussion groups. The industrious revolution and the eighteenth century's political changes were closely intertwined.

New examples for political change came from abroad, as an age of revolutions coalesced. Relying on the voluntary participation of citizen soldiers and elected officials, the American War of Independence created the largest republic since Ancient Rome, mobilizing its populace and developing alternatives to centralized, absolutist government. Tens of thousands of French soldiers witnessed the experiment firsthand. The new American states established Declarations of Rights and successfully managed regular elections. Democracy, previously a word of contempt in Europe for unstable mob rule, drew the interest of many reformers. While most in France were skeptical that American forms of government could be directly applied to their ancient, stratified society, Revolutionary War hero the Marquis de Lafayette became one of the late Old Regime's most celebrated advocates for reform.

Many came to believe that major, liberalizing changes could also be possible in European government, despite the many entrenched and wealthy aristocratic interests. In Britain, the American War led to the first concerted pushes for Parliamentary Reform—seeking to open an unequal and elitist political order—while in Ireland, the same years enabled the Irish to successfully push for political autonomy. The Dutch undertook a Patriot Revolution between 1780 and 1787, revolting against their authoritarian nobility and attempting to reestablish a representative republic. An Atlantic abolitionist social movement coalesced, with some northern American states abolishing slavery in liberty's name, while British activists gathered over 60,000 petition signatures to abolish the slave trade over the first half of 1788 alone. Many began to advocate for Britain and France to end slave trafficking together, after which they hoped the most exploitative forms of colonial slavery would wither and die. Projects abounded to reform or overthrow the era's worst abusers and abuses.

France, though widely considered the eighteenth-century Enlightenment's center, concurrently seemed the nexus of Old Regime excesses. The absolutist government continued being dominated by the nobility, while even the most talented commoners found the choicest routes to advancement blocked by those of higher birth. Officials' basic competency, however, appeared limited: France's debts became crushing (debt-servicing constituting two-thirds of the budget by the 1780s) after a series of ineffective wars, while periodic food shortages led to popular unrest and a continuing ministerial shuffle under an indecisive king at Versailles kept meaningful reform unachieved. Particularly amid an era of such possibilities, French absolutist incompetency appeared unsustainable.

The Rise of the Political Nation

The national debt—proliferating via profligate military spending, particularly during the American War—spurred France down the path to revolution. With finances growing dire, in 1787 Louis XVI convoked an Assembly of Notables, seeking to curtail tax exemptions for the nobility and clergy. The ensuing controversies broadcast elite dysfunction, as the king's handpicked nobles refused to make the royal ministry's desired changes. Attempts to enact new tax decrees by royal fiat were overturned by the regional supreme courts known as Parlements, while government attempts to override their decisions led to revolts in multiple provinces. A growing national consensus—a mix of opposition nobles, popular pamphleteers, and an increasingly politicized population, claiming to embody "popular opinion"—rejected the reform plans and demanded the King reduce his expenditures (the royal palace at Versailles consumed about 10% of France's annual budget). French groups increasingly joined forces against royal absolutism, while a growing number of reform proposals made the present order appear ridiculous.

This impasse led desperate officials to endorse calling an Estates General, assembling the nation (commoners as well as the two privileged orders) to directly participate in politics. The first such national parliament in 175 years, it drastically opened political possibilities for a growing number of ambitious would-be reformers. Proposals multiplied, with pamphlet publishing nearly quadrupling between 1787 and 1788. A motley crew of writers—"*Les Rousseau des ruisseaux* [The Rousseaus of the Gutter]"—oftentimes failed philosophers who under the Old Regime had lived off their pens by publishing royal libels, cheap novels, and/or pornography, now turned their attention to finding political solutions. A shadowy "Committee of Thirty" developed at Paris' Palais-Royal, diffusing liberal and sometimes radical pamphlets and newspaper pieces across France. Among the rising stars was the libertine turned prison reformer the Comte de Mirabeau, the America-traveling antislavery crusader Jacques-Pierre Brissot, and the disillusioned clergyman Emmanuel-Joseph Sieyès. As political options expanded, now only political stasis appeared impossible.

Rather than tampering down the growing expectations, the crown asked electoral assemblies to adopt Grievance Statements, stating what they believed was wrong in the kingdom and their plans for how to fix it. The French people, unaccustomed to being consulted, became empowered and emboldened, recommending a panoply of different (often contradictory) reform schemes. Yet, from the perspective of later years, their statements still seem moderate. Habituated to a closed political order ruled by hereditary vested interests, many remained incredulous that change could occur comprehensively. Popular unrest occurred in Paris, while tensions appeared high across the politicized nation. Though momentum mounted for significant changes, in spring 1789 it remained unclear what, if any, transformations would result.

Becoming a Revolution

Possibilities remained undetermined as the Estates General began on May 5, 1789. Seeking to manipulate public opinion, the crown had doubled commoners' Third Estate's representation (from a third to a half of seats), while keeping it unclear whether voting would be done by "head," giving commoners and reformist elites the advantage, or by "order," in which the nobility and clergy could block major changes. After six weeks of posturing—pushed by an emboldened Parisian populace and rural revolts—reformists made their move, forming a National Assembly of the majority of the Estates' members and beseeching the rest to join them. On June 20, after royal provocation, that majority met at the largest indoor venue available and took the Tennis Court Oath, pledging to remain in session until finishing a constitution for France. Three days later, the Third Estate successfully defied the King's call to revert to voting by order. Facing down threats from the still-dangerous aristocracy, legislators radicalized to become revolutionaries. Yet, most expected further trouble from a regime accustomed to absolute rule.

Only a broader people's revolution saved the fragile new National Assembly. When Louis XVI on July 12 fired Jacques Necker, his reformist minister, Paris revolted—forming a "Bourgeois Militia" that seized control of the capital and prepared to battle royal troops. Seeking gunpowder, crowds gathered outside the Bastille on July 14 and, despite volleys of fire from those stationed inside (killing ninety-eight attackers to only one defender), successfully pressured the fortress' surrender. More important than the actual taking of the Bastille was its symbolic value—a hated symbol of absolutism holding political prisoners that loomed for centuries over the capital city had fallen to the revolutionaries. Unwilling to execute a civil war against his capital, Louis XVI capitulated, recalling Necker and traveling to Paris to endorse the new revolutionary municipal authorities. Risking their lives, hundreds of thousands of Parisians had defied their king and won, after which little seemed impossible.

Paris' revolution was confirmed, in turn, by municipal revolutions and rural revolts across France. Across the provinces, peasants rose to burn chateaus and records, target aristocrats to demand they renounce their privileges, and confront royal officials over food prices. Urban residents, often under the pretext of reestablishing order, overthrew royal officials and abolished the police, appointing elected townspeople and organizing citizen militias in their place. Even the spread of the "Great Fear" across several provinces, fueled by wild rumors of imminent attacks by royal forces, foreign armies, or bands of thieves caused mass panics, sped up revolutionary mass mobilization. Having previously spent their lives subordinate to an aristocratic order dating back 1,500 years, peasants and townspeople now demanded a radically new regime of greater equality and participation.

With popular militants and seemingly the vast majority of the French people on their side, National Assembly authorities became emboldened to make radical changes. The legislators enacted the abolition of feudalism on August 4, ending noble privileges to make all French people legally equal (though confirming their property rights). On August 26, the assembly passed the Declaration of the Rights of Man and Citizen, enumerating the basic rights of French citizens, including "liberty, property, security, and resistance to oppression." Whereas previously "rights" had meant the privileges of specific groups, the French Declaration asserted, "All men are born and remain free and equal in rights"—suggesting they could be universally applicable to everyone. Whereas previously French society had operated through intricate tables of ranks—making almost no one inherently equal—now revolutionaries proclaimed formal equality for all beneath the royal family. With a rapidity that shocked all observers, the French were liberated from their history of hierarchical oppression and told the future represented nearly limitless opportunity.

A new regime took shape with remarkably little bloodshed—about 4,000 deaths across the nation—and the French by late 1789 sought to consolidate its gains. Legislators made compromises to ensure the King's executive powers, including a royal veto on legislation. A new Society of Friends of the Constitution network (better known as the Jacobin Clubs) arose, seeking to educate the populace and discuss political issues spread across the country. Federation ceremonies, in which thousands of national guardsmen (and soon the general populace) gathered to swear their fealty to the Revolution, multiplied across the provinces, reaching tens and then hundreds of thousands of attendees by spring 1790. Hope remained that the overwhelming majority of the French people would continue working together to craft a new regime of consensus and peace. By the time millions gathered to celebrate the first anniversary of the Bastille's fall on July 14, the Year I of Liberty appeared a spectacular success.

Destabilizing the Revolution

Most French people in mid-1790 wished for the Revolution to end amicably, with reconciliation and freedom for even their adversaries. The great contestations of 1789 had ended via compromise, with a low body count. The possibility of civil war, though widely feared in mid-1789, for over a year thereafter seemed remote. Many believed they had experienced a brief "Glorious Revolution" not unlike that which had solidified Britain's constitutional monarchy in 1688–9. Growing royal-absolutist opposition and divides among revolutionaries, however, opened monstrous new possibilities of the revolution being subverted from within, or trounced by its opponents from without.

Seeking to solve the debt crisis—the intractable issue that had begun the revolutionary progression itself—the National Assembly in May 1790 passed legislation to confiscate church lands and sell them to the public. The vast wealth of the church, including about 15 percent of France's arable land, became considered the nation's rightful property. "Contemplative" monasteries not engaging in public works were closed, while most other church institutions (charities included) had their funding diminished. Whereas many clergymen had previously supported the revolution, now a growing number denounced the new regime—leading the National Assembly later that year to demand the Civil Constitution of the Clergy Oath on the first Sunday of 1791 from clergy of their loyalty to the French state, even above obedience to the pope. Fifty-two percent took the oath, but the rest became outlaws—while many more retracted their support once the pope formally condemned participation (alongside France's Rights of Man, their 1787 religious toleration decree and freedom of expression in general). The *Chouan* guerilla movement supporting the refractory clergy began in Western France. As the religious split worsened, revolutionaries increasingly adopted the Voltarian anticlerical rhetoric of some Enlightenment writers, considering their opponents superstitious fanatics. Many of the faithful increasingly supported the nobility and monarchy in their counterrevolutionary machinations to limit, or perhaps overthrow, the Revolution.

Other groups, meanwhile, felt the revolution had not gone far enough. Peasant dissatisfaction spread at how little the abolition of feudalism had actually accomplished—though nobles had lost their formal privileges, they remained landowners able to raise rents to offset lost feudal dues. Many wealthier peasants bought former church properties at a discount—but declining finances impacted the Catholic charities many of the poor depended upon in hard times. Workers in the cities used the revolutionary spirit of mass mobilization, began to organize and bargain collectively—but in mid-1791 the National Assembly passed the Le Chapelier Law banning unions and guilds. The new constitution divided "active" and "passive" citizens, stripping voting rights from poorer Frenchmen. The moderate revolutionaries in power increasingly emphasized individual over collective rights, in ways favoring the middle class and wealthy over common workers—but in so doing, exacerbated popular discontents.

Politics destabilized under the weight of internal dissentions. The growing split with Catholicism alienated France's pious king. During Holy Week 1791, Louis XVI and his family attempted to leave Paris for a remote chateau, allegedly to receive communion from an oath-refusing priest. Parisian crowds, however, surrounded his carriage and prevented his departure. Louis thereafter resolved to flee the country, into the Habsburg-controlled lands of his in-laws. The royal family nearly succeeded the night of June 20–1 but were caught by revolutionaries in the frontier town of Varennes. This created an angry protest movement in Paris—the carefully crafted compromises of the past two years collapsed as tens of thousands of protesters sought to remove the traitorous king and possibly turn France into a republic. National Assemblymen, however, who had spent two years developing a constitution with a monarchical executive branch and feared further inflaming pious sectors of the provinces, instead disingenuously declared the king had been "kidnapped," and reconfirmed the monarchy. Parisian protesters, assembled for a petition-signing in favor of a republic, were violently suppressed in the Massacre of the Champ de Mars on July 17. National Assembly moderates wanted the revolution to be over.

The first French Constitution, enacted in September 1791, lasted less than a year. Louis XVI had no intention of abiding by the Revolutionary compact, but instead sought the revolution's defeat and his own reinstallation as an absolute monarch. The New Regime, having attempted to change so much so quickly, appeared fragile and vulnerable to attack, especially since most Old Regime military officers had left the country. Louis and Marie Antoinette corresponded with her Austrian relatives, colluding to provoke a war. Many revolutionaries also came to desire war for their own purposes: Jacques-Pierre Brissot, a leading abolitionist who had traveled extensively in both Britain and America, popularized the idea that a Franco-Austrian conflict could be a new war for freedom, in which revolutionaries would be greeted as liberators by oppressed peoples once they crossed the Rhine into German territory. On April 20, 1792, the National Assembly preemptively declared war on the Austrian Empire, believing their revolutionary spirit could overcome their forces' inexperience and overwhelm the "slave armies" of their opponents.

France's own slaves, meanwhile, revolted in their largest colony, Saint-Domingue. With the Declaration of Rights promoting liberty for "all men," rumors spread that freedom for slaves might have already been enacted (with greedy slave owners suppressing the news). Regional divisions grew on the island, while whites attempted to exclude free men of color from voting rights, leading to dissention and multiple revolts. Slaves rose to torch the plantations of the colony's northern plain in August 1791 and the ensuing multisided civil war lasted thirteen years. Many French revolutionaries became torn between principle and pragmatism: first, they sent troops to subdue the revolt, but by 1794, in an attempt to win rebel slaves back to their side, decreed the abolition of slavery (not just in rebel territories, but throughout the French empire), the first time any modern empire had done so. Only amid French Revolutionary contests over liberty and equality did history's only successful slave revolt occur, ultimately leading to the Republic of Haiti's founding.

On France's eastern frontier, the revolutionary armies lost their early battles, with terrible possibilities abounding should the front collapse and Paris be captured. Enemy commander the Duke of Brunswick threatened the capital's entire destruction if the royal family was harmed. The revolutionary army's own commanders openly sought to close the Jacobin Clubs, leading many to doubt the military leadership's loyalty. With Louis XVI vetoing war preparation measures, Parisians raised large demonstrations to voice their displeasure—and by August, unable to tolerate a treasonous executive branch in their own government, sought the King's overthrow. After the royal guards lured Paris National Guardsmen into battle on August 10, the monarchy was suspended and the royal family imprisoned. On September 20, 1792, the newly elected National Convention as its first act declared France a republic.

Attempts to craft a more moderate revolution failed due to counterrevolutionary intrigues and tensions among revolutionaries. The initial compromises of 1789–91 were for naught, as the crises of 1792 opened vast new precipices threatening the revolutionary project with ruin or annihilation. Refusing to relinquish the great hopes and possibilities glimpsed over the previous three years, revolutionaries sought to defend their gains and refine their new regime, creating an intensifying dynamic of radicalization.

The French Republic

A new era, soon (de)christened "The Year I," dawned. Less than three years after their revolution began, the French cut the cord with their past traditions—eliminating monarchy and aggressively reorganizing their new society on terms of greater equality. *Sans-culotte* working-class culture became celebrated, while revolutionaries sought to eradicate "aristocratic" vestiges and prejudices. Revolutionary authorities instituted universal manhood suffrage, artisans peopled the neighborhood-governing urban sections, while even small-town and village residents self-governed and founded local Jacobin Club branches. Social experimentation spread as a previously tradition-bound society discarded precedent to craft a new revolutionary order.

The Revolution was not only a political event but also a social rupture, altering the structures in which French people lived their lives. Revolutionaries struck against despotism not only in high politics but also in the home and marketplace. The new authorities legalized divorce, disregarding Catholic prohibitions. Primogeniture was abolished, granting all "natural children" equal shares of their parents' estates. Women attended political assemblies and clubs, in some winning the right to freely participate. Economic agitation increased as *sans-culottes* sought price controls and pressured the government to guarantee them the necessities of life. With a growing spirit of equality and fraternity, revolutionaries sought to establish an order of greater fairness, in place of ancient abuses.

In exchange, the French government demanded more from its citizens, particularly in wartime. France instituted the first modern military draft, the levée en masse, which more than quadrupled its armed forces to 800,000. France now took on all comers, combating not just Austria and Prussia but Britain, Spain, Portugal, the Netherlands, and Piedmont by February 1793. Having warned their citizens that the "fatherland is in danger," French officials fanned popular nationalism, inflaming blood-and-soil rhetoric alongside revolutionary idealism. Fighting smaller professional armies whose soldiers had sometimes been cashiered into royal forces against their will, France's borders soon expanded into Belgium, the Rhineland and Savoy. The revolution developed an energy and military force Europe's Old Regimes could not match.

Reverberations of the recent changes surpassed the revolutionary armies' front lines, particularly impacting politics in Britain and the United States. In early 1792 the London Corresponding Society had attempted to bring a Jacobin-style corresponding network to Britain, agitating for universal manhood suffrage and French-style egalitarianism. The movement would largely be forced underground the following year, however, as the British monarchy went to war against revolutionary France. In spring 1793, the French sent a new ambassador, Edmond-Charles Genet, to the United States, with directions to commence pirating and raiding against British and Spanish interests. So popular had the French cause already become in America, that Genet helped found a new Jacobin-style network, "the Democratic Club." The Democratic-Republican Societies that resulted organized American oppositional politics and led to the rise of the Democratic Party.

Despite the new era's kaleidoscopic hopes, revolutionaries nevertheless pursued unfinished business against their enemies. Fearing the deposed king's escape to aid the counterrevolutionary armies, the National Convention placed Louis XVI on trial for his life, under accusation of treason and collusion with the enemy Austrians. While the prior French constitution had declared the King to be inviolable, revolutionaries argued that his traitorous actions placed him outside legitimate legal protection. The proper penalty, however, remained controversial: despite a unanimous guilty verdict from the 693 legislators present, an immediate death sentence passed by a single vote. Only narrowly did violence against the revolution's enemies proceed over clemency. On January 21, 1793, before massive crowds, Louis XVI was guillotined, a clear signal to the revolution's enemies abroad and at home not to expect undeserved mercy.

With royalists now withdrawing from revolutionary politics, factionalization grew among dedicated revolutionaries—oftentimes former friends, allies, and fellow Jacobins. "Girondins" favoring free trade and regional autonomy withdrew from Paris' Jacobin Club, where the majority favored price controls and administrative centralization. The two factions sat on opposite sides of the Convention hall (the speaker's rostrum facing Jacobins on the left and Girondins on the right, creating the modern political designations), with both denouncing the other's leaders for allegedly masterminding conspiracies. The Jacobins held the support of many Parisian *sans-culottes* and organized an uprising to oust the Girondins, surrounding the Convention's hall with tens of thousands of protesters from May 31 to June 2, on the third day successfully demanding their removal from office. Numerous Girondin-supporting areas revolted—including the important cities of Lyon, Bordeaux, Marseille, and Caen—but were suppressed by French troops. Jacobin journalist Jean-Paul Marat was murdered by a Federalist sympathizer. A half dozen civil wars flared as the French combated five major kingdoms abroad. As revolutionaries increasingly turned on each other, factionalization—and fear of new conspiracies yet to come—grew endemic in French politics.

The Radical Revolution and Terror

Jacobins now dominated the National Convention, particularly the twelve-man Committee of Public Safety serving as its executive branch. Maximillien Robespierre, elected to the Committee in July 1793, became its most influential member. Though an enlightened humanitarian earlier in the Revolution, the austere lawyer from the northern town of Arras now became the unflinching "Incorruptible," pursuing and punishing those not embodying his conception of revolutionary virtue. The Committee sent "Representatives on Mission" across the countryside and military fronts, demanding strict revolutionary compliance and condemning backsliders. As the demands of revolutionary compliance increased, however, the new regime's sphere of liberty diminished.

The Convention finished a new constitution for the French Republic in October 1793 guaranteeing extensive freedoms. Under its terms, French citizens were granted universal manhood suffrage, guaranteed work, the right to a public education, freedom of the press, free assembly, and a right not just to "resistance" but indeed "insurrection" if authorities did not maintain public approval. This near-utopian popular-democratic regime, educating and politically enabling a vast populace to an extent unseen in world history, was never enacted, however. Given the stringencies of wartime and internal civil wars, the Convention deemed it necessary to suspend such rights until peacetime. Instead of the Constitution serving as a bulwark of the new regime, the resulting extralegal atmosphere enabled the slide toward terror.

Nevertheless, why revolutionaries pursued terror—amid a revolution embracing universal fraternity and initially seeking peace and reconciliation—remains widely debated by historians. Many (particularly those sympathetic to the revolution) have asserted that "circumstances" drove the revolutionaries to terror: that internal and external enemies required a ferocious response for the Revolution to survive. Others (often building their arguments from the counterrevolutionary tradition) believed revolutionary ideas made them inflexible and intolerant of opposition—that elements of Jean-Jacques Rousseau's *Social Contract* and "Classical Republican" thought from ancient Greece and Rome led revolutionaries to believe nonconformists were refusing to cooperate for selfish (likely conspiratorial) reasons. More recently, some have sought a psychological explanation, arguing a culture of fear and mistrust spread among revolutionary elites, leading them into extremism. Regardless, all sides remain struck by how, despite all revolutionaries had gone through together—and despite their having kept the revolution's early years predominantly peaceful—in fall 1793 they began killing each other. Twenty-two Girondin leaders, many members of the Jacobin Club earlier that year, after an expedited trial before a Revolutionary Tribunal were guillotined on October 31. Not just avowed counterrevolutionaries but now suspect revolutionaries became targeted.

Worsening battles with Catholic conservatives, including civil war in the Vendée region of Western France, led revolutionaries to pursue Dechristianization in fall 1793. In October, the Convention approved a new Revolutionary Calendar, measuring time not from the purported birth of Jesus but from the French Republic's proclamation instead. Weeks became ten days long instead of seven—to improve productivity and disrupt Christian practice. Churches were closed to Catholic services, with Festivals of Reason held in their place, as revolutionaries desired the development of a purer creed more reflective of nature. A cult of revolutionary martyrs arose to replace that of Catholic saints. Holy edifices suffered widespread destruction, for which critics invented the term "vandalism." The Revolution drew some of its most radical elements from the religious skepticism of the preceding Enlightenment era and implemented them in a more extreme form than their prior proponents would have thought possible.

After military reversals in late 1793 and early 1794 led to growing fears of revolutionary collapse before their many enemies, the use of terror became widespread. Groups arguing that the revolution was not going far enough (the Hébertists, centered around radical journalist Jacques-René Hébert) or that terror had gone too far (the "Indulgents" Georges Danton and Camille Desmoulins) were guillotined in turn. Though in some respects the Parisian terror remained limited to the political leadership, limited in scale when compared to the terrors of twentieth-century revolutionaries—2,639 were ultimately guillotined, including eighty-two Convention members, a significantly smaller body count than many of the era's military battles—the turn to political violence shocked many. Across France, approximately 40,000 died (in a nation of twenty-seven million) as a result of state-sanctioned extra-military political violence across the French Revolution. This figure does not count, however, the great bloodbath that took place in the Vendée civil war between royalists and revolutionaries in Western

France, where approximately 170,000 died in a region of 800,000, including widespread atrocities against noncombatants. Only in the Vendée did the French Revolution match or exceed the body counts per capita of twentieth-century revolutionaries in Russia, China, Cambodia, and elsewhere.

The excesses of the Year II suppressed much of the French Revolution's vibrant political culture. Newspaper debates ceased, as most surviving publications turned into organs for revolutionary propaganda. Most private letters, even from highly politicized correspondents, evince a newfound unwillingness to discuss issues openly, given the terrible penalties to be paid for dissent. Paris' *sans-culottes* ceased engaging in major protests after September 1793. As accused revolutionary factions were arrested, speedily tried and guillotined, even powerful legislators felt unable to express themselves freely. Fearing subversion from within, revolutionaries sought to shut down the very practices that had enabled and fueled the revolution.

The revolution's pressures proved nearly overpowering for many at its center, including Robespierre. The Incorruptible seems to have suffered multiple mental breakdowns and, after a terrible fight with fellow Committee of Public Safety members, refused to attend their meetings for weeks. Returning to the Convention on 8 Thermidor (July 25, 1794), he declared the revolution had not gone far enough, while claiming to have a list of "new conspirators" in the Convention. The next day, legislators shouted down his collaborator Louis Saint-Just and that evening marshaled army units against Robespierrists cornered at City Hall. Robespierre and his closest allies were guillotined the next day, quickly followed by the majority of legislators from the radical Paris Commune. While seen both then and since as embodying the radical revolution's search for purity and virtue, Robespierre became too destructive of a figure to endure. The radical revolution did not survive the Robespierrists' fall.

The Terror ended in part because it no longer appeared necessary, as the early republic's first crises had passed. In the Battle of Fleurus on June 26, France's revolutionary forces trounced the allied coalition, thereafter overrunning much of Belgium. With the frontier crisis over, revolutionaries had an opportunity to create their desired revolutionary order. Their armed forces were unmatched across Europe and the National Convention had established a strong, centralized government more powerful than what France's absolutist kings had ever possessed. With recruiting powers unlike any of their opponents, the revolutionary armies soon brought havoc and dynamic change to much of Europe.

The Revolution fell into the hands of corrupt moderates, who led a reaction against the prior era's excesses. "Terrorist" scapegoats were denounced—though the Thermidorian leaders themselves had often held leading roles during the Year II—while Jacobin Clubs were closed, Parisian protests suppressed, and the economic rights won by *sans-culottes* repealed. A revised Constitution of 1795 eliminated the social protections, free expression, and right of resistance guaranteed by the 1793 system. "Liberty" came to mean little more than free-market exploitation under corrupt administrators. The new Directory government replacing the National Convention inspired few.

Military Possibilities and Authoritarian Anticipations

Even as its political program faltered, revolutionary military campaigns remained strikingly successful. Brimming with manpower and increasingly confident (disproportionately young) military commanders, the revolutionaries overran Savoy, Belgium, the Netherlands, and German states between 1793 and 1795. The following year, 27-year-old Napoleon Bonaparte conquered much of northern Italy. A plunder economy developed that helped poison French politics. Revolutionary armies formally issued proclamations of equality and revolutionary rights—but in practice offered little opportunity for dissent or negotiation with foreign peoples who regarded the new French order with suspicion.

Despite the radical Revolution's repudiation, there were still many revolutionary changes French people remained passionate about preserving. Most wanted to retain citizen equality—to prevent the nobility's reimplementation and maintain a meritocracy. Much of the upper and middle classes had bought church lands on the cheap, and worried they would be confiscated if Catholicism regained its full Old Regime powers. The military machine produced fortunes for profiteering suppliers and those able to plunder foreign lands. The new political leadership, largely drawn from the legal profession and prosperous middle class, showed no signs of being willing to cede power back to exiled Old Regime elites.

Political instability continued plaguing the unpopular Directory. With its central figures becoming better known for corruption than any positive program, the regime faced challengers from the center, right, and left. Moderates protesting the automatic reelection of two-thirds of the Convention to the new legislature in 1795 were denounced as "royalists" and suppressed. Leading politicians joined forces with the army to purge another "royalist" wave from the national legislature in the coup of Fructidor (1797), while electoral victories of Neo-Jacobins seeking to reopen the political system were reversed by the coup of Floréal (1798). Nevertheless, decimating democratic opposition coalitions opened possibilities for a right-wing authoritarian coup, particularly if supported by the powerful military.

The Directory gambled by sending the popular Bonaparte on a mission to colonize Egypt. Seeking new territory for cash crops, particularly given the ongoing Haitian Revolution, they risked Napoleon returning as a conquering hero. The young general trounced the Egyptian military at the Battle of the Pyramids but struggled to subdue the Egyptian population. With his fleet destroyed by the British, Bonaparte attempted to march on the Ottoman authorities in Turkey, but an outbreak of plague decimated his forces in Palestine. The Directory, however, hearing only of victories in battle, ordered Bonaparte's recall. Leaving his troops behind, Napoleon returned to France, within weeks organizing the coup of 18 Brumaire Year VII (1799) and consolidating power as First Consul.

Bonaparte claimed to embody the French Revolution—but, as an enlightened pragmatist, discarded those portions he found unuseful. He firmly supported equality of opportunity, building a coalition of supporters ranging from former Jacobin terrorists to ex-nobles. The under-construction French Civil Code became the Napoleonic Code, consolidating men's legal equality (though often discriminating against women). A Concordat was negotiated with the Catholic Church, re-legalizing the faith while preserving revolutionary property confiscations and individual freedom of conscience. Napoleon, however, gave little real power to the national legislature, keeping real decision-making in the hands of himself and his administrators. Strong press censorship was enacted and spying on the populace increased. The Consulate can be described as Liberal-Authoritarian—upholding individual rights, but severely limiting political expression.

When Napoleon proclaimed his empire in 1804, crowning himself in a re-sacralized but minimally repaired Notre Dame Cathedral, France was a land greatly changed over the preceding fifteen years. France's people had gone from subjects of an absolutist king to citizens of their continent's most powerful nation. Despite political controversies and reversals, politics would never be limited to elite, hereditary coteries again. Liberty, equality, and fraternity remain the universal touchstones of good government. The tantalizing prospects of what French revolutionaries sought, if only fitfully accomplished, was not forgotten—while images of peasants and townspeople marching on the chateaux of unjust elites and storming the Bastille remain known throughout the world, as does the image of the retributive guillotine—inspiring generations of revolutionaries throughout Europe and the world. Unlike the Anglo-American tradition of liberty, which many proponents considered to require centuries of tradition and development, the most radical iterations of the French model declared rights and freedom to be immediately realizable for anyone, should a people combine their efforts to will it. Though the French Revolution lacked a clear conclusion, it embodied possibility itself.

FIGURE 1.1 *Vigée le Brun,* Portrait of Marie Antoinette with a Rose, *1783. © Wikimedia Commons (public domain).*

Marie Antoinette engaged in a long, difficult battle to win public opinion into her favor. An Austrian princess married into French royalty in 1770 to solidify an unpopular military alliance that had recently led to disastrous defeat in the Seven Years War, Marie Antoinette was unpopular before she stepped foot on French soil. Her carefree (to many, frivolous) personality won her further disdain. Elizabeth Vigée Le Brun, one of the few prominent female artists of her era, paints her formally in this 1783 portrait after a more informal portrait of her drew controversy, stylishly melding elements of rococo and neoclassicism. Retained by the queen as a court artist, Le Brun painted over thirty portraits of her queen and her family. None, however, effectively counteracted the scandalous rumors circulating about her in the French public.

1

Revolutionary Origins

No one saw the French Revolution coming, but the developing revolution drew upon the growing cultural and intellectual ferment in eighteenth-century France. Like its counterparts across the European continent, France was a society of orders, with the privileged aided by tax exemptions and preferential eligibility for administrative and military commands. Yet over the eighteenth century, much changed: domestic and colonial economic expansion created a prosperous and growing middle class, while an influx of new ideas, written by those known in France as "the Enlightened (*les lumières*)," altered the boundaries of what could be asked from government. Yet the path to revolution in France was much more complicated than it appears at first glance: most prosperous members of the middle class sought to buy or marry into the nobility, while more writers in France focused on strategies for Enlightened absolutist government than democratization. Revolution was only one of many potential outcomes from the era's ferment.

Grand structural changes combined with government mismanagement to make the revolution possible. Louis XVI, shy, indecisive, and maladroit, would have proven a mediocre king in the best of times. Queen Marie Antoinette demonstrated little ability to shape public opinion about herself or those around her, instead becoming a regular target for press attacks. Louis XVI's finance ministers failed to reform the kingdom's fiscal system, creating a regime-threatening crisis—though France's per capita debt remained significantly below their British rivals. The colonial system was rife with atrocities, as colonial officials had long refused to enforce the humanitarian Black Code and slave life expectancy upon arrival in the Caribbean little exceeded three years. Heavy-handed policing of the French people, especially in Paris, bred resentment—which soon incited explosions of collective anger once controls were relaxed. While most French people had long resigned themselves to governmental inefficiencies and abuses, the growing crisis of the 1780s led resentments to smolder anew.

The Enlightenment movement—an inescapable but incomplete explanation for the forms the French Revolution took—is still more paradoxical. Growing from a broader Scientific Revolution expanding across the Western world since at least the Renaissance, the Enlightenment is best characterized as a series of debates over how best to apply reasoned thought to human affairs. Whereas previously most people had expected society to remain in stasis, with "nothing new under the sun," the intertwined capitalistic and industrious revolutions (unlike political revolutions, a centuries-long process) evinced durable, positive change as cities gained population and consumer choices expanded. Literacy grew, the publishing industry—much of it trading in contraband—proliferated, and the ability to converse and debate on any sphere of knowledge highly prized. Scientific political management enabled the enlightened absolutist rules of Frederick the Great of Prussia and Catherine the Great of Russia, while European thinkers took note of the changes in the new United States and revolts in Corsica, the Netherlands, and elsewhere. While no consensus developed over the best method of government, most thinkers came to detest despotism (rule by whim without constitutional constraint) and superstition (recourse to supernatural explanation that contradicted scientific observation). The Enlightenment's inquisitive spirit defied boundaries.

The origins of the French Revolution are both too many and too few: scholars have identified manifold contributing factors, but none sufficiently explain the great rupture with tradition and precedent unleashed in 1789. It is impossible, however, to make sense of the French Revolution without some reference to the era's inefficient government, expanding economy, and growing ferment of ideas. Revolution was not inevitable, but it is retrospectively impossible not to see the combustible potential of eighteenth-century France.

Baron de Montesquieu, *The Spirit of the Laws*, 1748

A judge on Bordeaux's Parlement, a regional supreme court, the Baron de Montesquieu spent over two decades composing his massive *Spirit of the Laws*. Montesquieu saw the merits of both democratic and monarchical government, but detested despotism—which he defined as unchecked power, that abrogated reason and compromise in favor of an individual's caprice. In his erudite work, Montesquieu draws examples from across the known world, seeking to discover governing systems' foundations in human nature, helping lay the basis for modern political science. While he remained skeptical that laws could be directly transferrable from one nation to another—as this would violate the environmental specificity of laws' development and the existing system's spirit—Montesquieu asserts that new laws can be adopted and reforms instituted over time. Though controversial today for advocating environmental determinism (particularly his association of despotism with the heat of the tropics, while he asserted temperate weather enabled cooler reflection and balanced government), Montesquieu influentially advocated the concept of mixed government. Calling for flexibility and balance in the construction of legal systems, the book popularized the concept of "checks and balances," greatly influencing the framers of the United States' Constitution and those composed in France during the Revolution.

I have examined men, finding that, in the infinite diversity of laws and manners, they are not led by their fantasies alone.

I have hypothesized principles and seen specific cases comply with them; the histories of all nations are only their after-effects. Each specific law relates to another law or depends on a more general one. . . .

I have not derived my principles from my prejudices, but from the nature of things.

Thus, many truths cannot make themselves felt except once we see the chain connecting them to others. The more we reflect on such details, the more we feel the certainty of principles. . . .

Before all these laws are those of nature, thus named because they derive uniquely from the constitution of our being. . . .

In this state, everyone feels themselves inferior; thus, everyone feels equal. People do not attack each other and peace is nature's first law. . . .

As soon as men enter society, they lose their feeling of weakness and of the equality that existed between them. The state of war begins. . . .

The general force can be placed in a single person's hands, or in the hands of many. Some have thought that nature established paternal power, considering the government of an individual most conforming to the state of nature. But, the example of paternal power proves nothing. . . .

It is better to say that the government most conforming to nature is that whose particular disposition relates best to the disposition of the people for whom it is established.

Particular forces cannot come together, without all wills doing so. "The joining of these wills," Gravina well explains, "is what one calls the Civil State."[1]

The law, in general, is human reason, insofar that it governs all the earth's peoples, and the political and civil laws of each nation are only particular cases for applying this human reason.

They must be proper for the people for whom they are made, and thus it is a great hazard if one nation's are adopted for another's.

They must be in keeping with nature and the established government's principles, or those they want to establish . . .

They must relate to the country's environment, whether the climate is frigid, hot or temperate; to the quality of terrain, to how it is situated, to its height; to the lifestyle of its peoples, laborers, hunters, or farmers: they must correspond to the degree of liberty the constitution can suffer; to the inhabitants' religion, to their inclinations, to their wealth, to their number, to their commerce, to their morals, to their manners. In the end, all these relate. They have their origins, their legislative objects, the order of things over which they are established. All these perspectives must be considered.

Here is what I want to do in this work: I want to examine all these relationships. Together, they form what we call the spirit of the laws. . . .

There are three kinds of government: republican, monarchical, and despotic. To discover their nature, examine under which men are the least instructed. I suppose three definitions, or moreover three states: in the first, republican government is where the assembled people, or only part of the people, have the sovereign power; the monarchy, where a single person governs, but by fixed and established laws; whereas in despotism a single person, without laws or regulations, does everything by his will and caprice. . . .

It remains a fundamental law of democracy that the people make the laws. There are a thousand occasions when it is necessary for the Senate to pass statutes; it is even often necessary to try out a law before establishing it. The constitutions of Rome and Athens were very wise. Senate measures held the force of law for a year; they did not become perpetual except by the people's will.

Subordinate and dependent intermediary powers constitute monarchical government's nature; this is to say that which an individual governs by fundamental laws. . . . These fundamental laws necessarily suppose intermediary canals through which power flows: because if there was nothing in the state except an individual's momentary will and capriciousness, nothing would be fixed, and in consequence there would be no fundamental law.

It results from the nature of despotic power, that one man can only exercise what one man is capable of. A man to whom five hundred ceaselessly say that he is everything, while everyone else is nothing, is naturally lazy, ignorant and voluptuous. . . .

Madame de Campan, *Memoirs on the Private Life of Marie Antoinette*, published 1823

Marie Antoinette, already the symbol of an unpopular Austrian alliance when she arrived in France to marry the Dauphin (future Louis XVI), fell victim to increasingly vicious gossip and tabloids soon after she ascended to the French throne in 1775. As related by her lady-in-waiting Madame de Campan, summer nighttime soirées in the Versailles palace gardens, often lasting until two or three a.m., which she often spent with the King's brother the Comte d'Artois instead of her husband, gave rise to rumors of infidelity and questionable paternity of her children. Despite spending most of her time surrounded by courtiers and the public, stories flew of what might occur at less-supervised moments. Marie Antoinette became the subject of pornographic publications, alongside denunciations of her luxury, gambling, and absolutist political predilections. Royal counter-campaigns celebrating her as a virtuous mother accomplished little. Even as Louis XVI remained personally popular, Marie Antoinette was commonly held in low esteem. While Campan's *Memoires* were not published until after her death in 1823, and sought to defend her reputation along with that of the rest of Marie Antoinette's inner circle, they portray the frustration of a group besieged by often-unfair calumnies.

The summer of 1778 was extremely hot. July and August passed, but the air was not cooled by a single storm. The Queen spent whole days in closed rooms and could not sleep until she breathed the fresh night air, walking with the princesses and her brothers along the terrace by her apartments. These promenades at first inspired no remark, but some of the party suggested enjoying the music of wind instruments during these fine summer nights. The chapel musicians were ordered to play from the steps built in the middle of the garden. The Queen, seated on a terrace bench, enjoyed the effects of the music, surrounded by the whole royal family except the King, who joined them only twice, not liking to change his bedtime.

Nothing could be more innocent than these parties; yet Paris, France, nay, all Europe, were soon following them in a manner most disadvantageous to Marie Antoinette's reputation. The truth is that all Versailles' inhabitants enjoyed these serenades, while there was a crowd around from eleven at night until two or three in the morning. . . .

I do not know whether a few incautious women might have ventured further, wandering to the lower park; but the Queen, Madame [the King's aunt], and the Comtesse d'Artois were always arm-in-arm, never leaving the terrace. . . .

My advice was useless. Misled by the pleasure she found in these promenades, and securely believing her conduct blameless, the Queen could not anticipate the lamentable results that necessarily followed. This was very unfortunate; for, besides the mortifications they brought her, it is very probable that they prompted the vile plot that gave rise to Cardinal de Rohan's fatal error.[2]

Having enjoyed these evening promenades about a month, the Queen ordered a private concert within the colonnade featuring Pluto and Prosperine's statues.[3] Sentinels were placed at the entrances, and ordered to admit only those persons with tickets signed by my father-in-law. A fine concert was performed there . . . No music was played on the terrace. The crowd of inquisitive people, whom the sentinels kept at a distance from the enclosure went away displeased; the small number of people admitted no doubt occasioned jealousy, giving rise to offensive comments the public spread. I will not apologize for the kind of amusement the Queen indulged herself with during this and the following summer. The consequences were so lamentable that the error was surely great, but what I have said respecting these promenades' character may be relied upon as true.

By the time the season for evening walks ended, odious couplets were circulated in Paris treating the Queen in the most insulting manner . . .

Louis de Jaucourt, "Superstition" article, *Encyclopedia*, 1765

The great *Encyclopedie*, appearing in twenty-eight volumes between 1751 and 1772, featuring 71,818 articles, sought to collect human knowledge on all subjects, from philosophy and religion to government and the applied arts. Its article on "Superstition," written by French doctor Louis de Jaucourt—the enterprise's most prolific contributor, who authored over 18,000 entries—both defines the term and explains how the concept was then understood. As the Enlightenment movement sought to develop reasoned interpretations for all phenomena, "superstition" based on unproven belief and tradition appeared its antithesis. While not daring to attack religion itself, Jaucourt instead denounces overzealous fundamentalist interpretations propagating ignorance and persecution. Many Enlightenment leaders were Deists, believing God had set the universe in motion (to follow scientific laws) but then ceased intervening in human affairs. Atheism, while not explicitly endorsed, is considered preferable to zealotry. Many hoped that increasing scientific and humanistic knowledge would reduce human ignorance, preventing recourse to supernatural explanations. While most Enlightenment authors wanted to preserve religion as a way to teach morality, "superstition" became one of the major intellectual, spiritual, and political problems the movement contested.

SUPERSTITION (Metaphysics & Philosophy); all excesses of religion in general, following the ancient pagan saying:

> *Religentem esse oportet, religiosum nefas.* ["A man should be religious, not superstitious."]
>
> Aulus Gellius, vol. IV part. ix.[4]

In effect, superstition is a sort of religion, false, misled, filled with vain terrors, contrary to reason and the sane ideas one ought to have of the supreme being. Or, if you prefer, superstition is that space of enchantment or magic power that worry exercises on our spirit: unhappy daughter of the imagination, she strikes it with phantoms, dreams, and visions; it is her, Bacon says, who forged idols from vulgar, invisible specters, in days of happiness or pain, the invincible traits of love and hate.[5] She overwhelms the spirit, principally in malady or adversity; she changes good discipline and venerable customs into masquerades and superficial ceremonies. As soon as she has established deep roots in any religion, good or bad, she is capable of blocking natural light and troubling the sanest heads. Thus, this is humanity's most terrible scourge. Atheism itself (this says everything) does not destroy natural sentiments, makes no attack on the laws, nor on a people's customs; but superstition is a despotic tyrant that cedes everything to its chimeras. Its prejudices are greater than all others. An atheist is interested in public tranquility, by the love of his self-interest; but fanatical superstition, born from troubled imagination, overturns empires. . . .

Ignorance and barbarity introduced superstition, hypocrisy surrounded it with vain ceremonies, false zeal spread it, and interests have perpetuated it.

The hand of the monarch cannot go too far in chaining the monster of superstition and it is this monster, much more than irreligion (always inexcusable) that the throne must fear for its authority, and the country for its happiness.

Jean-Jacques Rousseau, *The Social Contract*, 1762

Few works had as much influence on eighteenth-century radical thought as Jean-Jacques Rousseau's *Social Contract*. Unlike John Locke or Montesquieu, Rousseau attempted not just to describe how society functioned but to prescribe an ideal state of affairs, loosely based on his native city-state of Geneva. The *Social Contract* called for direct democracy, in which all male property-holders could deliberate and vote on important matters. In an era when political parties were considered selfish factions, achieving consensus appeared necessary for a functional democratic government. Importantly, however, all involved would need to obey the majority's decision for the general good. If not, they would be "forced to be free," or cast out from society. An unorthodox, inconsistent, and often impulsive thinker, Rousseau later abandoned the more radical prescriptions of the *Social Contract* when called upon to advise Corsican and Polish constitutional projects. While it is debated how much influence Rousseau's political writings—instead of his bestselling sentimentalist literature or treatise on permissive parenting—specifically had over French Revolutionaries (particularly on Robespierre and fellow radical Jacobins during the revolution's most radical phase), Rousseau led many to imagine radical alternatives to the placid politics of Old Regime Europe.

Man is born free, but everywhere he is in chains. The more he believes himself the master of others, he becomes even more a slave than they are. How did this transformation occur? I ignore that question. What makes this legitimate? That I believe I can answer. . . .

As men cannot create new forces, but only unite and lead those already existing, they have no other means of save themselves except by forming an aggregate of the forces they can muster for resistance, to set them in play for a single motive, and bring them into concert.

This sum of forces can only be born from the agreement of many, but each man's force and liberty constitute their first instruments of preservation. How can they be engaged without harming themselves and neglecting life's necessities? This difficulty, applied to my subject, can be explained on these terms:

"Find a form of association that defends and protects with communal force the person and goods of each associated, and by which each, uniting himself with all, is only really obeying himself, thereby remaining as free as before." . . .

Let us reduce this balance to easily understandable terms. What man loses by the social contract is his natural liberty and an unlimited right to all that he could attain; what he gains is civil liberty and proprietorship of all he possesses. To not fool oneself in these compensations, one must distinguish natural liberty, which has no limits except the individual's force, from civil liberty, which is limited by the general will. Possession is only the effect of force or the right of the first occupant, while property is founded on a positive title. . . .

There is only a single law that, by its nature, requires unanimous consent: the social pact . . . When a state is instituted, residence signifies consent; inhabiting the territory means consenting to the sovereign.

Outside this primitive contract, the voice of the greatest number always obliges the others; this is a result of the contract itself. But, one asks, how can a man be free and forced to conform himself to wills unlike his own? How are opponents free while in submission to laws they did not consent to?

I respond that this is a poorly formulated question. The citizen consents to all laws, including those passed despite his opposition, even those punishing him when he breaks them. The constant will of all the state's members is the general will; they are thereby citizens and free. When one proposes a law in the people's assembly, what is asked is not precisely if they approve or reject the proposition, but whether it conforms to the general will, which is their own. Each gives their vote, which is to say their advice, afterwards, and from the voting tabulations are decided the declared general will. When thusly the advice contrary to my own carries, this proves nothing except that I was mistaken, while what I believed to be the general will was not. If my selfish advice had carried, I would have done something else than what I wanted, for then I would not have been free.

This supposes, it is true, that the general will's character is in its plurality: when it ceases to be, whatever side one takes, there will be no more liberty. . . .

For the social contract not to be an empty formula, it tacitly includes the following clause which alone gives force to the rest, that whoever refuses to obey the general will shall be required to do so by the entire body: which means nothing other than that he shall be forced to be free . . .

Louis-Sébastien Mercier, selections from *Panorama of Paris*, 1781–1788

Mercier's *Panorama of Paris*, published in nine volumes between 1781 and 1788, captures a vibrant city filled with dynamic tensions. Paris' approximately 700,000 residents lived under the patronage and surveillance of Europe's most powerful absolutist government, that over a century earlier had founded the world's first "police" force of secret undercover agents. Mercier—a playwright, pamphleteer, novelist and journalist—portrays a community ridden with suspicion, duplicity and tension, in which state repression made major revolts appear nearly "impossible," but many still feared potential breakdowns if such controls were removed. Alongside political tensions lay social ones, as the city drew both aristocratic high society and poor migrants from the countryside in great numbers, with the latter often struggling for the necessities of life and with the tensions of urban living. Yet, Parisians continued expressing themselves, sometimes heartily, in cafés, at theatres, or on the streets. While Mercier had no inkling of a coming revolution, scholars have often turned to his voluminous descriptions to explain the urban conditions that helped lead to the French Revolution's greatest uprisings.

Physiognomy of a Great City

Do you want to judge Paris' extent? Climb Notre Dame's towers. The city is round like a pumpkin; the plaster constituting two-thirds of the city's material, which is simultaneously black and white, announces that it is built of chalk and sits on chalk.[6] The continual flames rising from innumerable chimneys conceals from the eye the pointed summits of the clock towers, appearing like a cloud forming above so many mansions, whereby the city's perspiration can be perceived. . . .

I will quietly pass over its topographical position, and also the description of its edifices, monuments, and curiosities of all genres, because I am creating more of a panorama of its inhabitants' spirit and character, than of nomenclatures.

Excessive Size of the Capital

Viewed politically, Paris is too big. It is a head too large for the body of the state, but it would be more dangerous today to cut the boil than to let it subsist. It is a malady that, once rooted, becomes indestructible.

Great cities are much to absolute governments' taste, which do much to draw men there. They lure great landowners for luxuries and pleasure, while attracting crowds, like sheep into a pen . . . Altogether, Paris is an abyss . . .

I observe this city flourishing, but at the entire nation's expense. These buildings, six stories tall, filled with people, suck up the harvest and vineyard production for fifty leagues around them. These lackeys, these troubadours, these monks, these drummers of the pavement do not serve either the state or society . . .

The Spies

They are a vast mass of corruption. The police are divided in two: on one side are the spies and stool-pigeons; on the other are the roving agents, with immunity, who report the swindlers, crooks, thieves, etc. a bit like a hunter riles up the dogs against foxes and wolves.

The spies have other spies spying on them, who watch and see if they are doing their job. All reciprocally accuse each other, and devour each other for the vilest gain. It is from these appalling dregs that public order is born. . . .

Such is the admirable order reigning in Paris. A man suspected or targeted is not aware that his smallest movements are known until the moment they decide to arrest him. . . .

There are spies of the royal court, spies of the town, spies in the beds, spies in the streets, spies amongst the whores, spies amongst the wits; they are universally known as *mouchards* [flies] . . .

There was a time, under Louis XV, where the spies multiplied to such number, that it was impossible for friends who gathered together to mutually open their hearts on the issues deeply affecting them. The ministerial inquisition has set its sentinels at the door of all rooms and listeners in all cabinets; naïve confidences, made between friends and destined to die where they were heard, were punished like dangerous plots.

These odious researches have poisoned social life, depriving men of the most innocent pleasures, and transforming citizens into enemies who tremble to open up to each other.

Every man attached to the police, no matter under what denomination, can no longer be admitted into polite society, for good reason.

A quarter of servants serve as spies, and family secrets, believed most deeply hidden, are brought to the knowledge of the interested.

Government ministers have their own spies attached to them, separately from those of the police, and support them themselves. These are the most dangerous of all, because they are less suspected than the others, and most difficult to recognize. Ministers know by this method everything being said about them, but they do not profit from it. They are more concerned about ruining their enemies, to hold back their adversaries, than to take advantage of the wise part of the free and naïve notices that their multitude sends them . . .

What interests royal courts, especially our own, is that there is a degree of obscurity covering its operations. One wants to unmask what is hidden, one desires to know profoundly what is glimpsed . . . We only strongly attach ourselves to what requires great effort to penetrate.

The Night Watch

Paris' nighttime security is the work of the Night Watch and two or three hundred spies, who hit the pavement, reconnoiter, and follow suspect men. Nearly all abductions of spies are carried out at night.

The salvos heard here and there are only made to intimidate the criminals, but thereby Paris' streets are as secure at night as during the day, outside of some inevitable accidents . . .

Riots

A riot degenerating into sedition has become morally impossible. Police surveillance, the regiments of Swiss and French Guards in barracks nearby always ready to march, the Royal Household, the fortresses surrounding Paris, not counting the immense number of men attached to court interests, all seems proper for obliterating the chance of a serious uprising.

For more than fifty years, one can identify only two riots, both of which were promptly dispersed. The city has generally been tranquil since the time of the Fronde.[7] The rural police that can be deployed from all sides and the troops encircling the Ile de France region make it impossible for the seditious to rally. All maintain a calm that becomes the more assured the longer it lasts.

It is forbidden for the peasants to assemble in numbers; and where would they go? What would they do, supposing they were furious? The rural police would surround them; after the rural police would come regiments, after the regiments whole armies would arrive.

If the Parisian, in his moments of exuberance, mutinied, the immense cage he lives in would snap shut around him. Grain would be refused to him, and when the trough there is emptied, he would soon be reduced to begging for pardon and mercy.

Chancellor Maupeou marched with a weak escort to the Palace of Justice, to establish a Parlement after his own manner, on the ancient one's debris. He knew well no one would move against him . . .[8]

The cause of a sedition . . . would be soon known and extinguished. Paris is shielded from the alarm and terror that George Gordon recently caused in London.[9] . . .

Even at the theater, when standing crowds become passionate for or against a given line, or when taken by a given actor's gestures, the guard shuts up the noisy assembly, taking the side of a bad poet or flat actor, and in after some clamors, the reason of the rifle becomes supreme.

But if the People of Paris were abandoned to follow their first instincts, if they no longer felt the Night Guard on horse and foot behind them . . .

the populace, freed from the break to which they are accustomed, would abandon themselves to violence so cruel that they would not know where to stop.

It is perhaps because riots are so rare in Paris, that a serious riot (if it ever could happen) would bring alarming consequences.

Cafés

There are six to seven hundred cafés: they are the ordinary refuge of the lazy and indigent. They heat themselves there in the winter, to avoid buying wood for their homes. In some of these cafés, they hold academic sessions, judging authors and theater pieces, assigning their rank and value. Poets make their debuts there, they ordinarily make more noise, while those chased from such a calling by jeers become satirists, as the most unpitying of critics is always a misunderstood author.

Cabals for or against a work form there and become heads of party, who want nothing more than to render themselves formidable; they like nothing better than to tear apart a writer they dislike, from morning until night. Often, they have not understood him, but they always denounce, and a literary reputation needs to navigate such tempests.

In most cafés, the bragging is even more boring: it turns incessantly around the gazettes. Parisian credulity has no boundaries; it gobbles everything encountered, abusing it a thousand times over . . .

Such men arrive at the café at ten in the morning, and do not leave until eleven at night . . .

It is no longer decent to visit cafés, because this announces a lack of social connections, and an inability to frequent polite society. A café where instructed and amiable men assemble can nevertheless be preferable, by its liberty and gaiety, to the other circles that tend to be boring. . . .

Each café has its orator-in-chief. The role, in the suburbs, is taken by a tailor's boy or shoemaker's apprentice, and why not?

Markets

Paris' markets are poorly kept and disgusting. They are a chaos where all the foodstuffs are piled up haphazardly. Shabby sheds do not shield citizens' provisions from the intemperateness of the seasons. When it rains, the water falls from the roofs or drips into the baskets of eggs, fruits, vegetables, butter, etc.

The marketplaces are impracticable: their locations are small and narrow; horse-carts threaten to run the sellers over, as they negotiate prices with the peasants. . . .

The noise, the tumult is so considerable, that it takes a superhuman voice to be heard: the Tower of Babel could not offer a stranger confusion.

Twenty-five years ago, a depot for grain was built, which de-congested the market quarter a little, but this depot is quite narrow. It is suited to a third-rate town. It is insufficient for the capital's prodigious consumption. The sacks of grain are exposed to the rain . . .

Saint-Marcel Suburb

This is the neighborhood where the poorest, liveliest, and most undisciplined people of Paris live. There is more money in a single house of the Saint-Honoré suburb than in all Saint-Marcel put together.

In these dwellings, far from the city's central movements, ruined men, misanthropes, alchemists, maniacs, short-term renters, and several studious sages live, who really desire solitude and want to be entirely ignored and separated from the noisy theater quarters. . . .

Seditions and mutinies have their hidden origins in this den of obscure misery.

The houses have no other clock than the sun's passing; these men are held three centuries back from the reigning arts and manners. All private arguments become public, and a woman angry with her husband pleads her cause in the street to a tribunal of the populace, gathering all the neighbors and reciting the scandalous confessions of her man. Discussions of all natures finish with punches, while in the evening all is forgiven, when one of the two has a face covered in scratches. . . .

This suburb is the angriest, most inflammable, most querulous, and most disposed to mutiny of any neighborhood. The police are afraid of pushing this populace too far, managing them carefully, because they are capable of carrying themselves to the greatest excesses.

Abbé de Raynal, *History of the Two Indies*, Third Edition, 1780

The *History of the Two Indies* invented anti-colonialism. Europeans during earlier eras typically asserted that Europe had a civilizing mission to fulfill in the wider world (either for spreading Christianity or enlightened reason) and highlighted colonialism's advantages for economic development and statecraft. Those humanitarian tracts reporting colonial abuses typically called for better conditions and religious instruction for slaves. As abolitionism started to gain popularity, however, many began looking at colonial exploitation in a more radical light. Raynal—in a massive twelve-volume history of European overseas expansion around both the Indian and Atlantic Oceans first published in 1770, written with the un-credited aid of Denis Diderot and other philosophers—dissented from this consensus, openly condemning European colonial brutality and inhumanity. With the work a runaway bestseller, garnering over eighty printings, Raynal revised the study into a more radical Third Edition in 1780. Raynal foretold a coming race war, in which Africans would annihilate their outnumbered oppressors. While a common uprising across the colonies never materialized, Raynal was one of the few European intellectuals to anticipate the Haitian Revolution of 1791.

Nothing is more terrible than the condition of blacks across the American archipelago.[10] They begin by fixing an indelible symbol of slavery upon them by engraving with a hot iron on their arms or breast the name or mark of their oppressor. A narrow, unhealthy hut, without commodities, becomes their home. . . . Deprived of everything, they are condemned to endless work, in a burning climate, always under a ferocious conductor's whip.

Europe has developed more sane and sublime maxims of morality over the last century. The fraternity of all men is established in the most touching manner in immortal writings. We become indignant against the civil or religious cruelties of our ferocious ancestors, and look away from these centuries of blood and horror. Those of our neighbors, where barbarous men have chained them, obtain our aid and pity. Even imaginary pains bring our tears in the silence of our studies and particularly in the theater. It is only the unfortunate negroes' fatal destiny that does not interest us. We tyrannize them, we mutilate them, we burn them, we stab them, and we hear all this spoken of coldly, without emotion. The torments of the people from whom we owe our delicacies never reach our heart. . . .

Besides those differences drawn from the local colonial situations in the islands of America, each European nation has a manner of treating its slaves particular to itself. The Spaniard makes them the companions of their indolence; the Portuguese, the instruments of their debaucheries; the Dutch, the victims of their avarice. In English eyes, they are purely physical beings, which can either be used or destroyed as need be, but they never familiarize themselves with them, they never smile at them, they never talk to them. . . . The French, less proud, less disdainful, accord the Africans a type of morality, and these unfortunates, touched with the honor of seeing themselves treated like almost-intelligent creatures, appear to forget that a master impatient to make his fortune, forgetting the extent of their works, will often leave them without enough to eat.

Even the religious opinions of Europeans influence negroes' fate in America. The Protestants, who do not have the spirit of proselytism, leave them to live in Islam, or in the idolatry they were born into, under the pretext that they are incapable of keeping brothers of Christ in servitude. The Catholics believe themselves obliged to give them some instruction, to baptize them: but their charity does not extend further than the christening . . .

We will not offer proofs here to lengthen the ignominious list of those writers who use their talents to justify, by politics, what repulses morality. In a century when so many errors are courageously unmasked, it would be shameful to keep such important truths from humanity. All we have already said cannot diminish the weight of servitude . . . But in waiting for great revolutions to make the evidence of this truth felt, it is useful treat them better. Let us show in advance that there is no reason of state that can authorize slavery. Let us not worry about citing to the tribunal of light and eternal justice those governments who tolerate this cruelty, or who do not blush to make it the basis of their power.

. . . nations of Europe, hear me still. Your slaves need neither your generosity nor your counsels to break the sacrilegious yoke oppressing them. Nature speaks stronger than philosophy or interest. Already two colonies of negro fugitives are established, that treaties and force shelter from your attacks. These lightning strikes presage the thunder, and the negroes only lack a courageous enough leader to lead them to vengeance and carnage.

Where is he, this great man that nature owes to its vexed, oppressed, tormented children? Where is he? He will appear, do not doubt it, he will stand up, he will raise the sacred banner of liberty. This true signal will gather around it the companions of his infortune. More impetuous than a hurricane, they will strew about them the innumerable traces of their just resentment. Spanish, Portuguese, English, French, Dutch, all their tyrants will be delivered over to fire and the flame. America's fields will be mercilessly soaked with the blood they have long anticipated, and the bones of so many unfortunates, buried over three centuries, will shake with joy. The Old World will applaud with the New. Everywhere, they will praise the name of the heroes reestablishing the rights of the human race, everywhere they will raise trophies to their glory. Having disposed of the Black Codes, the White Code will be terrible, if the conqueror only consults the right of reprisals.

Jacques Necker, *Account Rendered to the King*, 1781

Jacques Necker's *Account Rendered* promised to be an unparalleled step towards enlightened administration. France had never previously possessed a unified budget and state finance remained a closely guarded secret. Amidst the War of American Independence, as French military expenditures grew exponentially, Necker—a Genevan Protestant banker and previous director of the French East India Company appointed to restructure the French government's poor finances—sought to increase confidence amongst lenders and the public by releasing what purported to be a thorough audit of the French treasury. Amidst the Enlightenment, economics became increasingly regarded as a science. Whereas previously moneylending had been considered an unsavory subject, unfit for nobles' concern, the national debt increasingly became a national problem. The pamphlet became a runaway bestseller, with

20,000 copies printed in several languages. However, the account Necker rendered was mostly fictitious: whereas he presented a positive outlook for state finances, in reality the state teetered on catastrophic bankruptcy. Louis XVI fired Necker in May 1781, but financial concerns remained at the forefront of French politics. After several successors also failed to reform state expenditures, the king recalled Necker to power in August 1788.

Sire, having devoted all my time and energy to serving Your Majesty since you called me to this position, I greatly esteem having a public account to render you of my works' success, showing the present state of your finances. . . .

What reward ought a servant to expect for this overview of his conduct? I have renounced such satisfaction and would have combined this new sacrifice with so many others, if I did not think such an authentic account's publicity could be infinitely useful to your Majesty's affairs. I cannot say if a similar permanent practice would not provide the greatest advantages. The obligation to enlighten all your administration would influence the first actions a Minister of Finance takes on his rightful path. Shadows and obscurity favor nonchalance; publicity, on the contrary, can only become an honor and recompense, insofar as he has felt such duties' importance and tries hard to fulfill them. . . .

In effect, if one fixes their attention on the immense credit England enjoys, and which today is her principal strength in war, one cannot entirely attribute it to their government's nature; now, whatever the monarch's authority in France might be, according to its properly defined interests, it will always respect fidelity and justice. It could be easy to forget, however, that it has the power to deviate from these principles, and it belongs to your Majesty, by his character and his virtues, to feel this truth by experience.

But there is doubtlessly another cause of England's great credit: the public notice to which the state of finances is submitted. Each year, this ledger is presented to Parliament and printed afterward. All the brokers thus regularly know the proportion maintained between revenues and expenses. They are not troubled at all by those chimerical worries and fears that are inseparable companions of obscurity.

In France, people have made a constant mystery of the state of finances. . . . It is important to found confidence on the most solid bases. I advise that in some circumstances, it is possible to profit from a veil being cast over financial affairs, to obtain amidst the disorder a mediocre and unmerited credit, but this is a fleeting advantage. Maintaining misleading illusions and favoring administrative indifference tends to be quickly followed by unfortunate undertakings, making enduring impressions that take a long time to recover from. This is not the first time that a great state displays itself, with light shone over its financial situation becoming embarrassing, but if this publicity can prevent disorder, what a service it renders! . . .

I will divide the account His Majesty has permitted me to deliver in three parts.

The first concerns the present state of finances and all the operations relative to the Royal Treasury and public credit.

The second will develop the operations that have spread important economies to the administration's advantage.

In the third, I will render account to your majesty of the general outlook, which can only have for its goal the greatest happiness of his peoples and the state's prosperity. . . .

Arthur Young, Account of a 1787 Salon Gathering, *Travels in France*, published in 1792

While visiting the Duc de la Rochefoucauld at his estate in the southern French province of Languedoc in August 1787, British travel-writer and agronomist Arthur Young experienced Old Regime high society in its last days. Young, a scientific fellow of the Royal Society in London and author of a controversial travelogue on Ireland, gave mixed opinions about the aristocracy—witnessing great cultivation, politeness, dexterous conversation, and worldly interest, but also indolence, frivolity, and a lack of respect for reason or learning. Whereas some scholars have placed elite "salons"—female-led elite discussion groups—at the center of Enlightenment sociability, more recent scholars (following Young's lead) have argued that they more commonly functioned as social circles for elites seeking to advance themselves in high society. Although some notable French writers served as guests at such gatherings, typically the mood and conversation remained light. Entertainment appeared more central to these gatherings than philosophical inquiry. The growing political fermentation in France had not yet altered this gathering. Young continued his travels across France until 1790, seeing the Revolution develop firsthand.

The ramble of the morning finished, we return in time to dress for dinner, at half after twelve or one: then adjourn to the drawing room of madam de la Rochefoucauld, or to the countess of Grandval alternately, the only ladies who have apartments large enough to contain the whole company. None are excluded; as the first thing done, by every person who arrives, is to pay a morning visit to each party already in the place; the visit is returned, and then every body is of course acquainted with these assemblies, which last till the evening is cool enough for walking. There is nothing in them but cards, trick-track, chess, and sometimes music; but the great feature is cards . . . In the evening, the company splits into different parties, for the promenade, which lasts till half an hour after eight; supper is served at nine: there is, after it, an hour's conversation in the camber of one of our ladies; and this is the best part of the day—for the chat is free, lively and unaffected; and uninterrupted, unless on a post-day, when the duke has such packets of papers and pamphlets, that they turn us all into politicians. . . .

What is a man good for after his silk breeches and stockings are on, his hat under his arm, and his head *bien poudrè*?[11]—Can he botanize in a watered meadow?—Can he clamber the rocks to mineralize?—Can he farm with the peasant and the ploughman?—He is in order for the conversation of the ladies, which to be sure is in every country, but particularly in France, where the women are highly cultivated, an excellent employment; . . . I am induced to make this observation, because the noon dinners are customary all over France, except by persons of considerable fashion at Paris. They cannot be treated with too much ridicule or severity, for they are absolutely hostile to every view of science, to every spirited exertion, and to every useful pursuit in life.

If I may hazard a remark on the conversation of French assemblies, from what I have known here, I should praise them for equanimity but condemn them for insipidity. All vigour of thought seems so excluded from expression, that characters of ability and of inanity meet nearly on a par: tame and elegant, uninteresting and polite, the mingled mass of communicated aside has powers neither to offend nor instruct; where there is much polish of character there is little argument; and if you neither argue nor discuss, what is conversation?—Good temper, and habitual ease, are the first ingredients in private society; but wit, knowledge, or originality, must break their even surface into some inequality of feeling, or conversation is like a journey on an endless flat.

FIGURE 2.1 In Times Past, Even the Most Useful Were Trampled Underfoot. *1789. © Christophel Fine Art / Universal Group / Getty Images.*

One of the many allegorical images capturing the Third Estate's plight during the months preceding the Estates General, "In Times Past" shows a nobleman and priest standing atop a rock crushing a commoner. The heavy boulder, representing the financial burdens commoners had to bear but nobles did not, reads "Taille [a property tax falling on commoners]," "Taxes," and "Corvées [unpopular forced work-gang labor required of many peasants]." Though the commoner is well-dressed, the rural setting suggests the experience's near-universality. Smarting at the grievances they had long endured, over a short series of months in 1789, the Third Estate would successfully combat the structural inequalities that had long enabled the privileged orders' dominance.

2

Towards the Estates General

Once Louis XVI approved the calling of an Estates General in August 1788, the three estates of the French nation—clergy, nobility, and commoners—began organizing and angling for power in the new assembly. All three orders had pretensions for leadership: the nobility believed it their natural and traditional role to command, the commoners asserted they could now make their collective power felt, while the clergy hoped they could arbitrate compromises (or, in the case of many parish priests, throw their weight behind the Third Estate).

Needing to build consensus for tax reforms that would eliminate noble and clerical privileges—previously, high social status had meant tax exemptions for "those who prayed" and "those who fought"—Louis XVI had called an Assemblies of Notables in 1787. Rather than holding open elections for representatives, however, the king's ministers hand-picked individuals believed favorable to their interests. Facing public outcry, both assemblies wound up vetoing the royal proposals. Attempts to force new royal tax edicts through without approval led to their being vetoed by France's regional supreme court system of Parlements. Revolts spread when the king attempted to override their decisions. Support for absolutism fell as French groups increasingly demanded constitutional limits on royal power, especially regarding unpopular finance proposals.

The Estates General's calling led to a great political awakening throughout the kingdom. This was exacerbated by unnecessary uncertainty over the format of the Assembly: the crown doubled the size of Third Estate representation, but left uncertain whether voting would be conducted by order (leaving the Commons with one vote of three) or by head (giving them fifty percent of the votes, a likely majority when combined with liberal nobles and parish clergymen). Despite attempts by the Parlements and a second Assembly of Notables to decree voting by order (ruining each group's popularity with most commoners), the Third Estate persisted in agitating for expanded representation. The moment appeared an opportunity not to be wasted. Pamphlet publishing skyrocketed, while public cafés and squares became sites of debate. The call for elections had included the request for each district to compose a *Cahier de Doléances* (Statement of Grievances) describing what they thought was wrong in France and how they would propose to reform it. Content analyses of the *Cahiers* is difficult—as no one knew how ambitiously it would be prudent to frame their proposals. Yet 84% of surviving Third Estate Cahiers wanted to abolish at least some aspects of the feudal system. For most French people, debates hinged on how many privileges ought to be overturned, rather than if changes ought to be made.

By spring 1789, ongoing debates led the Third Estate to radicalize. The slights and condescension of an unequal society increasingly weighed upon many politicized Frenchmen. The old order, particularly as it showed signs of cracking from within, came to appear unsustainable. The Third Estate, as pamphleteer and then Estates General representative Emmanuel-Joseph Sieyès memorably exaggerated, had been seen as nothing, while the productive contributions of the two first estates seemed small indeed. While no one fully conceived the many forms the French Revolution would take, a growing panoply of proposals for major changes circulated. Even amongst the privileged orders, many believed political power would take significantly different forms than before. Many French people who had not considered themselves broadly political before the revolutionary ferment became ready to risk their lives to secure major changes to the government by summer 1789.

Letters from the Marquis de Lafayette to George Washington, August and September 1787

In 1787, the massive national debt became publicly known, as the crown engaged in increasingly desperate measures to get new tax revenues. That February, the King called the Assembly of Notables, composed of hand-picked representatives of the Nobility and Clergy, hoping to convince them to surrender some of their tax exemptions. Noble reformers like the Marquis de Lafayette, a young military officer who had recently gained renown in the War of American Independence, influentially demanded full representation for all orders in a national assembly. With the nobility claiming to be the bulwark preserving the French people from royal despotism, all reform proposals were rejected by May. The crown next tried to force new taxes through by royal edict, but had their measures rejected by the regional supreme courts known as Parlements, who asserted the new taxes violated the rights and privileges of the King's subjects. Across the first year of what historians often refer to as the "Pre-Revolution," the government veered into a crisis of legitimacy, as the near-bankrupt absolute monarchy faced non-compliance on all fronts. To ambitious young reformers like Lafayette, opportunities—some inspired by recent revolutions abroad—appeared close at hand.

Paris, August 3, 1787

My Dear General,

I have received your first letter from Philadelphia with the greatest satisfaction. . . . I was not surprised to learn that you attended the Convention. Your refusal would have shocked me. The existence of the United States itself perhaps depends upon this gathering and you know how much your name adds weight to its decisions.[1] . . ..

The spirit of liberty spreads far in this country; liberal ideas are propagated from one end of the kingdom to the other. Our Assembly of Notables was a beautiful thing, except for those who conceived it.—You know that the personal quarrel I engaged in related to the gifts accorded to the favored, at the public's expense.[2] This gained me a great number of powerful and inveterate enemies, but been very well received by the nation. . . .

Presently, the Parlement, animated by the Notables' example, strongly resists the passing of new taxes. It will be forced to register the edicts, but it is good they have demanded a general assembly of the nation, and although this will not be realized immediately, I predict it will occur since the assemblies presently established in each province have acquired their proper importance and the feeling of their power. I hope the Protestant issue will be soon worked out according to the motion I made in the Notables on the eve of our closing.[3] . . .

Paris, October 9, 1787

. . . France's affairs remain in an always-indecisive state. An enormous deficit must be filled with new taxes and the nation is left to pay those they have not voted upon. Ideas of liberty have been propagated rapidly since the American Revolution. The Assembly of Notables has ignited combustible materials. Since it has been taken from us, we have needed to fight via the Parlements, which although simple courts of justice are charged with registering edicts and will not sanction any tax not consented to by the nation. Several of them have been exiled. A war of writings has followed. Parisians booed the Comte d'Artois when he went to carry out the King's orders.[4] They burnt several ministers in effigy. Finally, the Parlement has foolishly consented to an arrangement by which the two proposed new taxes are retired, so long as they register an increase of the old ones. The Provincial Assemblies have had their first meetings; the rules the king gave subordinated them entirely to the two Intendants of His Majesty in each province; we complained mightily and the regulation was changed.[5] You see that the King is often obliged to back down, without most people being thereby satisfied. The displeasure is so great that even the queen can no longer go to Paris, for fear of being poorly received. After everything that has occurred over the last six months, we at least managed to set in everyone's head that the King does not have the right to tax the nation, and that nothing of this sort can be stipulated except by a national assembly.

The King is all-powerful in France; he has all the means to contain, punish, and corrupt. The ministers are carried by inclination and believe themselves obliged by duty to perpetuate despotism. The court is filled with swarms of vile and effeminate courtesans; their spirits are enervated by the influence of women and the love of pleasure; the inferior classes are submerged in ignorance. On the other hand, French genius is lively, entrepreneurial, and inclined to despise those who govern. Minds begin to enlighten by the works of philosophers and the example of other nations. The French are easily excited by a noble sentiment of honor, and if they are slaves, they do not like being so. The inhabitants of distant provinces are disgusted by despotism and the court's expenses. There is a strange contrast between the oriental power of the king, the cares of ministers to preserve this intact, the intrigues and servility of a race of courtesans on one part, and on the other the general liberty to think, speak, and write despite the spies, the Bastille, and the regulations on bookstores. The spirit of opposition and patriotism spreads in the first class of the nation, including the first personal servants of the king, mixed with the worry of losing their positions and pensions; the mocking insolence of townspeople, always ready, it's true, to disperse when faced by a detachment of guards, and the more serious discontents of the people of the countryside; all these ingredients mixed together brings us little by little without a great convulsion to independent representation, and consequently, a diminished royal authority.

Gazette de Leyde Article on the Day of the Tiles, June 20, 1788

With the French government exercising censorship over the domestic newspaper press, many illicitly purchased smuggled newspapers from abroad. The *Gazette de Leyde*, headquartered in the Dutch town of Leiden but published in French, was the most popular, with a circulation exceeding ten thousand. Carrying the masthead *Extraordinary News from Diverse Places*, receiving letters from across Europe and the colonial world, while regularly reaching readers from St. Petersburg to Philadelphia, Lima, and Bombay, the *Gazette* featured frank discussion of the major issues facing the era's governments. As French unrest surrounding the Parlements and debates over the Estates General's format worsened across spring and summer 1788, the *Gazette* published numerous reports. Whereas *nouvelles à la main* (handwritten newsletters) had traditionally been a way of passing censored public news, the *Gazette* brought such intelligence to a wide audience. In Grenoble, a regional capital in the Alps on France's eastern frontier, an attempt to banish the Parlement of Dauphiné led to the "Day of the Tiles" on June 7, with insurgents taking to the streets and rooftops (some throwing roofing materials at the soldiers) to stop the judges from leaving. As seen here, the protest sought audiences in Paris and Versailles, trying to convince the government to change policy. Though still fighting largely for their traditional regional privileges, a growing spirit of popular insubordination worsened the governing crisis.

Letter from Paris, June 13, 1788.

The resistance Dauphiné brings against the new edicts is even more violent than the opposition in Brittany.[6]—A courier, dispatched from Grenoble by Monsieur the Duc de Clermont-Tonnerre, arrived here yesterday.[7] It was easy to perceive that he brought unfortunate news, confirmed by a second courier arriving four to five hours afterwards. Everyone was waiting for information, which they gave. The King's Ministers were called for as soon as it was announced that a revolt had erupted in Grenoble. Here is how the men in a position to know the details have recounted this sad event:

"The Commander in Chief received orders to exile the Parlement, but could not execute them without the people suspecting as much. They gathered in crowds before the magistrates' mansions, resolving to not let them leave town. The troops tried to disperse this motley group, but the most audacious climbed all the town's steeples and sounded the alarm bells. Peasants nearby, particularly the mountaineers, descended at this signal, numbering three to four thousand men: they entered town, some forcing the gates, which had been closed, while the townspeople aided others, opening several for them. The crowds, swelled by this reinforcement, then sought to arm themselves, trying to force open the Arsenal, but they were repulsed. Another group went to insult the Governor's Mansion: the apartments of the Commander and the Secretary were pillaged and sacked. From there, the rebels continued to the courthouse: the gates would have been forced, if the commander had not been pressured to surrender the keys, which he had kept since the new laws' registration. The people wanted to see their magistrates sit in session and none could refuse this invitation, or (to put it better) this order. The most mutinous, lacking arms, which they had not been able to seize from the Arsenal, took from their own homes or those of others all the guns, sabers, and swords they could find. Thus armed, they had no problem firing first on the King's Troops. The soldiers, since further indulgence would have exposed them to being smashed into pieces, repulsed force with force, and unfortunately an excess of blood was spilt. . . ."

"To avoid a greater effusion of blood, the commander judged it useful to suspend executing the King's orders and not insist on the Parlement's departure until he received new orders from the Court. That is what the two couriers came to receive. The second announced the departure of a third to follow, who will arrive today. We impatiently wait for private letters to give us more details on this strange revolt."

Statement of Grievances of the Secular and Regular Clergy of Forcalquier, April 7, 1789

The King convoked elections for Estates General deputies in January 1789, leading to debates within all three orders over the assembly's objectives and purview. The First Estate, constituting the Catholic clergy, appeared well-positioned to arbitrate between the demands of the nobility and commoners. The grievance statement drawn by the clergy of Forcalquier, a rural district in the Alpine mountains of upper Provence in southeastern France, was in many respects characteristic of nationwide trends in the clerical cahiers. Forcalquier's clergy were reformist on many issues: they supported lessening the financial burdens on commoners, broadcast their willingness to pay additional taxes, showed enthusiasm for reforming the ecclesiastical hierarchy, and sought to better help the poor. Yet, in other respects, they remained conservative and even authoritarian, calling for the strengthening of the Church. They demanded state repression against those who deviated from Catholic teaching, and called for bans on impious printed material and gambling be upheld, alongside strengthened enforcement of mandated holiday observances and the clerical monopoly over formal education. Enlightened skepticism appeared anathema to the clergymen, who wanted the state to remain active in preventing the diffusion of such ideas. Like each of the other orders, the clergy optimistically supported certain reforms, but hoped the Estates General would augment their own power.

Touched by the troubles afflicting his people, Louis XVI, the best, most just, most sensible of kings, calls his subjects to his throne. He wants to lower himself to the level of the least of you to hear your voice, receive your councils, search within his heart for the calm he is privileged to possess, and through the mutual confidence of a reciprocal love between the sovereign and his subjects, of the father with his children, bring the promptest remedy to the troubles afflicting the state. He asks with goodness the wishes and grievances of his peoples, seeking how to assure public happiness. Filled with sentiments of respect, love and recognition for so charitable a prince, the members of the clergy, who form this district's first order, have determined to approach the foot of the throne, via the deputies who will be elected for the Estates General. The present statement of grievances they have adopted displays their zeal for religion, the needs of the peoples, the interest of their order and their love for the fatherland.

RELIGION

The first object this assembly's members concern themselves with is religion. Afflicted by the progress of incredulity and deprivation of morals they regard as the source of the troubles saddening France, they humbly beg His Majesty and the Estates General to interest themselves in this important object, to stop the torrent of impiety, to maintain the dogmas and morality of our holy religion, the firmest supporter and the glory of the monarchy.

Our wishes in this regard are that impiety cease to triumph; that it carries at least the penalty of being shamed and ignored; that the friends of religion be treated as the kingdom's best citizens, and that they receive preference in the distribution of honors and recompense.

We see with sadness that there is no more respect for holy days, for the house of the Lord, for the sacred mysteries. The laws of the state, for such important matters, are almost entirely unenforced. We want them executed, as well as those against gambling and the cabarets that inevitably lead to impiety, indigence, and all vices.

DISCIPLINE

The liberty of the press, always harmful—especially in matters of religion, morals, and subordination—cries out for modification, so that it does not degenerate into licentiousness. The evils produced by bad books are inconceivable; this assembly's unanimous wish is for impious and libertine libels to be carefully proscribed. . . .

CONTRIBUTIONS

We cannot speak without emotion of the unanimity with which all the clergy of this assembly has testified their desire to contribute to every tax the Estates General will consent to, according to its members, in the same proportion as the other subjects of the King. Bishops, abbots, chapters, priors, parish priests, all support aiding the people, and showing obedience to the sovereign's will.

Our Estates General deputies, in bringing to the foot of the throne our sincere testimony of respectful submission, will also manifest our desire that the considerable debts the clergy has contracted to meet the state's needs be insured and progressively paid off in the manner least onerous to taxpayers.

BISHOPHRICS

His Majesty will be beseeched to form a Council of Conscience to enlighten him on the choice of Church ministries, and to favor, in the appointment of bishops and other ecclesiastical positions, service and merit more than birth.

The Estates General will solicit a law for bishoprics to be only given to those ecclesiastics useful to the Church, with a law renewing the ban on holding multiple dioceses, which if common practice is always contrary to the wise disposition of canons and the good of society.

Bishops' residence, as necessary as it is neglected, will be strongly recommended, and those absent from their diocese will be obliged to not lose sight of the local poor. . . . .

EDUCATION

Vice-ridden education has brought into our midst the destruction of morals. Our Estates General deputies will advocate the necessity of schools in village and country parishes. From their first years, we will set into young men's hands all the precepts of religion, simply and clearly developed, so that in learning to read, they will learn to render unto their God, to their fatherland, to their sovereign, to their parents, to all men, what they should.

Experience has made known how much the brothers of Christian schools are successful in this aspect of teaching.

The secondary schools and universities are worthy subjects of our grievances. The teaching, the instructors, the administration, all needs reform. The Estates General will be beseeched to establish more severe discipline and surer methods for improving studies.

The government will choose able persons, friends of religion and the fatherland, to charge with composing elementary books for uniform public education. . . .

Those girls who, in the diverse orders of citizens, need education, will be assigned to nuns. . . .

NUNS

The female religious, deputies to this assembly, in voting for common tax rules with all the other orders, have desired:[8]

1. That the *oblat* and other ten-percent taxes be suppressed;[9]
2. To have representatives freely chosen themselves in all the assemblies at the national, provincial, municipal and ecclesiastical levels;
3. That existing agreements be observed in everything concerning the regular clergy.[10]
4. That rural nunneries not be further exposed to the harassment of tax collectors. . . .

REFORMS

The people are overcharged, but taxes are necessary. Every good Frenchman in their heart desires that the national debt be repaid and eliminated. We ask for the lessening of taxes weighing disproportionately on poor people . . . the incredible and ruinous rights of domains, of customs.[11] The King does not know that his subjects cannot make contracts, without exposing themselves to ruin. If he was informed, would he suffer the impudent brigandage of the Farmers-General employees? Would he let stand the tariffs that torment our commerce, which chain our transportation?

Our deputies will obtain from our prince's good heart the removal of the *gabelle* and sagacious precautions against the excessive price of grains that, in many parts of the kingdom, and at this moment in Provence, overwhelm, blind and destroy the indigent class.[12]

Another of the kingdom's most pressing needs is judicial reform in both civil and criminal law. Attention surely will be paid to this important object, and we will have the consolation to see the statutes abridged and simplified, limiting detours into chicanery, which make such proceedings interminable. . . .

THE POOR

Parish priests are the fathers of the poor, whose sad state merits attention here. . . . Beggary is a terrible scourge: many have long spoke of making it illegal in France. Yet will there finally be an effective method of doing so, dictated by sage political thinking, which respects the rights of both religion and humanity?

The working day-laborer, the poor widow caring for her children, have no other resources but their pastors' charity. Our representatives will be our voices, and obtain aid for the unfortunate in all their difficulties. . . .

CONCLUSION

To these ends, Estates General deputies will carry and deposit at the foot of the throne, with the present cahier, the respectful engagements we contract to raise all our hands to the sky, and form, at the base of altars, the most ardent wishes for our charitable monarch, for the minister who as France's friend zealously occupies himself with the nation's happiness, the Estates General's success, the throne's glory and the prosperity of all the state's orders.

Statement of Grievances of the Nobility of La Rochelle, March 26, 1789

France's nobility, despite the growing threats to their order's privileges across the Pre-Revolution, considered the political crisis an opportunity. Most believed their order to be the natural arbiters of political power and thought that adept maneuvering in the crisis would end with the rollback of centuries of royal incursions on their privileges. The nobility of La Rochelle—a prosperous trading port and traditional dissident center of French Protestantism—portrayed themselves as reasonable and enlightened while simultaneously remaining proud of their status and traditions. The French "Constitution" for them consisted of the many concessions their ancestors had won from royal authority over centuries, and "liberty" in the unconstrained enjoyment of their own privileges and property. Rather than seeking to overturn precedent, they hoped to use centuries of negotiated compacts to fully restore their ancient chartered rights, which they believed would restore the French state's equilibrium. Some concessions, however, were proposed to the commoners: like the Forcalquier clergy, La Rochelle's nobility were willing to sacrifice tax exemptions to maintain their other privileges. Beyond taxation, local nobles hoped most concessions would come at the expense of church and monarch: the *cahier* attacks Catholicism's monopolies, demands greater freedoms of expression, and calls for limiting state powers of arbitrary imprisonment.

Amidst the state's misfortunes, a charitable prince calls his subjects to work with him for France's regeneration. There is great hope: the only need is to resurrect the proper constitution to remedy the evils subjugating it.

The French are so attached to their King, so convinced of the breadth of powers confided in him, that they have never permitted themselves to raise the slightest doubt about the authority they have given him. But, they have not forgotten that between the sovereign's powers and the nation's rights there exists no incompatibility, insofar as these rights, though long misunderstood, are imprescriptible in their nature and possess this constitutive principle: that the general interest is every society's first law.

The general interest extends over three objects.

1. The conservation of existence.
2. The conservation of liberty.
3. The conservation of properties, which naturally follows, and is the only means to enjoy the existence of liberty.

Such are the unique goals that the laws of all governments must serve. . . .

The monarchy's fundamental principle is that its constitutive laws result from the people's consent and their agreement with the King's will . . . We do not worry about invoking this principle. It has elevated the throne and what, for French happiness, insures the scepter between the fingers of our august sovereign.

It is a second truth written in our social contract and engraved in all the monuments of our history that no fiscal law can be executed without the prior consent of the taxpayers legally convoked and assembled, and approved by the prince. . . .

GENERAL DEMANDS

We declare the nation cannot be imposed upon without its consent, that this consent is absolutely necessary, and nothing can supersede it. Taxes and public contributions cannot ever be decided and enacted except after acts of legislation. All the national constitution's articles must be decided by the Estates General and sanctioned by the King. . . . .

The Estates General must audit and verify the public debt's amount; one of the assembly's first jobs is to consolidate this debt, guaranteeing in the nation's name that the principal, interest, and back payments of the recognized debt, as well as the reimbursements stipulated over fixed terms, will be henceforth and forever rendered punctually on their due date. For no reason, no matter the circumstance, can there be the smallest delay in payments. . . .

Taxes of any nature must be supported by all the state's orders; those affecting real estate must be direct, proportional, and unrelated to a person's standing. . . .

The order asks that the reduced stipends of parish priests, and the parishes of modest revenue be augmented to at least 1,500 *livres*. Why are the priests, pastors of divine right, deprived of the legitimate subsistence due to them? They alone take the heat and carry the weight of the day, in all the pains of their ministry. Meanwhile, those profiting from their work, those in rich monasteries, who have little interaction with the people, are those to whom the farmers give the first fruits of their labor. . . .

The order asks that the promptest measures be taken to reform the Criminal Code. While waiting for this useful change, the accused should be given a defense council, as in civil cases. We ask the arraignment be conducted publicly, that all arrests be made on fixed charges, to the end that current procedures' advantages or disadvantages be demonstrated by experience. . . .

The order asks that the Estates General abolish all privileged bodies, corporations or communities, every particular honorific, all evocation contrary to the national constitution, but with an indemnity accorded to those whose businesses will be reduced by this suppression. . . .

The order asks that all letters and private writings, when passing via the postal service, be treated as a sacred and inviolable trust; that all inquiries tending to carry the slightest menace, direct or indirect, to this trust be abolished forever; and that postal policing expenses be employed for useful objects.

The order beseeches His Majesty to accord freedom of the press, modified by the laws' wisdom. . . .

The order is infinitely convinced the Estates General cannot do everything in their first assembly, however long it must last. The most dangerous course would be to try to simultaneously remedy everything complained of. The proper choice of things to carry out immediately, versus those which ought only to be prepared, will be the most challenging choice to which an august assembly must apply its wisdom.

The order desires that the Estates General closely consider their views on the abuses about which they believe reforms must be made; that they depose, to this end, their thoughts in the Provincial Estates, that they charge them with conceiving ideas, developing projects, advancing their works, and consulting public opinion. . . .

The order asks that local elections be held for the Aunis lands independent of any other province.[13]

The order requests their number of representatives to the Estates General be double that of the clergy, and that the deputies to the three orders be, in the future, in the following proportion: one for the clergy, two for the nobility, three for the Third Estate.[14] It asks that this proportion be precisely followed in formulating the Provincial Estates.[15] . . .

That His Majesty be beseeched to promulgate a type of military constitution as wise as it is enlightened and that it might be permanent: perpetual changes are ruinous to the state, discouraging the troops who never form more than a new militia. . . .

GENERAL REQUEST

View of the nation.

Caring for the people is a serious occupation of the state; caring for the poor occupies all men. If it is difficult to find in the historical record an example of such a lengthy calamity, as terrible as that of which we currently discover the cruel effects, it is difficult to find a circumstance in which charity and humanity have been displayed with a more universal energy. Making a grievance article on this subject would outrage the nation's sentiments, but there must be more than relief given to the unfortunate . . .

PARTICULAR INSTRUCTION GIVEN BY THE ORDER OF THE NOBILITY TO THEIR DEPUTY TO THE ESTATES GENERAL . . .

As the Estates General's first order of business will be if voting is done by order or by head; as this question cannot be decided by the Estates General because, to decide this, one formation or the other must be first adopted. This order believes representatives ought to supplement their powers to those their compatriots lack. After having clearly enunciated their view that, following the ancient usages, one ought to vote by order, they are willing to consent to voting by head on all issues concerning taxes and fiscal laws, but maintain that everything concerning the constitution, the laws, and police regulations should be deliberated only by order. Their instructions are so precise and formal on this point, that they expressly order their deputy to protest and renew his protestations, without ever retiring from the assembly, every time ministerial authority, or the plurality of voices, even in the noble order, determine or consent to deliberations by head on issues not concerning taxes or fiscal issues.

This order is intimately convinced that France cannot exist without a monarchy, a monarchy with distinctions of orders or ranks, and that the kingdom's two first orders will cease to exist if they are confounded with the third and deprived of the distinctions acquired from the establishment of the monarchy. These two orders, in sacrificing all financial privileges in matters of taxation, in submitting themselves to all the costs necessary for bringing general good to the kingdom, reserve to themselves the rights essentially belonging to their station. They are unable to, and never will be able to, deprive themselves of the honorific privileges of which the maintenance is one of the monarchy's surest guarantors.

In a case where urgent need and the imperious law of necessity requires prompt and spontaneous aid, in this single circumstance, after a rigorous examination made by the Estates General of the reasons for its necessity, but never because of ministerial request or excuse, this order authorizes its deputy to consent to an *octroi* or a very limited loan, which could be accorded and fixed by the Estates General.[16] Excepting this sole case, this order expressly enjoins its deputy, as it is prescribed by this statement of requests and grievances, to not occupy himself with subsidies, before the constitution's principles and basis are determined by the Estates General and sanctioned by the King.

Statement of Grievances of the Third Estate of the District of Guéret, March 21, 1789

Even in the rocky volcanic mountain soil of the Massif Central, a region poorly connected with France's commercial centers, the Estates General's possibilities took deep root amongst the Third Estate. The District of Guéret's Statement of Grievances includes lively resentments against a tax system they felt disproportionally oppressed them, and at a government appropriations system that gave greater financing to more privileged areas nearby. Nevertheless, the Cahier also conveys a real sense of optimism in the Estates General's possibilities: they asserted a new order of equal opportunity to be close at hand, that could feature freedom of the press, fair taxation, and representative government. While calling for the end of noble privilege and confiscation of some Catholic property, Guéret's Third Estate nevertheless hoped to sway moderates with compensation for lost feudal rights, and the re-investment of clerical land revenues in parish priest salaries and church charities. Those debating the cahier concurrently betrayed their own privileged position within the Third Estate, calling for the elimination of common lands used by peasants so investors could increase their productivity. Despite the many interests and obstacles at play, it is difficult not to be struck by the confidence of this provincial Third Estate assembly as they considered how to reform France.

This province's Third Estate, filled with love and respect for the best of kings, carries to the foot of the throne the firm resolution to always remain united with the assembled nation's general views.

A topography spiked with mountains, an arid soil whose produce is soaked by taxes, makes it impossible for them to refuse means of working towards the public good. Their zeal will sustain them.

They could find plenty of grievances in their particular needs. But convinced that the union of the French will open the floodgates of public cooperation, establish the state's prosperity, and assure its constitution, they will only permit themselves some reflections relative to the general interest.

The province's deputies will make their best efforts to determine the Estates General's format, so their constitution can be determined and their periodic reunion irrevocably fixed.

They will ask that voting be counted by head, with the exception of circumstances in which the general interest calls for each order to give their opinions separately.

They will give their attention, in both their own order's and general assemblies, to conserve to the Third Estate the character of free men.

After occupying themselves with individual liberty, the most important thing, they will solicit that of the press.

They will ask that ministers be made accountable to the nation; nothing can better inspire them with confidence and assure their happiness.

The deputies will solicit the assembled Estates to work together to simplify taxes. This is the way to lighten the burden, but they should not to make any changes until the national constitution is established.

They must spread over the three orders all financial charges and contributions, without distinction or privilege, in taking the necessary precautions so that the capitalists support in a just proportion the public duty, to the end that the burden does not entirely weigh on the farmer and the businessman.

To end the Crown Domain's privileges and attribute to those there engaged non-transferrable property rights, financed at market prices.

To place on the open market the wealth of suppressed religious orders for liquidating the public debt, after such status is verified by the Estates. . . .

The deputies demand the suppression of salt-taxes, internal customs duties, and other interior restrictions. It is the nation's general view that they should not be replaced, even if circumstances demand their revenue be substituted by such means as the Estates General decides. . . .

They ask for the end of paying for municipal offices, to give communities the chance to govern themselves, by choosing their own officers.

The deputies beg His Majesty to advise in conjunction with the Estates General on the best means of distributing prompt justice regarding spending. . . .

Inalienable lordly rights and real forms of servitude have already been judged odious by the wisdom of the King's council, it will be necessary to solicit a law that authorizes buying out such privileges, in indemnifying the lords with money or a rent surcharge, following the regulations made by the Estates General.

It will be equally useful to abolish lordly monopolies on windmills, as present agreements enable fraud.

The dividing of common lands deserves to be considered. They include much terrain only offering minimal pasture. It would thus be in the general interest to develop some for agriculture and turn some into woodland.

The upper and lower Marche ought to only have a single unified government. It would be useful to solicit the establishment of common Estates for the province, to unite Combraille with the free lands.

In any case, the disunion of the upper Marche with the Bourbonnais is an issue of the greatest importance due to the disparities between local governments.

The Marche is overcharged with taxes, while the Bourbonnais province has found a pretext to free itself from the salt tax. The *corvées* annually undertaken in the Marche annually amount to around 100,000 *livres*, which only serves to improve the Bourbonnais roads. It is also in this last province where government indemnities and gratifications are distributed.

The deputies want to see parish priests' material conditions improved, asking they receive increased salaries from profits from the sale of ecclesiastical lands . . .

They will solicit the establishment of schools and hospitals, asking the revenues from suppressed religious houses be applied in the same province . . .

They ask also that the Third Estate be admitted to all positions and military grades, as well as to all charges and levels of the magistracy.

Having made the above statement, the Third Estate, filled with confidence in the wisdom and enlightenment of the deputies it has chosen, gives them general and sufficient powers to propose, debate, advise, and consent to all that could concern their estate's needs, the reform of abuses, the establishment of a fixed and durable order in all parts of the administration, and to employ the most efficacious means to obtain redress for the grievances heretofore explained, with specific attention to what this assembly has hereby decided, this twenty-first day of March, 1789.

Statement of Grievances of the Third Estate of Paris, 1789

Belatedly composing their Grievance Statement with the Estates General set to begin, the Paris Third Estate captured the optimism of a political movement coming to sense its potential. Paris' general assembly demanded a written constitution, as decided upon by the Estates General, that would give the French people permanent representation and reduce the King to the role of a constitutional monarch. Even more striking, they proposed a Declaration of Rights considering—not unlike recent American state declarations or that the French National Assembly would approve the following summer—that "all men are equal in rights," alongside enshrining such principles as no taxation without representation, freedom of religion, due process before the law, and a (mostly) free press. A later section calls for extensive municipal autonomy and, daringly, asks for Paris to become the permanent site for future Estates General meetings. Though it is uncertain how much of this programme Paris' electors expected to quickly achieve, one finds here many of the animating principles of the revolution to come.

The General Assembly of the Electors of the Third Estate of the City of Paris, vested with their powers, before proceeding to choosing representatives, express their regrets for having tardily convened, which has forced it to speed up its operations.

As Frenchmen, the electors will occupy themselves with the nation's rights and interests; as citizens of Paris they will present their specific demands. . . .

PREMIMINARY OBSERVATIONS

We ask our representatives to ceaselessly refuse everything that could offend the dignity of free citizens, who are coming to exercise the nation's sovereign rights.

Public opinion appears to have recognized the necessity of deliberating by head, to correct the inconveniences of distinction by order, make public-spiritedness predominate, and facilitate the adoption of good laws.

The representatives of the city of Paris remind themselves of the firmness they must maintain on this point; they regard it as a rigorous right, the object of a special mandate.

They are expressly ordered not consent to any subsidy, to any loan, should a declaration of the rights of the nation not be passed into law, and that the first constitutional bases not be agreed upon otherwise.

After fulfilling this first necessity, they will proceed to verifying the public debt and its consolidation.

They will demand every object of significant interest be entered twice into deliberation, at intervals proportional to the question's importance, and not be decided except by the absolute majority of voices, which is to say over half of all votes cast.

DECLARATION OF RIGHTS.

In every political society, all men are equal in rights.

All power emanates from the nation and cannot be exercised except through its happiness.

The general will makes the law; public force assures its execution.

The nation alone can concede taxation: it has the right to determine the quota, to limit its duration, to alter it, to designate its implementation, to audit it, and publish its results.

Laws only exist to guarantee each citizen their property and personal security.

All property is inviolable. No citizen can be arrested or punished without a legal judgment.

No citizen, even a solder, can be impeached without judgment.

Every citizen has the right to be admitted to all employments, professions, and honors.

Natural civil and religious liberty belongs to each man: their personal security, their absolute independence of every other authority except the law, excludes all research into their opinions, their speech, their writings and their actions, insofar as they do not trouble public order or harm another's rights.

In consequence of the declaration of the rights of the nation, our representatives expressly demand the abolition of personal servitude, without any indemnity; of legal servitude, via indemnifying their owners; of forced militia service; of all extraordinary commissions; of the violation of public law in the letters confined to the postal services; and of all exclusive privileges . . .

Following these principles, freedom of the press ought to be accorded, under the condition that authors sign their works and the publisher answers for them, with both responsible after publication.

The declaration of these natural rights, both civil and political, such as will be decided in the Estates General, will become the national charter and the basis of the French Government.

CONSTITUTION

In the French Monarchy, legislative power belongs to the nation, in conjunction with the king; to the king alone belongs the executive power.

Taxes can only be established by the nation.

The Estates General will be periodically held once every three years, not counting extraordinary meetings.

They will never separate without indicating their next session's time and place, and the season for their primary assemblies that will proceed to new elections.

On the fixed day, these assemblies will be convoked.

Every person convicted of having tried to stop Estates General's calling will be declared a traitor to the fatherland, guilty of the crime of treason against the nation, and punished by a tribunal the current Estates General will establish. . . .

The monarch's person is sacred and inviolable. Succession to the throne is hereditary amongst the reigning race, from male to male, by order of primogeniture, excluding the women and their descendants, whether male or female, and can only go to a prince born French in a legitimate marriage while reigning.[17]

At each new dynasty's establishment, the previous Estates General's deputies have the right to reassemble, without a new convocation. A regency, in all cases, cannot be conferred except by them. . . .

In each new reign, the king will swear an oath to the nation, as will the nation to the king, the content of which will be fixed by the current Estates General.

No citizen can be arrested, nor his domicile violated, with *lettres de cachet* or any other order from the executive power . . .[18]

The ministers, regulators, and chief administrators of all departments, will be responsible to the nation assembled in the Estates General, for all misconduct, abuse of power, and misuse of funds.

The kingdom will be divided into provincial assemblies composed of that province's residents, freely elected by their orders, and in the proportion to be established. . . .

All cities, towns and villages will have elected municipalities, administering their local interests. . . .

Judiciary power must be exercised in France, in the king's name, by tribunals composed of members fully independent of the executive power. . . .

Nobles will be able, without losing status, to engage in commerce and all useful professions.

There will be no more ennobling, either for merit or otherwise.

The Estates General will establish an honorable, civic recompense, purely personal and not hereditary, to be conferred by royal presentation to citizens of all classes meriting it by the eminence of their patriotic virtues, and by the importance of their services rendered. . . .

The Constitution to be decided in the present Estates General, following the principles we have developed, will be the nation's property, and cannot be changed or modified except by the constitutive power, which is to say, by the nation itself, or by its representatives nominated ad hoc by all citizens, working only to compliment and perfect this constitution.

The constitution's text will be engraved on a public monument raised for this purpose. It will be read in the king's presence upon his taking the throne, to be followed with his oath, and recorded. All those serving under the executive power, whether civil or military, magistrates of superior or lesser tribunals, the officers of all municipalities in the kingdom, before beginning to exercise the functions confided upon them, will swear to observe this national charter. Each year, on the day of the sanction's anniversary, it will be read and posted in the churches, courthouses, schools, military barracks, and ships, and the day will be a day of solemn festivities in every French dominion. . . .

MUNICIPALITIES

The city of Paris, because of its size and population, its commerce and industry, from the twin excesses of luxury and poverty, from its richness and every-growing needs, from the assiduous yet insufficient care taken for its provisioning, is, without comparison, the city of the kingdom needing the most active and vigilant administration, requiring the most sagely organized and best concerted efforts.

In consequence, the Third Estate asks for the city of Paris an administration composed of members freely elected by all citizens, and reelected every three years, formed on the provincial assemblies' example, charged with the same functions, and having the same relations with the Estates General, the administration of which will take on, following the regime to be established, the functions of a municipal body charged with managing city properties, etc.

Provincial administrations, including that of Paris, will carefully examine if it is useful to maintain, reform, or suppress guild corporations.

It will be similarly sent to the assembly of Paris to examine if it is proper to maintain, reform, or suppress the privileges the houses of the king and princes possess, and those of corporate bodies.

The Estates General will hereafter assemble in Paris, in a public edifice dedicated to its use.

Emmanuel-Joseph Sieyès, *What is the Third Estate?* 1789

Of the many political pamphlets published over the months leading to the Estates General, none offered such a confident blueprint for revolution as Emmanuel-Joseph Sieyès' *What is the Third Estate?* Though written by a clergyman, the pamphlet polemically attacked the privileged orders, claiming commoners did the nation's productive work while virtually all political and administrative power remained in the hands of a "fainting class" of nobles. Moreover, the pamphlet enunciated a positive program for change: demanding the Third Estate receive half of all votes in the upcoming Estates General, calling for meritocratic job opportunities in the government, and the overturning of noble privileges. Sieyès valorized the work and contributions of common people, while refuting traditional arguments for their political exclusion. Though some historians have exaggerated the pamphlet's immediate impact—Sieyès barely gained election to the Estates

General as the twentieth of twenty deputies elected for Paris—virtually all of his radical views became mainstream across the Third Estate as the French Revolution gained force. At least in hindsight, no other pamphlet so successfully captured the growing radicalism of the Third Estate: all state power appeared rightfully theirs, while the privileged orders appeared useless.

The plan of this piece is fairly simple. We have three questions to address:

1. What is the Third Estate? Everything.
2. What has it been until now in the political order? Nothing.
3. What is it asking for? To become something.

We will see if our reasoning is just. We will then examine the means tried, and those we ought to take, for the Third Estate to become, in effect, something. Thus, we will discuss:

4. What the Ministers have *tried*, and what the Privileged Orders themselves have *proposed* in its favor.
5. What one *ought* to do.
6. Finally, what the Third Estate *still* needs to do to take its due place. . . .

The Third Estate is a complete nation.

What must be done for a nation to subsist and prosper? Private work and public functions.

One can enclose in four classes all such works:

1. Earth and water produce the first needs of man; the first class, in our analysis, will be those families attached to the land.
2. From the first sale of goods for consumption, a new means of work, more or less multiplied, adds a greater or lesser value. Human industry thus perfects nature's yield, and the raw product thus doubles, or even increases a hundredfold, in value. Such are the works of the second class.
3. Between production and consumption, as between the different degrees of production, there are intermediary agents, as useful to the producers as the consumers; these are the merchants and traders. The traders ceaselessly compare the needs of place and time, speculating on the profits of retention and transport; the merchants, in the last analysis, accrue capital, whether through bulk, or in specialization. This type of utility designates the third class.
4. Outside of these three classes of laboring and useful citizens who constitute the proper object of consumption and usage, there must still be in a society a multitude of specific jobs directly useful or

> agreeable to people. This fourth class encompasses those from the most distinguished scientific and liberal professions to the services of the least valued servants.

Such are the works that support society. Who carries them out? The Third Estate.

Public functions can equally, at present, range themselves under four known denominations: Sword, Robe, Church, and Administration. It would be superfluous to examine them in detail to see that the Third Estate does about ninety-five percent of the real work. With this in mind, remember it is charged with everything really difficult, with all tasks the Privileged Order refuses to do. . . .

If this exclusion is a social crime towards the Third Estate, can one at least say it is useful to the public good? Do the privileged not know monopoly's effects? That it discourages what is pushed out of the way, never mind that it renders useless what is favored? Do they not know that every work deprived of its free course is done more expensively and worse? . . .

It suffices here to feel that the pretended utility of a privileged order for public service is only a chimera; that without them, everything condemnable therein could be better accomplished by the Third Estate. Without it, the superior places would be much better filled, naturally becoming a reward for talents and recognized services. If the privileged have usurped all the lucrative and honorific posts, this is both an odious iniquity for the great mass of Citizens and treason against the public good.

Who would thus avoid saying that the Third Estate does not have everything in it to form a complete Nation? It is a robust man with a chained arm. If one took away the Privileged Order, the Nation would not be something less, but something more. Thus, what is the Third? Everything, but a complete being that has been hindered and oppressed. What would it be without the Privileged Orders? Everything, a totality free and flourishing. Nothing can be done without them; everything would be infinitely better without the others.

It does not suffice to demonstrate that the privileged, far from being useful to the Nation, can only weaken and harm it, it must still prove that the Noble Order cannot join the social organization; it could well be an electric shock for the nation, but it does not know how to play a role.

Henceforth, it is not possible amidst all the building blocks of a nation to find a place for the Noble Caste. I know there are too many infirm, incapacitated, incurably lazy, and poorly mannered amongst them, making them strangers to society's work. . . . Such a fainting class is assuredly foreign to the nation. . . .

What is a nation? A body of associates living under a common law, and represented by the same legislature.

Is it really certain that the Noble Order has privileges, expenses, even rights separated from the rights of the great body of Citizens? . . . .

We will not examine the state of servitude under which the People have suffered for such a long time, nor their constraints and humiliation. Their civil condition has changed, and it must change further: it is quite impossible that the nation as a whole or any particular order become free, if the Third Estate is not. One does not become free via privileges, but by the rights of citizenship: rights that belong to everyone. . . .

For our goal, the Third Estate must be understood as the ensemble of citizens who belong to the Common Order. Everything privileged by law, in whatever manner, must be eliminated from the Common Order . . . . We have said: a common law and a common representation is what makes a nation. . . .

It is important not to judge their demands by the isolated observations of several authors more or less instructed in the rights of man. The Third Estate is still quite backwards in this regard, and I do not only mean the insights of those studying the social order, but that mass of common ideas that form public opinion. One cannot appreciate the Third's petitions apart from the authentic reclamations the kingdom's great municipalities have addressed to the government. What do they show? That the people want to be something. Truthfully, that is the least due them. They want to have real representation in the Estates General, this is to say deputies drawn from their Order who are able to enunciate their views and defend their interests. But what will they gain by participating in the Estates General, if the interest contrary to theirs predominates? They will only by their presence consecrate the oppression by which they will be the eternal victim. Thus, it is quite certain they will not be able to effectively vote in the Estates General, if they do not have an influence at least equal to that of the privileged, and they ask for a number of Representatives equal to the two other Orders combined. . . .

The privileged fear the Third Order having equal influence; they declare it unconstitutional. This conduct is even more striking when one considers that they have been until now two against one, without finding anything unconstitutional in this unjust superiority. They feel a strong need to conserve the veto on all that could go against their interest. . . .

In every free nation—and every nation ought to be free—there is only one means of ending differences which arise regarding the constitution. Such recourse belongs not to the Notables, it belongs to the nation herself. If we lack a constitution, one must be made; the nation alone has the right. . . .

One closes their eyes in vain to the revolution that time and the force of events have operated—it is real. Before, the Third were serfs, the Noble Order was everything. Today the Third is everything, Nobility is only a word; but by this word has developed a new and intolerable aristocracy, and the People have every reason to not want aristocrats. . . .

What is the nation's will? It is the result of individual wills, as the nation is the assemblage of individuals. It is impossible to conceive a legitimate association that does not have for its object common security, common liberty, and the common good. . . .

It is now impossible to say what place the two Privileged Orders ought to occupy in the social order: this is asking what place one ought to assign in a sick person's body to a malignant humor that torments them. We must neutralize it, we must reestablish good health and the working of all the organs well enough that they cannot form more deadly combinations, capable of sapping the most essential means of vitality.

FIGURE 3.1 *Jacques Berthaut,* Camille Desmoulins Harangues the Crowd in the Palais-Royal, *July 12, 1789. © Heritage Images / Getty Images.*

On a sunny summer Sunday afternoon, the French Revolution's great uprising began. Announcing the king's dismissal of Jacques Necker, journalist Camille Desmoulins climbed atop a picnic table in the garden of the Palais Royal and fired a pistol in the air. Parisians formed a protest-march, gathered followers across the theatre district, then headed west towards Versailles, hoping to confront royal authorities. The image captures the French Revolution in its early stages of hope and passion—as people rushed to risk their lives to defend the threatened National Assembly. First printed in 1791, reaching five updated editions by 1817, the *Tableaux de la Révolution française* produced high-quality engravings of some of the French Revolution's greatest moments. Though we do not know if the engraver saw this actual scene, this is how the beginning of the Bastille insurrection became remembered.

3

Sparking the French Revolution

Despite the fermentation convulsing France in the period approaching the Estates General, no one fully expected the great changes that followed over late-spring and summer 1789. Receiving little leadership from the King and his ministers, the Estates General remained in stasis over its first six weeks—with neither of the privileged orders willing to approve a common assembly with the Third Estate. That the great ferment of ideas in France would be for naught—and the Estates General possibly dissolved as the Assemblies of Notables had been—helped spur the Third Estate to take radical action.

On June 17, the Third Estate declared themselves a National Assembly, representative of the great majority of the nation. With the king having doubled the number of Estates General representatives (without deciding the voting method, leaving uncertain whether they would constitute one-third or one-half the total), attention turned to him as arbiter. The crown announced a speech from the throne for June 20—but then postponed without telling the Third Estate. Finding their meeting hall locked, the legislators feared their dissolution, but resolved to march across town to the royal tennis court (the largest indoor gathering space they could procure) and take an oath to remain constituted as a National Assembly until France was granted a constitution. When the king, three days later, demanded that the three orders continue meeting and voting separately, the Third Estate defied them—refusing to disperse and keeping the National Assembly in place.

The Third Estate still feared royal reaction and found their worries confirmed by Jacques Necker's removal as finance minister on July 12. This time, common Parisians rose to the revolution's defense. A peaceful demonstration that afternoon was dispersed by a royal cavalry charge, after which the city rose in insurrection. A bourgeois militia enrolled propertied citizens and gathered weapons to prepare for the city's defense. Insurgents seized a large armory at the Invalides military hospital the morning of July 14—while Parisians learnt that great gunpowder stores existed in the Bastille, the hated political prison in eastern Paris. Crowds gathered in the courtyard and, after several hours of low-level fighting, the fortress surrendered. Though Parisians still faced tens of thousands of troops surrounding the city, Louis XVI (no longer certain whom the troops would side with) decided against trying to re-take his capital by force and capitulated. Necker was recalled, and Paris' municipal revolution, functioning through self-governing districts and an elected town legislature, confirmed. First National Assembly legislators and then Louis XVI ventured to a capital thronging with newly armed National Guardsmen, feeling the fervor of newfound liberty.

Popular revolutions followed across France. Rural insurrections became endemic in the countryside: uncertain if the National Assembly would fulfill their demands, peasants rose up against their feudal lords, burning chateaus and archives, while townspeople carried out their own municipal revolutions on the Parisian model. Nobody knew what the future would bring, with word of the Bastille's fall helping set off a Great Fear spreading rapidly across many regions (ca. July 17–August 3), in which worries of bandit gangs profiting from the unrest merged with fear of foreign armies invading to reestablish the old regime. This led peasants and townspeople to arm, organize, and in some cases destroy what they could of the Old Regime before the feared repression arrived. Yet amidst such uncertainty and disorder, the French created a shockingly new regime, mobilizing the populace across the nation and organizing new local governing structures in defense of electoral representation and citizens' rights.

June and July 1789 became a time of rapidly expanding possibilities for the people of France. All prospects, from emancipation to subjection, seemed close at hand. Feeling they had everything to win or lose, common French people rose in unparalleled numbers to shape the New Regime they desired. The French Revolution came to embody such great hopes of so many that in 1789 it appeared irrepressible.

Jacques Necker, Speech at Opening of Estates General, May 5, 1789

Finance Minister Necker's speech at the Estates General's opening, following brief welcomes by Louis XVI and the Keeper of the Seals, deserves a prominent place in the history of failure. Despite having the King's confidence, the respect of most elected to the Estates General, and a formidable reputation as a reformer from his earlier time as finance minister, Necker failed to present a comprehensible plan for reform—limiting himself to describing the debt and financial crisis facing France, and encouraging the new deputies to develop their own plans for addressing it. Even the key question of whether the deputies would vote by head or order remained unaddressed. Necker's voice gave out while reading the two-hour speech in the large *Menus Plaisirs* gathering hall, at which point he gave it to an assistant to finish. By the performance's end, the power vacuum at the center of the French government became apparent. France faced many problems, but solutions remained unclear.

Messieurs, what a day this is! What an ever-memorable era for France! To see here, after such a long time, these deputies called around the throne from a nation so celebrated, from a nation that has filled the universe with its renown, and which can call history's incorruptible testimony to attest its great acts and warrior values, or retrace the picture of its progress and triumphs in all genres of war and rivalry! . .

Yet this is not presently an easy regeneration, to which you need only bring your ideas and ambition. There must be a constant, durable, and useful order resulting from your investigations and work. Your path must respond to your mission's grandeur. The purity, nobility, and integrity of your views must match the importance and gravity of the confidence deposed with you. . . .

I must, Messieurs, following the King's orders, begin by rendering you an honest account of the state of finances. An expensive war and a series of unfortunate circumstances have introduced a great imbalance between our revenues and expenses. You will examine, Messieurs, the means the King has ordered me to propose to you to reestablish an equilibrium if necessary; you will research the best solutions, indicate them, and respond to a watching Nation and a waiting Europe, in bringing all your efforts together to establish in the finances of the greatest Empire an order that must be always assured. . . .

The deficit, according to the accounting of 1788, is 160,827,492 *livres*.

But if one counts in this sum all the reimbursements amounting to 76,502,367 *livres*, and all the extraordinary and passing expenses payable in 1788, it grows another 29,395,585 *livres*. . . .

His Majesty finds much grandeur and satisfaction in uniting with you, Messieurs, to consecrate the immutable principles of justice and probity. He finds more satisfaction in respecting them, than in all the pleasures of regal pomp, or the unlimited exercise of an authority that loses its value, if it is not destined to maintain and defend justice against all sorts of attacks. In the end, Messieurs, France's political power is perfectly compatible with the conservation of these principles. Wartime expenses became immense because it was necessary to cover all the seas just for defense, and since deploying prodigiously large armies was needed to establish equality with the military forces of Europe's other nations. In this state of affairs, it is absolutely impossible to undertake such great efforts via extraordinary taxes: one must necessarily mix revenue sources to obtain such considerable capital via an annual and moderate sacrifice by taxpayers. . . .

We will set under your eyes, Messieurs, this year's projected expenditures and revenues. You will see that, after relying on the most likely projections, extraordinary revenues of 80 million are needed. There will be proposed to you loans or other resources, as will appear the most suitable to you, and during this, Messieurs, you will remark with satisfaction that the interest on the necessary loan to balance this year's needs is included in the accounting of revenues and fixed expenses of which we have already made you aware, in such fashion so this interest will not augment the deficit at all. . . .

We end, Messieurs, by returning to the loveliest of ideas, since, in concert with your august Sovereign, you will have laid the foundation of France's happiness and prosperity, and moreover set the first stones on the vast highway of the public good. . . . A nation blindly unhappy with an administration's faults or abuses does not hesitate to complain through every method of opposition and resistance, but such a spirit must change . . . as the march of government must always remain united on the principles assuring public happiness. The King passionately desires that everything just in his administration be known, determined, and invariable . . .

The King, Messieurs, in thinking about this important edifice of happiness and power you can help him elevate, truly desires its establishment on more solid foundations: find them, indicate them to your Sovereign, and he will grant the most generous assistance. The King, Messieurs, enlightened by long ordeals and precipitous events that have doubled his years of experience, loves reason more than ever, and he is a good judge. . . .

What would happen, Messieurs, if from your first moments a striking disunion appeared? What would become of the public good amidst these divisions, should the interests of order, state, and personality occupy all your thoughts? . . .

But do not doubt at all, Messieurs, that there must be a good and salutary constitution, cemented by the power of the public spirit, and this public spirit, this patriotism, does not consist in a passing fever, in the blind desire of a new encounter; such desire, such agitation, always subsides . . .

Yes, Messieurs, the King in reassembling the Estates General, the King, in uniting around himself the Nation's representatives, the King, in calling to his aid such a great concourse of enlightened men, has already satisfied his glory; but he needs you to obtain the dearest desires of his heart. . . . .

Declaration of the National Assembly, June 17, 1789

A stalemate endured for the Estates General's first six weeks, as the majority of the two privileged orders refused to endorse proceeding as a common body, while the Third Estate refused to accept separate deliberations that would have left it a minority voice. By mid-June, radical voices in the commons convinced an overwhelming majority of the order to declare the Estates reorganized as a National Assembly, hoping at least significant portions of the two privileged orders would wind up joining them. In so doing, the new body declared themselves sovereign—legitimated by the people's will and not subject to royal veto or restriction. Absolutism perished. While leaving open the possibility of future reconciliation, the revolutionary declaration asserted that the National Assembly was France's new governing power. In perhaps the largest political shift of the French Revolution, sovereignty effectively passed from the king to the people's representatives.

The Assembly, deliberating after the verification of their powers, recognizes that this assembly is already composed of the representatives directly sent by at least eighty-six hundredths of the Nation.

Such a massive deputation cannot remain inactive because of the absence of deputies of several districts or some classes of citizens; now the absent who have been called cannot prevent those present from exercising their full rights, especially since exercising these rights is an imperious and pressing need.

What's more, since it only belongs to the verified representatives to unite and form the national view and since all the verified representatives must be in this assembly, it is all the more indispensable to conclude that it belongs to them and only them to interpret and present the nation's general will; there cannot exist between the throne and assembly any veto, any legislative power.

The Assembly thus declares that the common work of national restoration can and must begin without delay, by the deputies present, and that they ought to pursue it without interruption or obstacle.

The name National Assembly is the only one suiting the assembly in the present state of things, because its members are the only legitimately and publicly known and verified representatives, because they are sent directly by the near totality of the Nation, and finally because representation is one and indivisible, no deputies, in whatever order or class they are chosen from, have any right to exercise their functions separately from the present assembly.

The assembly will never lose hope of reuniting all the deputies absent today; it will not cease to call them to fulfill their obligation to participate in the Estates General. At whatever moment the absent deputies present themselves over the ensuing session's course, the assembly declares in advance that it will enthusiastically receive them and share with them, after the verification of their powers, the results of the great works that must procure the regeneration of France. The National Assembly decrees that the present deliberation's motives will be immediately drawn up for presentation to the King and the Nation.

Louis XVI, Speech to the Estates General, June 23, 1789

Three days after a cancelled royal speech had led suspicious legislators into taking the Tennis Court Oath, pledging to persist until France had a constitution, Louis XVI attempted to recapture control of French politics in his June 23 address. Deploying the full weight of his royal authority, Louis declared the political body he had called just months earlier would remain the Estates General, voting by order, and not an undifferentiated National Assembly voting by head. From Louis's perspective, he had already made more concessions than any absolute monarch before him, and now needed to rein in the growing revolution before it overturned French hierarchy, laws, and property. Louis and his advisors failed to grasp, however, how much politics had changed in a few short weeks: now, the Third Estate refused to remain subordinate to the King and privileged orders, and defied the simplest of Louis' instructions: to disperse at the end of his speech. The Count of Mirabeau stood up to the King's men, declaring the commoners would only be dispersed by the force of bayonets. The King, just hours after the most resolute speech of his reign, again changed his mind and backed down. The King's programme was never enforced, and French politics moved on to revolutionary measures.

Messieurs, I believe I have done all in my power for the good of my peoples, since I resolved to call you together, since I overcame all the difficulties your convocation raised. For this reason, I exceeded the nation's views, in creating the change I wanted to make for its happiness.

It seemed that you only had to finish my work. The nation waited with impatience for the moment when, by combining the charitable views of their sovereign and the enlightened zeal of their representatives, they were going to enjoy the prosperity this union would bring.

The Estates General has been in session for nearly two months and have not been able to fulfill their preliminary operations. A perfect intelligence ought to create a singular love of the fatherland, while a dreadful division throws alarm into all spirits. I want to believe, and like to think, the French are not changed. But, to avoid making reproaches against any of you, I consider that the renewing of the Estates General after such a long time, the agitation preceding it, the goal of this convocation—so different than that which brought your ancestors together, the restrictions of its powers, and several other circumstances, necessarily required opposition, debates, and exaggerated pretentions.

I must, for the general good of my kingdom, I must for myself cease these dreadful divisions. It is in this resolution, Messieurs, that I bring you newly together around me; I do this as the common father of all my subjects, I do this as the defender of my kingdom's laws; I recapture their true spirit, and punish the attacks made against them.

But, Messieurs, after having clearly established the respective rights of the different orders, I wait for patriotic zeal. From the two first orders, I anticipate their attachment to my person. I wait for their recognition that there are urgent problems in the state; that in the affairs affecting the general good, they will be the first to propose a reunion of advice and sentiments that I see as necessary in the present crisis, to work for the health of the state.

[read by one of his secretaries]:

Declaration of the King, Concerning the Present Holding of the Estates General.

The king wants the ancient distinction of the state's three orders to be conserved in their entirety, as essentially connected to the constitution of his kingdom; that the deputies freely elected by each of the three orders form three Chambers, deliberate by order, and may, with the sovereign's permission, convene to deliberate in common, can only be considered the body of the representatives of the nation. In consequence, the king has declared null the deliberations taken by the deputies of the Order of the Third Estate, the 17 of this month, as well as those that might follow, as illegal and unconstitutional. . . .

[The King rose again to speak]

I have also wanted, Messieurs, to bring before your eyes the many benefits I have given my peoples. This is not to limit your zeal within the circle I am tracing, because I will adopt with pleasure every view of the public good the Estates General proposes. I can say, without deluding myself, that never has a king done so much for any nation; but what other could have so merited his sentiments as the French nation! I do not fear to say that those who, by their exaggerated pretentions or by inopportune difficulties, delay further the effect of my paternal intentions, render themselves unworthy of being considered French.

[Read by one of the King's secretaries]

Declaration of the King's Intentions:

No new tax can be established, no ancient one can be extended beyond the term fixed by law, without the representatives of the nation's consent. . . .

The table of revenues and expenses will be made public each year, in the form the Estates General proposes, and His Majesty approves. . . .

All properties without exception will be constantly respected, and His Majesty expressly understands the term 'properties' to include tithes, title taxes, rents, feudal and seigneurial rights and duties, and generally all useful or honorific rights and prerogatives attached to lands and fiefs, or belonging to individuals. . . .

The King, desiring to assure all citizens' individual liberty in a solid and durable manner, invites the Estates General to find and propose the most useful means of conciliating the abolition of those orders known as *lettres de cachet* with the maintenance of public security, and with the precautions necessary, whether for respecting family honor in certain cases, or for swiftly punishing the beginnings of sedition, or for protecting the state from the effects of a criminal conspiracy with foreign powers.

The Estates General will examine and inform His Majesty of the most appropriate method to reconcile freedom of the press with the respect due to religion, manners, and the honor of citizens. . . .

The King invites the Estates General to consider raising militias under its command and discuss methods for conciliating what is necessary for the state's defense, with the caring reforms His Majesty desires to procure for his subjects. . . .

His Majesty, after having called the Estates General to occupy themselves, in concert with him, with the great objects of public utility, and all that which could contribute to his people's happiness, most explicitly declares that he wants to fully retain, without the smallest concession, command of the army, along with all police and military power, such as French monarchs have constantly enjoyed.

[The King rose to give a third speech]

You come, Messieurs, to hear my disposition and views: they conform to my strong desire to further the public good; and if, by a fatality outside my thinking, you abandon me in such a beautiful enterprise, I will work for the good of my peoples alone. Alone, I will consider myself their true representative, and knowing your statements of grievances, knowing the perfect accord existing between the general view of the nation and my charitable intentions, I will maintain the confidence inspiring such a rare harmony, and I will move towards the goal I want to reach with all the courage and resoluteness that ought to inspire me.

Remember, Messieurs, that none of your projects, none of your dispositions can have the force of law without my special approbation. Thus, I am the natural guarantor of your respective rights; all the orders of state can rest easy in my equitable impartiality.

All defiance on your part would be a great injustice. It is I, until now, that has made all my peoples' happiness; and it is perhaps rare that the unique ambition of a sovereign be to obtain from his subjects what they finally tell him to accept in benefits.

I order you, Messieurs, to separate yourselves at once and report tomorrow morning to the respective rooms reserved for your order, to recommence your sessions there. I thereby order the Great Master of Ceremonies to prepare the rooms.

Jean-Baptiste Humbert, *Insurrection of Jean-Baptiste Humbert, Watchmaker, Who was First to Climb the Towers of the Bastille*, 1789

The capture of the Bastille fortress, a hated prison on the eastern edge of Paris, was not pre-meditated. Rather, it organically developed on the third day of a Parisian insurrection opposing the King's dismissal of reformist minister Jacques Necker. As seen in the published personal account of Jean-Baptiste Humbert, a humble journeyman watchmaker, the Bastille's taking developed from a plan to forage gunpowder to stop both the King's troops rumored to be planning an invasion of the city and lower-class Parisian rioters considered a threat to property. Humbert's July 14 is chaotic in the extreme: he is nearly suffocated by overzealous fellow insurgents, shot by friendly fire, helped by one of the Swiss Guards defending the Bastille, hospitalized with a flesh wound, and almost lynched by a confused revolutionary crowd, yet still continues fighting for liberty. Despite the complicated machinations of politics, alliances, and loyalties in mid-1789, common Frenchmen came to strongly identify with the National Assembly and Revolutionary cause, risking their lives in its defense. The concrete act of seizing such a symbol of despotism led partisans to believe they were now undertaking a Revolution beyond all precedent.

Frenchmen, my compatriots, I am a native of Langres.[1] I learned to be a watchmaker in Geneva, Switzerland, where I was a journeyman when that Republic lost its liberty.[2]

I peacefully slept on a cot in a guardhouse when French troops seized that city after several traitors opened the gates.

I witnessed the consternation of the *bourgeois* residents, and heard the complaints they made against a Minister of France who, they said, had misled my king,[3] I heard their sighs, complaints, and regrets, that I will long hold in my heart against this Minister, a part of the sad sentiments I felt for the unfortunate Genevans.

I came back to Paris in 1787. There I became accustomed, without feeling it, to carrying the yoke weighing heavily on my compatriots, the brave Parisians.

Like them, on the twelfth of July [1789], at the news that the armed populace attacked *bourgeois* residents instead of defending them, I went to the electoral district of St. André des Arts to offer my services.[4] I believed what I heard there: the attack near the Tuileries by the Prince of Lambesc, and several other well-known incidents, had raised *bourgeois* alarm and led them to take arms. I submitted myself to the commanders they named.[5]

In my labors, I strongly believed in only doing my duty, never glorifying myself or taking advantage of a situation. I am content to make six *francs* a day, what I need to support myself. But I am still pleased to have helped France recover her liberty, and hope to make my parents happy by recounting my actions.

Serving the district of Saint-André-des-Arts, I reported to the parish Monday morning [July 13, 1789], just like all the citizens with whom I patrolled the day and night of Monday to Tuesday, carrying swords, as the district did not have any rifles, and only several involved did.[6]

Deprived of sleep, fatigued, and needing food, I left the district at six in the morning [on July 14, 1789]. I learnt that rifles had been taken from the Invalides for the districts. I returned to warn the *bourgeois* of Saint-Andre, who assembled around half past noon.[7] Monsieur Poirier, our commander, realized the news' importance and prepared to lead the citizens. But, held back by different considerations, unable to see these were of little importance compared to getting rifles for the *bourgeois*, he would not leave. I grabbed M. Poirier and along with five or six *bourgeois* forced him to go.

We arrived at the Invalides around two in the afternoon and found there a great crowd, which separated us. I do not know what the commander or his troops did thereafter.

I followed the crowd into the basement where the guns were.

On the staircase, I encountered a man carrying two rifles. I took one from him and went back up; but at the top the crowd was so great that those who tried to go up tumbled back down the stairs. Not injured and only feeling annoyed by the fall, I took a rifle that lay at my feet, and gave it to someone without one.

Despite the crowd, others kept trying to come in, while nobody could get out. People pressed so tightly in the basement that everyone cried out for fear of being smothered.

Many people were already acting foolishly; thus, those in the basement who had arms decided to force the unarmed crowd to retreat by threatening to bayonet them in the stomach. That worked. We profited from a moment of terror and retreat to force them out.

The crowd gone, we started moving the crushed people onto the grass between the dome and the graveyard. After transporting them, seeing the uselessness of my presence, armed with my gun, I looked for my commander in vain and then set off for my district.

I learned on my way that powder was being distributed at City Hall. I moved light-footedly there. They gave me a little, but no bullets, saying they didn't have any.[8]

In leaving City Hall, I heard it said they were planning to besiege the Bastille.[9] The regret of not having bullets suggested to me an idea I quickly accomplished: buying small nails from a spice seller at King's Corner near the square, I loaded them into my rifle.

Leaving the spice store with my weapon, I was stopped by a citizen who told me that they were now distributing bullets at City Hall. I went here and received six small *chevrotine* musket balls.

I soon left for the Bastille, loading my rifle on the way.

Arriving via the riverbanks at the Arsenal's second courtyard, I joined several persons wanting to join the siege.

We found several nightwatch soldiers armed with their guns. I encouraged them to join the siege. After responding that they had neither powder nor lead, we made a collection for them and gave each two shots. They then went enthusiastically.

At the moment we passed before the Hôtel de la Régie, someone opened two cases of bullets, which we distributed discreetly. I took a pocketful, to give to those lacking. I still have more than three pounds' worth.

Several steps away, I heard a woman's cry for help. When I approached, she exclaimed "they will set fire to the gunpowder shop!" She added this was "an injustice," because this store was open and selling to the *bourgeois*. This woman brought me in, where I found a wigmaker carrying in each hand two lit torches to set the fire. I rushed this wigmaker and gave him a great hit to the stomach with my rifle, which knocked him down. Seeing the saltpeter supply already in flames, I quickly smothered it.

Meanwhile, two servants from the house upstairs helped me force out the bad men who had already entered the premises, and made their way into the records room. I also chased from the apartments several individuals who had broken armoires, under the pretext of searching for powder.

I then left the house, after many thanks, and found the nightwatch soldiers to whom I had given power and bullets. One said he would guard the shop door.

I started toward the Bastille, via the Arsenal courtyard. It was about half past three. The first bridge had fallen, its chains cut, but the portcullis barred the passageway. The insurgents occupied themselves with advancing the cannons, extremely difficult work. I entered via the little bridge, and I helped bring two cannons forward.

Once we recommenced the assault, everyone participating fully and voluntarily, we formed columns of five or six, and I found myself in the front row.

Thus arranged, we marched to the castle drawbridge. There, I saw two dead soldiers, one on each side. To my right, one wore a Vintimiglia regimental uniform. I could not distinguish the uniform of the soldier on the left.[10]

We aimed the bronze cannons towards the great drawbridge, and the smaller one, with silver lining, towards the small bridge.

This situation obliged me to leave my column to see if presently, from the castle's high tower, they did not give any new signs of peace (that all desired). I charged myself with crossing the terrace.

During this mission, others decided to commence a rifle attack. I quickly attempted to return to my post, but a crowd barred my route despite the peril. I returned along the wall's ledge, and retook my post. I had to return to the ground by stepping on the Vintimiglia soldier's cadaver.

We each fired about six shots. Then there appeared from the wall a paper, through an oval hole, of several inches. We ceased firing. One of us went nearby eatery to find a plate to receive the parlay. We set the plate on the ledge. Many people gathered below to make a counter-attack. As a man went to get it, he was hit by a rifle shot, falling dead into the moat.

Another person, a flag-carrier, went to take the communication, the contents of which he read in a loud, clear voice.

The paper's terms did not satisfy our demand for their capitulation. We decided to fire the cannon. Everyone moved out of the way to let the cannonball pass.

At the moment we fired, the small drawbridge fell. Once lowered, it was swarmed. I was only about the tenth to cross it. We found the door behind the drawbridge closed: after about two minutes, a veteran soldier came to open it, and asked what we wanted: "that we take the Bastille," we all said. Then he fell back. My first task was to cry out that the passage was open.

I entered the great courtyard (about the eighth or tenth person to do so). The veteran soldiers took positions to the right and left of the Bastille's Swiss Guards. We cried "lower your guns," which they did, except for a Swiss officer.[11] I menaced him with my bayonet to force him to, telling him again, "put down your gun!" He responded, "*Messieurs*, I assure you I didn't fire."

"How can you tell me you did not fire?" I said to him. "Your mouth is still black from your gunpowder." While speaking, I tried to grab his sword, while at the same instant, someone else did so too. As we fought over it, my view turned to a staircase on the left. I saw three *bourgeois* who had climbed five or six stories and then descended with haste. I left the saber, and, with my rifle, which I never left, I moved rapidly to the staircase, to help the *bourgeois*, who told me not to go up.

I ascended rapidly to the high tower, without seemingly being followed by anyone. I arrived atop the staircase without encountering anyone else. I found a Swiss soldier crouched with his back to me. I aimed at him, shouting, "lay down your arms." He was surprised, and put down his rifle, telling me "Comrade, do not kill me, I am of the Third Estate, and I will defend them until the last drop of my blood. You know I must do my service, but I have not fired."

During this speech, I took his rifle. Then I commanded him, with a bayonet to his stomach, to pass me his cartridge pouch, which he did.

Soon after, I made it to the cannon perpendicularly above the Bastille drawbridge, hoping to spike it so it could not fire on the assailants. But as I turned my right shoulder under the cannon's mouth, I took a bullet, the ball hitting me in the neck. I fell unconscious. The Swiss, whose life I spared, carried me to the staircase along with the guard's rifle, but I lost the one from the Invalides.

Regaining consciousness, I found myself sitting on the staircase. The Swiss helped revive me and stop the blood flowing in abundance from my wound. He cut off a piece of his shirt to wrap around it.

Feeling weak, I decided to go down the stairs, begging the Swiss to help me, which he graciously did.

Halfway down the staircase, we encountered armed and unarmed *bourgeois* going up. Seeing me covered in blood, they thought the Swiss had wounded me. They wanted to kill him; I beseeched them not to. They believed my explanation, and I continued, helped by the Swiss, to descend.

We arrived together in the courtyard, but they would not let the Swiss leave. I was thus obliged to go by myself. They let me through once they saw my bloody wound.

Near the Bastille, I encountered a surgeon, who convinced me to let him tend my wound. After an examination, he told me the musket ball was lodged in my neck. He decided he could not remove it, saying I should go to a hospital, which I did.

En route, I encountered a man leaving the Minimes monastery, where he had just been treated for a sprained wrist. He took me there, where they helped me. They could not find a musket ball.[12]

Pressed by a violent thirst, they gave me a tin of wine and water. That restored my forces. I rose up joyously, intending to go back to the Bastille.

I dressed quickly, taking my gun and ammunition, but I was beseeched to change my mind by the Minimes who had bandaged me. They told me that movement could render my wound life-threatening and urged me that it was absolutely necessary to retire to my room to rest. They wanted to help me, but I thanked them instead.

Heading back, I thought of several friends, who lived on rue de la Ferronnerie. I had left them in the morning, when they were worried about the same dangers as myself. I went towards their home, and four armed *bourgeois* led me by rue du Hurepoix. I received thanks all around as I passed. By when we got to Quai des Augustins, a crowd followed us, believing me an enemy, and two of them threatened to kill me. Unable to respond to all their charges, I was seized, but at that moment a Quai bookseller recognized me.[13] He pushed me into the building, and saved me from the hands of the crowd. I lay down in his house, receiving there the care I needed.

I rested until almost midnight, when I awoke by repeated cries of "To arms! To arms!" I could not resist the desire to be useful. I got up, armed myself, and went to the guardhouse, where I found Monsieur Poirier, Commander, under whose orders I had placed myself the previous morning.

Adrien Duquesnoy, Personal Journal, Entry of July 16, 1789

Despite many legislators' ambivalence about popular violence, the National Assembly embraced the success of the Bastille insurrection. The populace had risen to support the legislature's survival (considering Necker as its guarantor) and the king was forced to submit to Paris' municipal revolution to regain the confidence of the people in his capital. Adrien Duquesnoy, a deputy from Nancy in Lorraine, was part of the assembly's deputation sent to Paris on July 15, less than twenty-four hours after the Bastille fell. He found the city fundamentally changed: no longer made meek by absolutism, Paris' *bourgeois* residents had armed themselves, seized military installations, and asserted their freedom. The people realized their collective power and now sought to show their force to visiting national authorities. Two days after the National Assembly legislators visited, Louis XVI traveled to Paris, proceeding without escort through even greater crowds to recognize the new revolutionary municipal authorities. Suppressing a revolution backed by popular unanimity appeared virtually impossible. Now Paris—and France—would govern themselves.

As everything changes, everything succeeds! Yesterday [July 15] . . . at two p.m., forty carriages of legislators left for Paris, escorted by armed guards. An immense number of people lined the route: all repeated, "Long live the King!" but even more loudly "Long live the nation!" At the city gates, a Bourgeois Guard stopped the carriages, wanting to know who we were and why we came, and slowed the vehicles to a trot until reaching Louis XV Square. There, it was necessary to disembark and traverse the streets on foot to City Hall. All the streets were lined with crowds of people, all intersections filled by men of all conditions, and despite the apparent tumult, there reigned such order that the middle of the street was completely clear. We heard shouts of "Long live the nation! Long live the National Assembly! Long live liberty! Long live the Constitution! Long live the Fatherland! Long live the French!"

Finally, after a very long walk, we arrived at City Hall. No one has ever seen a more imposing spectacle than that on Grève Square: a crowd of peaceable and disarmed citizens, mingled with their brothers in arms for their defense: French Guards, Swiss guards, soldiers of all regiments, Knights of Saint-Louis, men of all ranks, of all arts, of all conditions, integrated, united for public defense. The greatest policing, the greatest order, the crowd of people awaiting the first order they would receive. What a nation! What a shocking love of liberty! This is not licentiousness, this is not a passing effervescence, this is a profound and durable sentiment, because it is accompanied by calm and reflection. . . .

In leaving City Hall, accompanied by the same cortege, each of us having close to him a militia officer, we went to Notre Dame, where a Te Deum was chanted.[14] We were led from there to the Palais-Royal, where an immense crowd awaited us: we could not escape the crowd that disarmed us with their applause, cries, caresses and the enthusiasm of this good people.

It is impossible for me to paint all the sensations I felt this day, which is certainly the most beautiful that a man who has contributed something to the operation of such a revolution can have. Words fail and now I can little explain it to myself. There are a thousand details one cannot grasp, a thousand fugitive sensations that cannot be described. But this idea: *they are free, and I have worked for this*, such a thought fills the heart with a soft satisfaction, a pure joy, all the more since it follows stressful situations and horrible worries . . . . Yes, certainly, we are free, our hands can no longer carry chains . . .

It is not without worry that one envisages 200,000 Parisian men in arms, 200,000 men little accustomed to discipline, proud of their liberty, perhaps already altered by bloodshed. May the spirit of moderation and peace always reign! May the people understand that, to be and always remain free, there must be order and justice!

I do not consider without fright that there still exists quite a dangerous fury against the nobility; it has been muffled a bit, but who knows what will prevent it from being reborn more terrible than ever?

Relation of a Part of France's Troubles, During the Years 1789 and 1790, 1790

In the countryside, France experienced a revolution as profound as those occurring in Paris and Versailles. Rather than simply waiting for legislators to abolish feudalism, alter the tax code, and improve rural life, peasants took matters into their own hands, engaging in a broad variety of protests. Many of these acts were peaceful (such as rent strikes and processional demonstrations), others utilized intimidation (attempting to coerce nobles and clergy to renounce their local privileges or forgive back rents), some attacked property (burning records, pillaging food-stores in moments of shortage and/or sacking the homes and castles of their opponents), and a few violently attacked recalcitrant opponents or squared off against rural police, soldiers and even fellow revolutionaries in the new National Guard. While, unfortunately, we possess only limited sources detailing the rural insurgency, with very few from the insurgents' own perspectives, this anonymous *Relation of a Part of France's Troubles*—albeit from a hostile viewpoint—chronicles the sheer diversity of dissenting acts peasants and their allies engaged in as they attempted to win redress for their grievances, and advance their vision of a more equitable France.

Around 400 inhabitants of the Parish of Maligny, close to Tonnerre, forced the fiscal agents to follow them to the chateau of M. Daguesseau to seize its archives.[15] They demanded his clerk release all licenses and tax receipts: they mistreated him and he only owes his life to the courageousness of a woman who grabbed the arm of a man trying to plunge a sword into the clerk's body.

They next went to the home of M. Maillard, notary, then to the bailiffs and all the archives; they seized the papers and titles and burned most of them.

They reassembled under the covered market; they forced the curate and municipal officers to approve taxing the price of grain at six pounds for each 100 pounds. These excesses continued three days and only ceased as Chably and Ligny's militias approached, along with three brigades of the rural police, who arrested eighteen ringleaders and led them to Tonnerre's prisons. . . .

We know the forests of Compiègne, the woods of Rambouillet, and those of Orvillers and Choisy-le-Roi have been devastated by bands of brigands, up to the moment when national militias arrived, imposed themselves, and dispersed them.[16] . . .

M. de Salunces, Lord of Drugeac, soon became the object of the parish inhabitants' furors. As he left church after mass, the seditious seized him, dragged him into one of his farmers' homes, where after a thousand prolonged outrages continuing until four in the morning, they forced him to sign away all the back rents owed him. They brought him to his castle where they ransomed him for a considerable sum, at which price he bought his life. . . .

The parishes of Aulx, Chambourney, Belle-vaux, Naizy and Hérincourt en Comté, were in full insurrection during the months of April and May 1789; armed bands controlled all the roads, seized all the grain carts they found, and inflicted on the drivers all imaginable forms of violence. . . .

[N]ear Besançon, the two rebel leaders were arrested by the rural police, and deposed in Ornans' prisons, awaiting transfer to Besançon's: at the moment of transfer, the inhabitants of Etalans and Ornans forced open the prisons and set the detained at liberty. . . .[17]

The 8th of [May 1789] over 3,000 rioters arrived at Verger Abbey, located between Douai and Cambrai. The nuns tried in vain to stop them from pillaging; the furious refused to listen to reason. They forced open the doors, broke open the armoires, pillaged the grain destined for the convent's consumption, stole the furniture, drank the wine, and devastated the entire monastery.[18] . . .

Few chateaus in Périgord were not attacked and pillaged: their charters and titles were thrown into the flames. The region's nobility took refuge in Sarlat; eight parishes in the surrounding area threatened to burn the town down; a plot to abduct at the gentlemen formed to foment a riot on market day. But the municipality, informed of this plot, took adequate measures to foil it. . . .

In the Agenois and Sarladois regions, the brigands adopted a regular plan of pillage and devastation; they banished all false friends and closed the church storehouses. They forced restitution for rents paid, and all castles to give them alcohol and money. . . .

From the month of August 1789, fermentation grew in the Bourbonnais province, and the town of Guéret was the theater of the first disorders. There, the people declared war on the distinguished inhabitants; they beat the general alarm, raised gallows on the public square, and marched around town searching for those that jealousy, resentment, or interest designated for victims. The bourgeois finally took arms, and it was not without difficulty that they imposed order on the seditious. . . .

The 27th [of July 1789], a seditious gathering formed in the town of Bourges. The rebels carried themselves to all excess despite the efforts of the rural police and a regiment from Piedmont. The most powerful bourgeois were threatened and did not dare appear. The seditious went to the merchant M. Tourangin's house; they forced open the doors and windows with hatchets and levers; they broke the furniture, forced open the armoires and discarded what they could not carry; the stores were pillaged. The insurrection's next stages would have been even more disastrous if not for the good work of the rural police and Piedmont soldiers.[19] . . .

The twelfth of September, a gang of peasants stopped a grain convoy destined for Paris at Orléans' gates. The national militia and garrison troops gathered to protect the convoy were attacked by the seditious and had to repulse them by force. Three of the rioters were killed, and nine arrested and taken to jail. . . .[20]

In the month of November, the people and workers of Saint-Etienne-en-Forès rose up. They terribly mistreated the National Guard commander and carried off five to six thousand rifles and several powder barrels. They pillaged and extorted money from the better off, while flying the red flag.[21] . . .

Discord, hatred, their agents, their attacks, the spirit of independence, the spirit of insurrection, their impetuous and devastating movements are thus the main things sullying our vision, breaking the heart of a patriotic and fidelitous historian, as such torments to his sensibility lead him to go to his country's aid.

Decree on the Abolition of Privileges, August 11

The National Assembly began one of its most radical lurches forward on the night of August 4, 1789, audaciously abolishing the social structure that had defined France for over a millennium. Disquieted by the rural insurrections gaining strength across much of the nation, legislators—barely possessing quorum at an evening session after many noble and clerical deputies had left for dinner parties—began voluntarily renouncing their own privileges, then proceeded to renounce those of their regions and privileged groups. Over the following week, the vast edifice of exemptions and preferences that had defined Old Regime French society were abolished. The right to collect feudal dues, the exclusive privilege of hunting game (including animals that preyed on peasant crops), and office-selling were eliminated. Yet, the National Assembly also specified that the title-holders would be compensated for certain lost revenues—leading to significant contestations, continued peasant obligations, and rural disorder over the following years. Only in 1793 was feudalism comprehensively eliminated. Nevertheless, a new order arose in which all French citizens were formally equal, obliterating the distinctions and discriminations commoners had previously faced.

The National Assembly entirely destroys the Feudal Regime. It decrees that, in the rights and duties as much feudal as customary, including those holding "death-rights" real or personal,[22] or to whom personal or representative servitude is owed, are abolished without reparation and all others are declared re-purchasable, with the price and method of repurchase to be fixed by the National Assembly. Those of the said rights that are not suppressed by this decree will continue nevertheless to be received until reimbursement. . . .

The exclusive right of hunting during rabbit season is also abolished. Every owner has the right to destroy or have destroyed, on his possessions only, every type of game, unless it does not conform to police laws relative to public safety. All game keepers' offices and all hunting reserves, under whatever denomination, are equally abolished . . . The President is charged with asking the king to recall the galley slaves and men banished for the simple act of hunting, the release of prisoners presently detained, and the abolition of existing procedures.[23] . . .

The tithes of every nature, and the fees tied to them, under whatever denomination, known and perceived, even by subscription, possessed by either the secular or regular clergy, or by beneficiaries, enterprises, and all feudal holders, even by the Order of Malta, and other religious and military orders, even those abandoned to the laity, if replacing and if optioned for the fixed share, are abolished . . .

Office-selling of judiciary and municipal positions is suppressed immediately. Justice will be rendered freely. Nevertheless, those holding these offices will continue their functions and collect their salaries until the Assembly has decided the means to procure their reimbursement.

The secondary rights of rural parish priests are suppressed and will cease to be paid as soon as the augmentation of fixed salary and to the pension of curates. Other regulations will be made to fix the town clergy's compensation.

Financial privileges, personal or collective, on the level of subsidies are abolished forever. Taxes will be collected from all citizens and on all properties, in the same manner and same form, and we will advise the best practices for enacting proportional payment of all contributions, even for the last six months of this fiscal year. . . .

All citizens, without distinction of birth, can be admitted to all employments, including all ecclesiastical, civil, and military dignities, and no useful profession requires dispensation. . . .

An account will be rendered to the National Assembly on the state of pensions, gifts, and wages, about which it will occupy itself in concert with the King, for the suppression of those that are excessive, without determining the future sum the king can dispose for this object. . . .

The National Assembly solemnly proclaims King Louis XVI "Restorer of French Liberty."

The National Assembly will go together to the King, to present His Majesty its decided decree, carrying him their most respectful recognition and homage, beseeching him to permit the Te Deum to be chanted in his chapel, with him in attendance. The National Assembly will occupy themselves, once they finish the Constitution, with deciding the laws necessary for developing the principles they fix with the present decree, which will be soon sent by its deputies into all provinces, with the decree of the 10th of this month, to there be printed, read from the pulpit of parish churches, and hung everywhere necessary.

FIGURE 4.1 *Jean-Jacques le Barbier,* Declaration of the Rights of Man and Citizen. *© Wikimedia Commons (public domain).*

French Revolutionaries celebrated the Declaration of the Rights of Man and Citizen as one of their greatest accomplishments. Created shortly after the document's August 1789 approval, Jean-Jacques Le Barbier's *Declaration*, dedicated "to the representatives of the French people," places the text against a background filled with Roman and Enlightenment symbols upon tablets resembling depictions of the Old Testament's Ten Commandments. One female figure sits atop triumphal arches holding broken chains, while an angel points at an enlightened triangle (representing God in Masonic iconography). The text is strewn with laurels (Roman signals for victory), while between the columns lies a Roman fasces (suggesting the need for unity, later borrowed as the symbol for fascism), topped by a Phrygian hat (which Roman freed slaves wore as a sign of their liberty). Reason, god, and ancient tradition are thus brought together to support a document making strikingly new claims about universal human rights.

4

Revolutionary Freedoms

While the revolutions of June and July leapt into the unknown, revolutionaries spent the rest of 1789 attempting to build the foundations of a new order. A power vacuum widened, worsened by urban and rural revolts, discrediting royal authority as it failed to effectively intervene or arbitrate France's interconnected crises, leading legislators to rush through new structures and plans for the revolutionary future. In their optimism, the National Assembly's members hurriedly created a system reflecting the era's greatest ambitions, enunciating principles of liberty more extensive than those permitted anywhere else in the Western world.

Inspired by the principles of natural law they witnessed both in radical Enlightenment tracks and recent American examples, revolutionaries developed a Declaration of the Rights of Man and Citizen to provide the basis for their new Constitution—not as a post-facto addendum like the United States' Bill of Rights composed the same year. Whereas prior American declarations of rights, passed by several states during the Articles of Confederation era, had mostly enshrined principles already well established by British law, the French declaration enumerated audacious new freedoms, granting the French people broad rights and permission to resist if they were not enforced. Moreover, these rights were asserted to belong to the French not by virtue of their nationality, but rather for being human beings—providing a powerful vision of human rights for the world.

After defining the people's rights, the National Assembly (more problematically) tried to define the rights of the king. Louis XVI was reduced from having theoretically unlimited, absolute powers (outside of specific rights granted particular groups of subjects) into being a presidential-style executive power. The extent of the veto to be accorded to the crown—various factions supported an absolute veto, a suspensive veto slowing down implementation, or no veto at all—divided revolutionaries. The National Assembly, now seeking to slow the revolution's momentum, took the middle course. The king could not stop the legislative process, but he could slow it by suspending measures for up to five years. Some wondered, however, if this would prevent the revolution from effectively responding to crises requiring quick governmental action—particularly as many still feared a counterrevolutionary offensive.

Continued concern over the fragile revolution's progress—together with food shortages and a counterrevolutionary gala at Versailles the King and Queen attended—led to the famed October Days. Thousands of Parisian market women coerced first municipal leaders and then National Guardsmen into marching with them on Versailles, besieging the king's palace and demanding the royal family permanently return with them to Paris. After a standoff in which at least four of guards were killed—and Parisians broke into the palace to chase the Queen from her apartments—the royal family acquiesced, proceeding to Paris as near-prisoners and finally sanctioning the Declaration of the Rights of Man and Citizen. Only with the royal family's compliance did Parisian protesters believe the revolution could become secure.

By late-1789, a new revolutionary order had taken shape. It sought to secure personal liberty, grant French people the necessities of life (particularly affordable bread), and—hopefully—defend the revolution against its enemies. Many revolutionaries by late October hoped the revolution was over, that the gains achieved could be consolidated, and the revolution's aristocratic enemies would be eventually reconciled to the new order. For over a year longer, most believed that the revolution had essentially stabilized, with only the details to be arbitrated. The passions unleashed by the year's events, however, only temporarily ebbed.

Thomas Jefferson, Richard Gem and Marquis de Lafayette, selections from letters and documents concerning the drafting of the Declaration of the Rights of Man and Citizen, January–July 1789

Amidst a letter to his Virginia neighbor James Madison also discussing Native American vocabularies, Algerian pirate captures, and an inventory of recent European publications, Thomas Jefferson noted his collaboration with the Marquis de Lafayette on a new sort of document for France: a declaration of rights. Building off state declarations of rights adopted during the American Revolution, as well as the English Bill of Rights of 1689, the French document constituted an unprecedentedly radical declaration of universal rights. With neither of the co-authors (Lafayette and Jefferson's English doctor Richard Gem) having otherwise composed much of note, Jefferson's primary authorship is probable—though difficult to prove.

Regardless, this exchange shows an important cross-fertilization of ideas between American and French Revolutionaries. As Jefferson alludes to, Madison was then composing the American Bill of Rights, which he would introduce in the House of Representatives of the First Congress in July 1789. Lafayette introduced his declaration in the National Assembly July 11, 1789—just hours before the king fired Jacques Necker, and the day before the Bastille insurrection began—and the final declaration contained several of his version's key ideas, including full equality under the law and the right of "resistance to oppression."

Thomas Jefferson to James Madison, Paris January 12, 1789.

There has been little foundation for the reports and fears relative to M. de la Fayette. He has from the beginning openly taken part with those who demand a constitution: and there was a moment that we apprehended the Bastille: but they ventured on nothing more than to take from him a temporary service on which he had been ordered; and this more to save appearances for their own authority than any thing else; for at the very time they pretended that they had put him into disgrace, they were constantly conferring and communicating with him. Since this he has stood on safe ground, and is viewed as among the foremost of the patriots. Every body here is trying their hands at forming declarations of rights. As something of that kind is going on with you also, I send you two specimens from hence. The one is by our friend of whom I have just spoken. You will see that it contains the essential principles of ours accommodated as much as could be to the actual state of things here. The other is from a very sensible man, a pure theorist, of the sect called the oeconomists, of which Turgot was considered as the head. The former is adapted to the existing abuses; the latter goes to those possible as well as to those existing. . . .

Proposed Declarations of Rights drawn by the Marquis de Lafayette and by Dr. Richard Gem.

Nature has made men equal, and the distinctions between them necessitated by the monarchy have for their basis, and ought to be measured by, their general utility.

The rights of man ensure his property, his liberty, his honor, and his life itself. No limitation can be placed upon them except by virtue of the laws consented to by himself or his representatives previously chosen, and applied by an equal tribunal.

All sovereignty resides essentially in the nation. The government divides itself into three powers: the legislative which ought to be principally exercised by a numerous representative assembly, freely and frequently elected; the Executive, which belongs exclusively to the King, whose person is sacred and the ministers responsible; the Judiciary, which ought to be confined to the tribunals of which the only function must be to guard the depository of the laws, and to apply them freely to the affairs submissive to them, and of which the organization and the regime assure to the judges their independence, to the public their impartiality, to all parties the means of justification, and an easy distribution of justice.

Taxes ought to be consented to for a short term, and proportionate to the real needs of the tax district, and to the real abilities of the area to pay.

The commanding of troops belongs to the king alone, and their obedience has no limits except those that guarantee public liberty.

A man gifted in speech and thought cannot be bothered either for his opinion or for the communication of his ideas, at least if they have not violated the social order or private honor, in which case it will be subordinate to the law.

And as the progress of enlightenment and the introduction of abuses necessitates from time to time a revision of the constitution, there must be spread out but fixed times, for a convocation of deputies whose single object must be to restore to the nation all its rights in reforming its government.

General principles relative to a political state:

1. No arbitrary distinction can be made between citizens, neither nobility, nor power, nor hereditary charge.
2. The right of electing the body of representatives must reside in the property-owners of the territory: thus the citizens who possess a certain revenue in lands will exclusively enjoy the Right of the City.
3. The state must be homogenous, having a perfect unity in all its parties, the same constitution, and the same legislation, and not have any subjects.
4. The state must not make alliances with foreign nations, except in times of war.
5. The civil and criminal codes, like all institutions of whatever nature, must conform to universal justice.
6. All bodies of citizens must form militias.
7. Full religious liberty.
8. Full liberty of industry and commerce.
9. Liberty of the press.
10. The law of habeas corpus.
11. Judgments by juries.
12. Territorial taxes only.
13. The property of the parents must be inherited equally by their children.
14. No substitutions.
15. Divorce, or dissolution of the marriage contract.

Lafayette's draft of the Declaration of Rights [late June/early July 1789]

Nature has made men free and equal; distinctions can only be founded on general utility.

Every man is born with inalienable rights; these are the rights of property, maintenance of his honor and his life, the full disposition of his person, of his industry, of all his faculties, caring for his well-being, and resistance to oppression.

The exercise of natural rights has no limits except those that assure the same rights to society.

No man can be troubled for his religion, nor for his opinions, nor for the communication of his thoughts by speech, writing or publishing so long as they do not trouble citizens' peace by engaging in calumnies.

No man can submit except to the laws consented to by himself or his representatives previously chosen and legally applied.

The principle of all sovereignty resides imprescriptibly in the nation.

All government has for its unique goal the common good; the legislative, executive and judicial powers must be distinct and defined: no body nor any individual can have an authority that does not expressly emanate from the Nation.

The legislative power must be essentially exercised by the deputies chosen in all the districts via free, regular and frequent elections.

The executive power is exercised by the King whose person is sacred, all the individual or collective agents are accountable and responsible to the nation whatever authorization they may have received.

The judicial power must be used for applying the law; trials must be public and the distribution of justice easy and impartial.

The laws must be clear, precise and uniform for all citizens.

Subsidies must be freely fixed and proportionally distributed.

And like the progress of enlightenment, the introduction of abuses and the right of succeeding generations necessitates the revision of all human establishment, the constitutional means must be indicated to ensure in certain cases an extraordinary convocation of representatives whose only object must be to examine and modify, if necessary, the form of government.

Lafayette to Jefferson, Versailles July 9, 1789

To Morrow I present my bill of rights about the middle of the sitting. Be pleased to Consider it Again and Make Your observations.

They are very Angry with me for Having supported the Motion Against the Coming of the troops. If they take me up You Must Claim me as an American citizen. . . .

Declaration of the Rights of Man and Citizen, August 26, 1789

No document embodied the French Revolution's universalist hopes better than the Declaration of the Rights of Man and Citizen. The first portion of France's inaugural constitution, designed to provide the principles for its contents, the constitution declared its basis to be not historical precedent (as English and American declarations largely justified themselves) but rather natural right. By declaring "All men are born and remain free and equal in rights," revolutionaries created a new inclusive ideal of human rights—though one not easily applicable to their colonies, where hundreds of thousands remained enslaved. Moreover, the document emboldened citizens to defend their rights, making "resistance to oppression" expressly protected should other portions of the document (including free association, speech and press) be infringed. Though buttressed by other articles demanding obedience to the law and submission to the general will, revolutionaries trumpeted the achievement of core rights applicable to all. When the United Nations adopted a global Declaration of Human Rights in 1948, they took France's 1789 declaration as their model.

The French People's representatives, constituted in the National Assembly, considering that ignorance, forgetting or contempt for the rights of man are the sole causes of public misfortune and the corruption of governments, have resolved to expose in a solemn Declaration, now presented to all the members of the social body, ceaselessly recalling to them their rights and duties, to the end that the acts of the legislative power, and those of the executive power, can be at each instant compared with the goal of all public institutions. Thereby, they will become more respected, to the end that the reclamations of citizens, founded from this point forward on simple and incontestable bases, will always turn to the maintenance of the constitution and the happiness of all.

Consequently, the National Assembly recognizes and declares, in the presence and under the auspices of the Supreme Being, the following rights of Man and Citizen:

Article 1. All men are born and remain free and equal in rights. Social distinctions can only be founded on the basis of common utility.

Article 2. The goal of all political association is the conservation of the natural and imprescriptible rights of man. These rights are liberty, property, security, and resistance to oppression.

Article 3. The principle of all sovereignty resides essentially in the nation. No body, no individual can exercise authority not expressly emanating from it.

Article 4. Liberty consists in the ability to do anything that does not harm another: thus, the exercise of the natural rights of each man has no limits except that which assures to the other members of society the enjoyment of the same rights. These limits can only be determined by law.

Article 5. The law can only forbid those actions harmful to society. All that which is not forbidden by law cannot be prevented, and no one can be forced to do what it does not order.

Article 6. The law is the expression of the general will. All citizens have the right to contribute personally, or via their representatives, in its formation. It ought to be the same for all, whether it protects or punishes. All citizens thus equal in its eyes are equally admissible to all honors, positions and public employments, according to their potential, and without other distinction than their virtues and talents.

Article 7. No person can be accused, arrested, or detained except in the cases determined by law, and according to the methods it prescribes. Those soliciting, expediting, or executing arbitrary orders ought to be punished; but every citizen called or seized in the name of the law ought to obey instantly: one becomes guilty by resisting.

Article 8. The law ought only to establish penalties strictly and evidently necessary, and no one can be punished except in virtue of a law established and promulgated before the violation, and legally applied.

Article 9. Every man shall be presumed innocent until proven guilty, if it is judged indispensable to arrest him, all unnecessary severity for securing his person shall be severely punished by law.

Article 10. No one ought to be bothered for his opinions, even about religion, as long as their enunciation does not trouble the public order established by law.

Article 11. The free communication of thoughts and opinions is one of the most precious rights of man: every citizen can thus speak, write and publish freely, with the exception of needing to respond to the abuse of this liberty in those cases determined by law.

Article 12. Guaranteeing the rights of man and citizen necessitates a police force: that force is thus instituted for the advantage of everyone, and not for the private utility of those to whom it is conferred.

Article 13. To maintain the police force, and for the expenses of administration, a communal contribution is indispensable: it ought to be divided equally amongst all citizens, adjusted for their ability to pay.

Article 14. All citizens have the right to certify, personally or through their representatives, the necessity of public contributions, to consent to them freely, to follow their implementation, and to determine their level, the assessment method, how they are collected, and their duration.

Article 15. Society has the right to demand accounts from every public agent of his administration.

Article 16. Every society in which the guarantee of rights is not assured, nor the separation of powers determined, does not have a Constitution.

Article 17. Property is an inviolable and sacred right, no one can be deprived of it, unless in the case of public necessity, legally certified, makes it evidently necessary under condition of a just and fair indemnity.

André de Sinéty, *Proposal for a Declaration of the Rights of Man and Duties of the Citizen*, 1789

Numerous National Assembly deputies proposed, and some published, alternative Declarations of the Rights of Man and Citizen as the legislature considered what rights to include—most of which were more moderate than the final version approved. André-Louis-Esprit de Sinéty de Puylon, a noble deputy from Marseille, proposed a declaration in which both French citizens' rights and duties would be made explicit. Sinéty's version attempts to balance the rights of individuals with their duties as part of society. Such a measured approach was much more in keeping with Anglo-American charters of rights—indeed, many Americans did not favor a Bill of Rights in 1789 because they believed such a statement would circumscribe their freedoms. France's 1795 Constitution of the Year III would draw from Sinéty's example by including a Declaration of Duties. Formally enshrining "inequality" alongside "equality" never rhetorically appealed to legislators, however. By choosing a more open-ended Declaration of Rights than what Sinéty and numerous other legislators proposed, revolutionary legislators permitted further radicalization.

The French people's representatives, united in the National Assembly, having the state's regeneration as their principal goal, considering that the social order and all good constitutions ought to have immutable principles for their basis; that man is born free and only submits himself to the regime of a political society to set his natural rights under the protection of a communal force; that the man-citizen has sacred duties to carry out towards his peers and society; that a corresponding just reciprocity of needs and assistance limits the rights of man for the happiness of all, and amply compensates for the sacrifices all citizens must make of part of their natural rights to society, which exercised individually and without considering others, would be detrimental to all; wanting to consecrate, and solemnly recognize, in the presence of the supreme Legislator of the Universe, the natural rights of man and the duties of citizens, and expose them to public veneration by a table showing the correspondence of each article, one with the other, that can inspire in all individuals just confidence in their rights, and sacred respect for their duties; declare that these rights and duties rest on the following truths:

Article I.

Rights of Man: Each man draws from nature the right to protect himself and the desire to be happy.

Duties of the Citizen: The true happiness of man cannot exist except through intimate knowledge of the supreme being who created him, protects him, enlightens him, consoles him, and assures him recompense for his virtues.

Article II.

Rights of Man: To assure his conservation and procure his wellbeing, each man draws from the nature of his faculties: liberty consists of exercising these faculties.

Duties of the Citizen: The wellbeing and liberty of man cannot be assured to him except via patriotism, the reciprocity of duties between fellow citizens, and the always-active charity between them.

Article III.

Rights of Man: From the use of man's faculties derives the right of property. Each man has an equal right to his liberty and his property.

Duties of the Citizen: The use of faculties cannot be free and full, or the right of property inalienable, except by the respect of each for the liberty and properties of others, and by their submission to society's laws.

Article IV.

Rights of Man: The life of man, his liberty, his honor, his work and the things he has the exclusive right to dispose of, compose all his properties and all his rights.

Duties of the Citizen: Each citizen must respect the properties of others; the laws must guarantee them to everyone. All attack on others' properties is a capital crime.

Article V.

Rights of Man: Each man has not received from nature the same ability to use their rights. Inequality is born among men: inequality is thus part of nature.

Duties of the Citizen: Men cannot preserve themselves from the dangers of inequality except by the social connections that shelter the weak from the enterprises of the strong. They need the mutual aid of humanity and fraternity to correct this inequality.

Article VI.

Rights of Man: Society is formed by the need to maintain the equality of rights amidst unequal means. The goal of all society is thus the establishment of laws.

Duties of the Citizen: The relationship between mutual rights and duties cannot be maintained except by laws; it is thus respect for the laws alone that can assure citizens' rights and hold them to their duties.

Article VII.

Rights of Man: The first wish of man in society ought to be service according to his capacity and talent; he has the right to be summoned to any public employment.

Duties of the Citizen: The sole title that all citizens have to the exercise of public employments ought to be virtue, patriotism, and talent; the greatest and most scandalous stain on honor ought to be exclusionary desires.

Article VIII.

Rights of Man: Law being the expression of the general will, every citizen has the right to cooperate in its formation, whether by themselves or via their freely elected representatives.

Duties of the Citizen: The laws established by the citizens' legitimate representatives are obligatory for everyone. None can subvert them and no political authority can command and coerce, except in the law's name.

Article IX.

Rights of Man: No citizen can be accused or troubled in the use of their property, nor disturbed from their liberty, except in virtue of the law, in its prescribed forms and in those cases specified.

Duties of the Citizen: The law alone protects public security and in prosecuting crimes, no one can serve justice by themselves; the magistrate, the law's only executor, has the sole right to investigate public and private crimes. No one should be tempted to shield a criminal from the law's pursuit.

Article X.

Rights of Man: Every person convicted should only submit to a penalty proportional to the crime they have committed, as pronounced by law.

Duties of the Citizen: The law being obligatory, no rank, state, or fortune can shield the guilty from the penalty pronounced.

Article XI.

Rights of Man: As the law cannot regulate everything, it must be supplemented by morality and religion. Man is ultimately accountable to God and his conscience.

Duties of the Citizen: Religion is the most powerful regulator. It must be engraved in all hearts. Not respecting it essentially injures society and good order.

Article XII.

Rights of Man: Maintaining religion requires a public faith; each citizen who does not trouble the public faith will not be bothered.

Duties of the Citizen: God alone has the right to scrutinize hearts and the ability to enlighten men. No one ought to be able to trouble fellow citizens in their religious opinions, but all ought to have absolute respect for the public faith.

Article XIII.

Rights of Man: Free communication of thoughts is a right of man, it ought not to be restrained except when it impinges on the rights of others.

Duties of the Citizen: No one ought to attack the good order of society or their fellow citizens' honor by their words or writings. Public and private calumny should be punished by law, which should develop ways of preventing it by deterring and punishing calumnious and dangerous writings. . . .

Pierre-Victor, Baron de Malouet, Speech on the Royal Veto, September 1, 1789

For all the radicalism of summer 1789, the National Assembly sought a moderate course by September. As the Declaration of Rights had declared that all sovereignty resided in the nation, the role of the King's executive power had to be redefined. Seeking to re-solidify authority, many deputies became known as "*Monarchiens*," attempting to stabilize the monarchy as a bulwark against both absolutists and democratizing radicals—thus creating a system of "checks and balances" on the Anglo-American model. Such a figure could temper the passions of the Assembly and avoid rash future changes. Louis XVI's authority was recast as that of a useful, disinterested person, who without personal ambition (monarchs claimed to have only the interests of their country at heart) could arbitrate for the good of the nation. The Assembly granted him a powerful "suspensive" veto, which could prevent revolutionary legislation from being enacted for up to five years. In practice, however, Louis' machinations would prevent him from ever capably fulfilling this role—and the hypothetical right of peoples to resist oppression would be put into action.

Messieurs, what is the royal sanction? Should we have one?

How should it be determined? The solution to these questions ought to follow the principles you have already consecrated, or which the French people unanimously recognize, by the power belonging to them and that which their king possesses. I begin by remarking that, of all powers, sanctioning the laws is the only one despotism cannot allow . . . The despot desires, he acts, he oppresses, he executes his will, but not through laws; no free people can voluntarily accept such actions; no public power can sanction them. The despot's will, always errant in his lands like a storm on the horizon, has no character, no inviolable asylum . . .

In a country where one man is considered master of the law, superior to the law, superstition and ignorance announce their power as emanating from celestial power; then, religious formulas were imagined to sanction their will and this impious doctrine has made despotic government a veritable theocracy. But amongst those people submitted to it, society's primitive sovereignty is manifested without obstacle every time the multitude manages to unite itself: an imperishable instinct carries its establishment as supreme judge of tyranny, to break the oppressive force it has created without knowing how to regulate it, to submit to a new blindness . . . Thus in Asia, in Africa, and within Europe's confines, unforeseen revolutions shake the thrones, frequently showing princes their weakness and peoples their force.

It is thus true that everywhere the people want to be free; this can only occur by an act of their sovereign will.

It is thus true that all sovereignty resides in the nation; this is the principle you have consecrated.

Now, given this principle, Messieurs, what can the royal sanction be? It is an act of sovereignty, by which the law is pronounced; this is a power communicated by the nation, which possesses everything.

To better judge this, we must examine to what end the supreme magistrate has been instituted, to whom the right of sanctioning the laws can be confined.

It would be absurd to believe the crown's prerogatives serve the monarch's personal satisfaction and pleasures; there are none not finding their origin and end in general utility. . . .

Such is amongst us the origin and the end of royal authority. The nation, in instituting it, has only given that portion of its sovereignty it cannot exercise by itself, which can best be exercised by a single person. Likewise, they have delegated to the legislative power, and confided the exercise to their representatives freely elected. . . .

The people, Messieurs, who want, who determine the utility of having a king, who make him the center of all powers, as the conservator of all their rights, take precautions to preserve a single authority they will defer to, while ensuring he will not abuse them.

This last intention is fulfilled, on the people's part, in reserving to their representatives the exercise of legislative power and the surveillance of executive power. But, the people have equal interest in defending royal authority from all unjust initiatives by their representatives . . .

Thus, society's general happiness cannot exist except through the harmony of the powers working together for it, without being troubled by discord; thereby, the nation wanting a monarchical government would only have an uncertain government that could slide precipitously towards either aristocracy or democracy!

The royal sanction is thus the only means of fixing the principles of security and inviolability in the forms of government, and this important prerogative, making the nation's leader independent from its representatives, can never render it stronger than the general will, as soon as it makes itself clear . . . .

The royal sanction is thus useful for national serenity. It is necessary to the monarch to peacefully manage the public power. It is no less important to the security of the legislative body's members.

Madame Chéret, *Events of Paris and Versailles, by one of the Women who had the Opportunity to be in the Deputation*, 1789

In a short pamphlet, Madame Chéret, one of the leaders of the March on Versailles, gives her own account of the events of October 5 and 6. While male-led marches from Paris had been repulsed on July 12 and August 30, amidst worsening fears of food shortages and royal reaction, in early October Parisian women mobilized. The Women of the Markets (*Dames des Halles*) held the Old Regime privilege of access to the monarch to inform him of common people's complaints and problems. This time, however, they recruited several thousand women for a mass-march and motivated tens of thousands of male Parisian National Guardsmen to follow them. With the soldiers between Paris and Versailles declining to fire on the women, the crowds arrived at the National Assembly and royal palace by evening and, after bloody confrontations with the king's guards, pressured the return of the royal family to live in Paris by the next morning. The march's leaders asserted the King's presence in the capital would both assure its provisioning (the royal family being called "the baker, the baker's wife, and the baker's apprentice" amidst the march) and prevent future counterrevolutionary plots. In so doing, they made Paris the revolution's undisputed center.

Towards half past eight in the morning, many women arrived at City Hall: some demanded to speak to Messieurs Bailly and Lafayette for an explanation of why it was so difficult and expensive to have bread; others desired the King and Queen to come to Paris and take residence in the Louvre, where they would be, the women said, infinitely better off than at Versailles. Others asked that those sporting black cockades be sent away, that the Regiment of Flanders and Bodyguards be recalled, and that their Majesties have no other guards than the Parisian National Guard.[1] During this interval, Major-General Gouvion, Second Commander of the Volunteers of the Bastille Richard du Pin, and Distributor of Powder, Arms and Equipment Lefévre ran the greatest peril, since the multitude, furious at not finding arms and munitions, wanted to hang them. Their avoiding this was nothing short of a miracle.

Towards midday or one in the afternoon, Monsieur the Marquis de Lafayette, who seemingly found no advantage in trip to Versailles, finally decided he needed to accede to the citizens' ardent desires. . . . .the citizen-women went to Versailles, under the command of Hulin, Maillard and other Volunteers of the Bastille, those heroes who wanted to add to their laurels of July 14 the honor of telling the National Assembly the cause of the people's troubles, without which the greatest of monarchs was nothing. Arriving at the Point-du-jour, our capital's citizens halted to set themselves in order: the men at Sèvres forced the merchants to sell them foodstuffs, but paid them and then continued to Versailles.[2] During the trip, at least two or three people invoked the king's name: they were stopped, had their black cockades pulled out, and were forced to join the march.

When reaching the entry to their Majesty's estates, the Bourgeoisie of Versailles, the Regiment of Flanders, and the Dragoons (we will not speak of their officers) clapped their hands, showing their satisfaction with acclamations of joy, applauding their arrival, and prayed them to work for the general good. Can one make such a prayer of women born French, and who had at their head the Heroes of the Bastille? Several minutes afterwards, around four in the afternoon, our citizen-women were taken by Hulin and Maillard to go to the National Assembly, which required careful negotiations to enter. What an imposing spectacle for them! Nevertheless, their appearance displeased certain members of an order that ought never to have existed, if our fathers had the wisdom to reflect and feel that there had not been, before the invasion of the Francs against the Gauls, two sorts of people, the conquerors (the nobles), and the vanquished (the commoners). It is the greatest absurdity to admit amongst the representatives of a nation like ours those men who were only the false owners of properties that blind credulity afforded them. Whatever it might be, despite the spirit of worry our good friends have spread amongst the faithful, of which several have raised the siege, the honorable members of the National Assembly wanted us to believe they had firmly decided not to stop, that nothing was finished forever. They accorded to our twelve deputies: 1. A new law against exporting grains; 2. A promise to tax wheat at 24 *livres*, an honest rate to make bread plentiful and help the less prosperous citizens; 3. That meat would not be sold for less than eight *sous la livre*.

At this juncture, the Bodyguards and National Guardsmen amused each other, they said, by firing their rifles; we still do not know who fired first, but word spread that we lost some people. The king proved, the fifth of October 1789, that he merits more than ever the title accorded him on July 17, of "Restorer of the French Nation." Our female citizens, covered in glory, were at His Majesty's expense brought back to city hall in carriages, where we were received as the female liberators of the Capital. This event ought forever to abort the designs of present and future aristocrats.

Reading of a Letter from the London Revolution Society in the National Assembly, Followed by the National Assembly's Response, Presaging the Jacobin Club's Founding, November 25, 1789

French Revolutionaries enthusiastically responded to offers of aid and friendship from outside groups—and looked to profit from others' examples. The London Revolution Society was primarily composed of Protestant Dissenters (Baptists, Quakers, Unitarians and others) denied full civil and political rights because they refused to swear to all the Church of England's articles of faith. Enthused by the universalism French revolutionaries espoused, they wrote to the National Assembly hoping for future Franco-British alliances and the further elaboration of universal human rights. The address led to an upsurge of Anglophilia amongst French political elites, who soon founded their own *Société de la Révolution* in an old Dominican "Jacobin" convent on the rue St. Honoré, several blocks west of the National Assembly, that soon changed its name to the Society of the Friends of the Constitution, retaining the English-style nickname "*Club des Jacobins* [Jacobin Club]." This new organization hoped to build consensus among revolutionaries in France through discussion and debate, while educating the French citizenry and others abroad on civic principles and the practices of representative government. As on many other occasions, some of the revolution's most radical leap forward resulted from creatively adapting international examples.

The Society for commemorating the Revolution in Great Britain, disdaining National partialities, and rejoicing in every triumph of Liberty and Justice over Arbitrary Power, offer to the National Assembly of France their Congratulations on the Revolution in that Country, and on the prospect it gives to the two first Kingdoms in the World, of a common participation in the blessings of Civil and Religious Liberty.

They cannot help adding their ardent wishes of an happy settlement of so important a Revolution, and at the same time expressing the particular satisfaction with which they reflect on the tendency of the glorious example given in France to encourage other Nations to assert the unalienable rights of Mankind, and thereby to introduce a general reformation in the governments of Europe, and to make the World free and happy.

Response, written by the Duc de la Rochefoucauld:

It belonged that great apostle of liberty, Dr. Priestley, to propose a motion promoting the most beautiful homage to liberty, that of national sympathies.[3] The address of felicitation that the Count of Stanhope has given the honor to send to the Duc de la Rochefoucauld, was received by the National Assembly with the most lively applause.[4] They have seen the aurora of a beautiful day, when the two nations that have always respected each other, despite their political divisions, will contract an intimate liaison by the similarity of their opinions, and by their common enthusiasm for liberty. They charge their President to write to Stanhope, but as the many duties of the presidency have not yet permitted the sending of the letter, the Duke de la Rochefoucauld impresses upon himself the perpetual honor of responding the Dr. Price.[5]

FIGURE 5.1 *Lesueur Brothers,* Planting the Tree of Liberty. © *Photo Josse / Leemage / Getty Images.*

Popular print-makers seeking to capture revolutionary events, the Leseur brothers' work gives us some of the most detailed and memorable images surviving from the revolutionary period. In this scene from ca. 1790, we witness the planting of a liberty tree—a symbol taken from the ancient Roman Republic and popularized during the American War of Independence. On the left are a detachment of National Guardsmen, parading with bayonets attached, while on the right stand a crowd of civilians—women in white dresses of purity, men wearing red "Phrygian" liberty caps, children looking on expectantly, and revolutionary officials in the background with tricolor cockades attached to their hats. The print highlights the sense of excitement and fraternity as revolutionaries came together to commemorate their new compact.

5

Revolutionary Radicalization

Between the great uprisings of 1789 and the terrors of 1792–4 lay a period of vast possibilities. 1790 has often been described as the "peaceful" year of the French Revolution, in which the French overwhelming pledged to work together to forge a new order of responsible liberty. At the Federation Festivals of 1789–90, French people swore ecstatically that they would defend the revolution, while working to complete and uphold the national constitution then under construction. With the formidable popular power unleashed by the Revolution organized into festivities featuring hundreds of thousands, the New Regime appeared to be solidifying into a powerful and capable government.

The under-construction constitution was only the most dramatic portion of the administrative reconstruction of France achieved over the revolution's first year. Local elections were successfully held for offices in 44,000 municipalities, opening what had previously been a closed aristocratic preserve to common citizens. The ancient provinces, as unequal in size and power as American states, were re-districted into eighty-three largely equal departments. Whereas previously each province boasted of its ancient privileges and distinctiveness, the National Assembly re-drew the administrative map to encourage parity, uniformity and centralization. Backed by citizen-soldier National Guardsmen, the new regime possessed a popular mandate wholly unlike that of the Old Regime.

Even in this era of good feelings, the revolution still possessed worrying features. The Jacobin Club network affiliated revolutionaries across the country, to communicate intelligence to strengthen socio-political bonds and defend the revolution against its enemies. Though claiming to only desire the public good, the Jacobin network—particularly the central Paris branch caucusing National Assembly members—often pushed for more radical changes than the legislature's majority supported. They did not lack real opponents, especially among the ranks of the privileged who had lost status and power from revolutionary changes. Many could identify with publications like the *Friend of the King*, not just espousing conservatism but seeking to inspire a conservative counterrevolution that could undermine or overthrow the revolution.

The National Assembly in late-1790, fearing counterrevolutionaries' influence, passed legislation requiring priests to swear their fidelity to them (even over their loyalty to the Pope). This alienated many devout revolutionaries, including some clergymen in the Assembly who had helped sponsor some of 1789's most radical changes. Some previously radical regions like Brittany increasingly grew conservative (with many taking up arms against the government in the *Chouan* guerilla movement). The growth of popular counterrevolutionary movements gave displaced elites new hope, who sought to conflate religious piety with support of the nobility and royalty.

Many aristocrats remained in exile, lobbying foreign kings to invade France and reestablish the Old Regime. At no stage could the French Revolution develop without an eye turned to events abroad. The specter of foreign intervention heightened conservative hopes and encouraged plotting against the new French authorities. Revolutionaries, angered, heightened their rhetoric against counterrevolutionaries further.

While all sides realized the potential for future civil war, some revolutionaries argued the New Regime could best be defended by furthering a new vision of peace, social justice and fraternity. Maximillien de Robespierre's proposal to abolish the death penalty in 1791 built from some of the ongoing revolution's principal themes—seeking to abolish injustice, arbitrariness, and barbarism in favor of enlightened humanitarianism. If a new social order could be crafted to allow French people's talents to flourish, the French Revolution could outpace its counterrevolutionary competitors and triumph. If brutality could be discredited, fraternity might reign.

Most revolutionaries in early 1791 would not have predicted the approaching foreign and civil wars, much less the use of terror between revolutionary factions, but social cleavages had opened. Even while revolutionaries clung to the rhetoric of unanimity, real and enduring opposition to the revolution developed. French recourse to a 'second revolution' bringing democracy and terror was not inevitable, but developed from the many pressures revolutionaries continued to face.

Arthur Young, selection from *Travels in France*, account of an early Jacobin Meeting, published in 1792

The evolution of French Revolutionary politics led to the development of new forms of organization. Clubs had played only marginal roles in the early French Revolution, but in late 1789 the Jacobin Club developed as an influential caucus for radical National Assembly deputies. Club members typically spent their evenings at the old monastery on the rue Saint-Honoré, socializing, debating, and testing speeches they intended to give in the National Assembly. The heady atmosphere could push speakers to more radical conclusions than they had initially envisioned. Returning from provincial travels, Young in January 1790 visited the new Paris club and found the new organization disconcerting—little respecting French monarchical traditions, organized in opposition to conservative factions, fanning rumors of conspiracies, and attempting to decide great questions before the National Assembly did. Though a somewhat exaggerated account—republicanism would remain rare until the King's flight a year and a half later, the Jacobins only incorporated a dedicated minority of the Assembly, and actively worked to build national consensus through an affiliated network of provincial clubs—Young's account correctly predicted the direction of the Revolution's coming radicalization.

The violent democrats, who have the reputation of being so much republican in principle, that they do not admit any political necessity for having even the name of a king, are called the *enragés*. They have a meeting at the Jacobins, called the revolution club, which assembles every night, in the very room in which the famous league was formed, in the reign of Henry III; and they are so numerous, that all material business is there decided, before it is discussed by the National Assembly. I called this morning on several persons, all of whom are great democrats; and mentioning this circumstance to them, as one which favoured too much of a Paris junto governing the kingdom, an idea, which must, in the long run, be unpopular and hazardous; I was answered, that the predominancy which Paris assumed, at present, was absolutely necessary, for the safety of the whole nation; for if nothing were done, but by procuring a previous common consent, all great opportunities would be lost, and the National Assembly left constantly exposed to the danger of a counter-revolution. They, however, admitted, that it did create great jealousies, and no where more than at Versailles, where some plots (they added) are, without doubt, hatching at this moment, which have the King's person for their object: riots are frequent there, under pretence of the price of bread; and such movements are certainly very dangerous, for they cannot exist so near Paris, without the aristocratical party of the old government endeavouring to take advantage of them, and to turn them to a very different end . . . I remarked, in all these conversations, that the belief of plots, among the disgusted party, for setting the King at liberty, is general; they seem almost persuaded, that the revolution will not be absolutely finished before some such attempts are made; and it is curious to observe, that the general voice is, that if an attempt were to be made, in such a manner as to have the least appearance of success, it would undoubtedly cost the king his life; . . . In a word, the present devotion to liberty is a sort of rage; it absorbs every other passion, and permits no other object to remain in view, than what promises to confirm it.

The Friend of the King newspaper, selections from "Preliminary Discourse on the State of France," June 1, 1790

Soon to become the most popular conservative newspaper in Revolutionary France, *The Friend of the King* used its first issue in June 1790 to propagate their vision of a revivified monarchism that could effectively respond to recent changes. Though decrying Old Regime abuses and celebrating some revolutionary transformations, the paper denounced the checks the National Assembly placed on monarchical power, blaming such changes for the destabilization of French politics and society. Amidst much revolutionary rhetoric that to the editors—clergyman Abbé Thomas-Marie Royou and nobleman Galart de Montjoie—seemed drunk on liberty, they attempted to bring public opinion back to supporting the traditional hierarchical pillars of French society: church and king. In their exasperation with the revolution's course, the journal radicalized over the next two years, regularly defending counterrevolutionary schemes, encouraging foreign invasion to crush the revolution, and antagonistically debating Jean-Paul Marat's *The Friend of the People*. Fighting repression from Revolutionary authorities and radical protesters, the journal appeared under multiple editors (though retaining the same title) over the following two years, before finally being suppressed following the monarchy's fall in August 1792.

The editors of the *Literary Year*, horrified like the sane part of the public, have seen the innumerable array of broadsides and periodical pamphlets, in which one can find everything except truth. We the authors, breaking without modesty or restraint from those of another party who spread errors and lies while circulating calumny and blasphemies, now think it our duty to contest this impure torrent.

A lamentable conspiracy is formed against the altar and throne. The principles of justice, fidelity, morality, and political sanity are attacked daily by a legion of incendiary writers whose scandalous audaciousness needs to be stopped. Their frenzy is evidently the work of false and cunning philosophy that for over half a century has aroused peoples against what is most important for them to respect. Their sacrilegious and seditious views do not escape Fréron, who, in unveiling them, predicts the revolution this pride-filled sect and enemy of all dependency has made will one day succeed, if not encountering insurmountable obstacles.[1]

These predictions are proven correct today. This estimable writer's successors, penetrated by his principles, jealous to follow the path he traces for them, will have, like him, the firmness to unmask the enemies of the public good. The attacks of fanatical philosophy are at their height; it now becomes necessary to double our courage to combat them. As the attacks occur daily, they must be repulsed as often. . . .

People have been strangely misled about our intentions, if one only looks to find, in this new journal we offer the public, a censure of great changes that the pressure of circumstances have brought. The old regime had its problems, including intolerable abuses; but in lamenting the faults of times past, the misfortunes of Louis XIV . . . the operations of finance, whether inept or shameful, that under Louis XV's long reign exhausted the public treasury and prepared all the evils now afflicting us; in applauding the suppression of arbitrary arrest warrants, for holding the executive power's agents accountable, for the right finally rendered the nation to decide and vote on taxes; in recognizing that obedience to the National Assembly's decrees, sanctioned by the King, is our first duty, all this does not distract us from the deplorable state to which the French Monarchy is reduced to today. We exaggerate nothing, but will tell all the truths that may be useful.

Moreover, we owe our readers an honest explanation of our principles and cannot give them that before tracing the revolution's trajectory. . . .

The opinions, prejudices, manners, laws, the form of the government itself, have all changed. Before 1789, France was a tempered monarchy, in which the sovereign, restrained by fundamental laws, saw himself further limited in exercising his authority by the resistance of orders and bodies. Clothed with all the force of executive power, holding in his hand all means of improvement, interested in the happiness of his peoples . . .

Today, what is the condition of the most beautiful empire of the universe? This is no longer a monarchy; all its foundations are destroyed. This is a sort of royal democracy, in which the chief obeys and no longer commands, he promulgates the laws but does not make them. He monitors their execution, and only has a vain influence on the legislative body's will. He heads the troops, but he does not organize the army, and they do not take an exclusive oath of obedience to him. Simply, though it takes courage to say it, there are no more subjects, and apparently no more masters.

All the throne's foundations have been struck at the same time. The two first orders, the ancient corps of the state, have seen themselves simultaneously attacked by a legion of enemies. In this unprovoked war, it is uncertain if one ought to be more distressed about injustice than shocked by the ferocity of those alleging it. . . .

These changes occurred amidst the convulsions that work on the constitution began and continues. Seditious writers have preached a murderous doctrine; priests have been insulted, calumniated in a thousand pamphlets. Every dream of impiety has found apostles. Attacks against the altar have inspired attacks against the throne . . .

Agitation, promises, impostures, the gold of the factious has managed to mislead the multitude. Like an epidemic illness, the bloody mania of proscriptions has spread from the capital into the provinces. Properties have been violated, chateaux burned, almost everywhere French blood has reddened this land that was for so long one of peace and happiness. . . .

Who can say now what will follow this new order of things? . . .

Ah, generous and loyal people! . . . You idolize your kings, you whose country is covered with the great works of a house fertile in heroes, and whose chief will repay with love your fidelity! You to whom heaven has given a king exempt from all vices and vested with all virtues. A citizen king, your father, your friend, who has addressed to you these touching words: "I cannot be happy except through my people's happiness," can you profit from the rights you would not enjoy if he had not given them to you, to turn against the conditions of the pact that united you to him, to enrich yourself on prerogatives, on proprieties that the possession of fourteen centuries assured him! And you could, Frenchmen, without your hearts breaking in sadness, hear the best of sovereigns say until his last moments, to the successor of his long line: "My son, I have done everything for my people . . . and my people have taken everything!"

Jean-Marie Goujon and Pierre-François Tissot, Account of Federation Festival, July 14, 1790

The July 14, 1790 Federation Festival at Paris' Champ de Mars, celebrating the first anniversary of the Bastille's fall, captured the early revolution's fraternal spirit and led to a great outpouring of collective joy. Building from a series of "federation" National Guard rallies across the country from summer 1789 onwards, soon expanded to include the general citizenry, hundreds of thousands of French citizens gathered to take oaths to the Revolution. Paris' July 14 event, featuring King Louis XVI swearing to uphold the still under-construction French Constitution, drew hundreds of thousands. Despite rain and long delays, many described the oath-takings in ecstatic terms, believing the Revolution had consolidated French support and would triumph over its foreign and domestic enemies. Cities and towns held satellite events at the same hour throughout the nation, as did sympathetic radicals abroad. Jean-Marie Goujon and Pierre-François Tissot, respectively twenty-two and twenty-four years old and both future National Convention legislators, attended the ceremony, writing afterwards to their parents of the new era of fraternity they believed the gathering embodied. That afternoon, the revolution appeared overwhelming, sublime, and unstoppable.

Goujon to His Mother:

My dear mama, I saw the federation and encountered no trouble! I still live! I did not perceive the least disorder, nor the least sign of displeasure, nor the lightest murmur from this people that some would so like to anger! I saw 500,000 men assembled, their hands upstretched towards the Supreme Being, raising themselves into free spirits worthy of virtue. I saw, I joined myself to them; my beating heart wondered if nature possessed a more beautiful title than that of French citizen, and I took glory in its being reserved for me. I could not speak a word, but the tears escaping my eyes attested to what I felt at the bottom of my heart. The drunkenness of virtue seemed to carry me into a new universe; I felt worthy of being a man. Ah! I took the oath and I will never forget it. I will live free or I will die.

I embrace you all.

Tissot to his Father:

This day, forever memorable to history, passed without trouble or misfortune. My eyes have seen the most beautiful spectacle of the universe, five hundred thousand people animated by the same spirit, the same intention, swearing in the name of an entire people, turned towards God living on the Altar of the Fatherland, to live free and die free and loyal to the law. I cannot attempt to give you this patriotic festival's details, one must have seen it to have an idea of it, and one cannot attempt to retrace it. Imagine the Champ de Mars surrounded by thirty-two rows of seats filled by an immense multitude that rose up to the trees surrounding this immense space, wherein the extremities were occupied on one side by the king's tribunal and the other by an arch of triumph, with both surrounded by an innumerable multitude. Amidst all this was the altar, at the steps of which one saw thousands of National Guardsmen that seemed to form a single mass . . . The procession took at least two and a half hours to enter, there were, I believe, sixty thousand National Guardsmen in the Champ de Mars, and all these people were arranged in an admirable order without accident. Perpetual applause filled the air, and joined with cries of "Long live the nation and liberty!" which spread from rank to rank. The moment of the oath created the liveliest enthusiasm. Monsieur de La Fayette stepped atop the altar and, supported by those surrounding him, exposed and visible to the eyes of all the spectators, took it first.[2] Instantly, all the soldiers raised their arms into the air, all the other citizens with their hands high repeated it, there is no expression for painting such a spectacle's effects. Personally, I was in a rapture from which I still have not fully recovered, and I am now more than ever convinced that the revolution will not be stopped. I consider the federation the rampart of liberty; this is quite a beautiful idea . . . to have united and connected with an oath all the citizens of a great state. One gains the impression that a simultaneous reunion unites all hearts! I do not doubt there will be times it will be more difficult to feel the revolution's happy effects, but whatever happens, I count now on the courage and patience of the French. Let us now only see liberty and happiness. We already have one, may the other follow . . . For myself, my sentiments and opinions have been unequivocal since the revolution began. They are always the same and I do not worry that truly wise men will reproach me for enthusiasm in saying that yesterday they acquired a new degree of force and energy. The Federation assuredly is the surest guarantee of our felicity and of the reality of our regeneration. I am persuaded, my dear papa, that you would be perfectly content with the future of the public good if you could have seen like me this ravishing spectacle that no nation in the universe could have matched.

Protest against Refractory Clergyman refusing Civil Constitution of the Clergy, *Universal Gazette*, January 19, 1791

The Constitutional Oath of the Clergy, requiring all priests to swear their loyalty to the unfinished French Constitution and government (even above allegiance to the Papacy), went into effect the first Sunday of January 1791. All priests were required to take the oath before their congregations, yet nearly half of all across France refused to. While most across the Paris region did, the parish priest of Saint-Roch (a church just blocks from the National Assembly) refused. The following account, taken from the Paris newspaper the *Universal Gazette*, shows the local protest against the priest continuing to carry out his functions at a funeral and baptism. Revolutionaries remained divided on the extent of the penalties to enact against "refractories" refusing the oath; however, the priest on this occasion is defended and preserved from potential harm by the local Paris Section forces. Some revolutionaries were not radical on every issue and many desired to preserve Catholicism's autonomy from the political order. The schism opened by the Oath never healed, motivating growing resistance to revolutionary authorities by devout Catholics and revolutionaries' ultimate embrace of dechristianization. Although the clergy had been key allies of the Third Estate in 1789, they increasingly fell afoul of the radicalizing revolution.

The priest of Saint-Roch did not take the oath last Sunday, so the people consider him dispossessed of his position.[3] Yesterday, this pastor wanted to lead a burial, but a crowd gathered in the church and openly opposed his carrying out this clerical function, which was finished instead by the Abbé Fauchet.[4] Then, M. Marduel saw a baptism begin, and went to the baptismal founts to administer the sacrament. The people followed to oppose him, and took the baptismal shell from him. This opposition irritated the pastor, who haughtily reclaimed his right, and no one knows how many excesses would have been committed against him, if the local section, then assembled in the church, did not come to his aid, and only got him to retire after some efforts. Amidst this scandal, the people said, "he taunts us, he provokes us, but nothing bad has befallen him beyond being chased from his functions, as an official not obeying the law."

Maximillien de Robespierre, Selections from Speech favoring the Abolition of the Death Penalty, May 30, 1791

The French Revolution did not finish where it started, even in the minds of those who would (in time) find themselves at its center. On May 30,

1791, Maximillien Robespierre's political prospects remained mediocre: a provincial legislator from the northern town of Arras, he would soon successfully introduce a "self-denying clause" into the upcoming National Assembly elections, which refused himself and his fellow legislators the ability to stand for re-election. Yet Robespierre saw himself as a virtuous idealist, having built over the previous two years a reputation as "The Incorruptible": a man unwilling to bend to pragmatism if it meant sacrificing his principles. Extending Enlightenment-era calls to reform "barbaric" Old Regime justice systems from philosophers like Voltaire and the Italian jurist Cesare Beccaria, Robespierre proceeded with a speech calling for the death penalty's abolition. Such a measure would embody the humanitarian hopes many revolutionary legislators still held in 1791—the possibilities of a better world free of state-sanctioned atrocities and needless suffering. Rather than seeing the concept as totally new, however, Robespierre builds from Ancient Greek and Roman precedents, as well as from Asian traditions, to rebut more recent European practices. Robespierre's fellow legislators, however, did not find the measure sufficiently pragmatic, and the death penalty remained in French jurisprudence. Even Robespierre notes in his speech that there are circumstances that could make killing necessary. Two years hence, "The Incorruptible" would become the principal leader of a new system of state-sanctioned terror.

When the news was carried to Athens that citizens were condemned to death in the town of Argos, Athenians ran to the temples and conjured the Gods to turn Athenians away from such cruel and dreadful thoughts.[5] I come to pray, not to the gods, but to the legislators, who have to be the oracles and interpreters of the eternal laws that divinity has dictated to mankind, to erase from the French legal code the bloody laws that command judicial murder, sickening their morals and the new constitution. I will prove: 1. That the death penalty is essentially unjust. 2. That it is not the harshest reprimand for crimes, while multiplies crimes more than it prevents them.

Outside civil society, when a fierce enemy attacks my life, or when, after being chased off twenty times, he returns to again ravage the field my hands have cultivated, because I cannot oppose him except with my individual force, I must either kill or be killed, and the law of natural defense justifies and approves my action. But for a society, when the collective force is armed against any individual, what principle of justice could justify them killing him? What necessity could absolve them of it? A conqueror who kills his enemies is called a barbarian! A man who slits the throat of his child, who he could disarm and punish, appears a monster! A defendant that society condemns is no more than a beaten and powerless enemy: he becomes before her weaker than a child before its parent.

In this manner, in the eyes of truth and justice, these scenes of state-ordered death with so much fanfare are nothing but cowardly assassinations, solemn crimes, committed not by individuals but by entire nations with legal forms. How cruel, how extravagant are these laws. Do not be shocked by them any longer. They are the work of tyrants, they are the chains that damn the human race: they were written with blood. “It is never permitted to put a Roman citizen to death.” Such was the law the people approved . . .[6]

The legislator who prefers such atrocious penalties as death to gentler means in his power outrages public delicacy, dulls the moral sentiment of the people he governs, similar to a bad tutor who, by frequently using cruel punishments, stunts and degrades his student’s spirit. In the end, he will use up and weaken the government’s power by trying to give it greater force. . . .

If the death penalty most effectively prevents the greatest crimes, it must thus be quite rare for the peoples employing it. Now, the situation is precisely the contrary. Look at Japan: torture and the death penalty are widely used; nowhere is crime so frequent and atrocious. They say the Japanese rival in ferocity with barbarous laws the acts that outrage and irritate them. In the republics of Greece, where the punishments were moderate, where the death penalty was quite rare or absolutely unknown, did they suffer more crimes or less virtue than the countries who govern by laws of blood? . . .

Listen to the voice of justice and reason: she cries to us that human judgments are never so certain that society can bring death on a man condemned by other men subject to error. Can you imagine the most perfect judicial order, where you have found the most honorable, enlightened judges? You will always find room for error and wrongful detention. Why do you forbid the means to make this right? Why do you make it impossible to extend a helping hand to oppressed innocence? What do sterile regrets matter, these illusory reparations you accord to a vain ghost, to unfeeling ashes? They are the sad testimonies of your penal laws’ atrocious barbarity. Give men the chance to expiate their crime by repentance or acts of virtue. Why without pity close to him all return to virtue, to self-respect, to lead him down, so to speak, into the tomb already covered by his crime’s fresh stain? This, to my eyes, is the most horrible refinement of cruelty.

The legislator’s first duty is to develop and conserve public morals, the source of all liberty, source of all social happiness: when, for a particular objective, he departs from this general and essential goal, he commits the greatest and most terrible error.

The laws must thus always present to peoples the purest model of justice and reason. If, in place of this powerful severity, of this moderating calm that must characterize them, they sow anger and vengeance, if they lead to human blood flowing that they could have prevented and do not have the right to take. . . . The idea of killing inspires much less fright, when the law itself gives the example and spectacle; the horror of crime diminishes when one cannot punish it except by another crime. Be careful not to conflate penalties’ efficacy with the excess of their severity: one absolutely opposes the other. Everything favors moderate laws; everything conspires against cruel laws.

One observes that in free countries, crimes are rarer and the penal laws more lenient. It’s true: the free countries are those where the rights of man are respected, and where, in consequence, the laws are just. Everywhere they offend humanity by excessive rigor proves that the dignity of man is unknown there, that citizenship does not exist; it is proof that the legislator is only a master commanding slaves, and that he punishes without pity according to his own fantasy. I conclude that the death penalty must be repealed.

FIGURE 6.1 *Léon Cognlet,* The National Guard of Paris Departs for the Army in September 1792. © *Photo Josse / Leemage / Getty Images.*

The coming of the French Revolutionary Wars excited a new spirit of patriotism and possibility. Though painted several decades afterwards in 1836 for a French history museum in the Palace of Versailles, academic artist Léon Cognlet's composition captures the ardor of the new French forces perhaps better than any other work. A spirited volunteer battalion appears poised to depart, while women offer garlands and urge them forward. The Paris cityscape is centered on a revolutionary monumental space, with the statue of King Henri IV having been removed from atop its pedestal amidst a general purge of royalist symbols after the monarchy's overthrow on August 10, 1792. The French tricolor hangs in its place. Further downriver, the southern edge of the Tuileries Palace—recently emptied of Louis XVI and his family—is visible at the end of the Louvre complex. The soldiers face eastwards, ready to go fight the counterrevolutionary "slave armies" of their Germanic opponents.

6

Overthrowing the Monarchy

Revolutionaries in 1789 had not sought a republic. The French monarchy dated back to the sixth century and the king was a sacred figure, ordained by the church. In establishing a constitutional monarchy, revolutionaries wanted the king to play an active role so he could legitimate their rule and help them maintain peace throughout the nation. When the King took an oath to uphold the forthcoming constitution amidst hundreds of thousands of cheering French citizens on Paris' Champ de Mars, most believed the constitutional monarchy secured.

It took a series of crises, largely instigated by the royal family, to destabilize this consensus. Feeling trapped and coerced by revolutionaries in Paris, Louis XVI increasingly listened to extremist voices around him, desiring that he flee the country to take command of a counterrevolutionary army poised to annihilate the revolution by force. The night of June 20, 1791, Louis and his family made their escape, slipping out of Paris undetected and nearly making it to the Germanic border before National Guardsmen in the small eastern town of Varennes captured them and forced their return to Paris, amidst throngs of thousands jeering subjects.

As Louis could not make it to a counterrevolutionary army, he asked the crowned heads of central Europe to march their armies to him. He and Marie Antoinette beseeched their Austrian relatives to incite a war with France. The National Assembly, believing the peoples of central Europe would rise up in support of revolutionary freedom, came to desire a war too. While both sides believed the war that began on April 20, 1792 would quickly end through crushing victories, in practice it continued (with only short breaks) for twenty-three years. The Austrian-led Holy Roman Empire was immediately joined by Prussia—the most feared army in Europe—while Britain, Spain, and northern Italy's Piedmont-Savoy laid groundwork for joining the counterrevolutionary coalition (which all would by early 1793). France's New Regime now had to vanquish the combined forces of surrounding Old Regime kingdoms. The thrones came to consider the French Revolution antithetical to their own existence.

Alongside the terrifying tremors of battle came exhilarating new possibilities. Renouncing compacts with the royalty, aristocracy, and church led to a new upsurge in political radicalism. Unpropertied citizens were now actively needed for the war effort—and no longer accepted the "passive citizen" subordinate status authorities had relegated them to under the Constitution of 1791. Common French people demanded full participation in revolutionary governance, while *sans-culotte* working-class culture—glorifying simplicity, directness, and the virtue of labor—became a touchstone of national politics. No longer willing to compromise with the aristocrats still seeking their destruction, a new degree of fraternity and collective purpose spread in the revolutionary ranks.

The conflict's stakes led both sides to increasingly terroristic rhetoric. Prussian commander the Duke of Brunswick, ignoring distinctions between soldiers and civilians, threatened the wholesale destruction of Paris if any harm came to the royal family. Capturing revolutionaries' fighting spirit, the "Marseillaise" anthem captures the roar of a threatened people willing to spill "impure blood" and defeat the "horde of slaves" wanting to return them to chains. Whereas under the Old Regime war was commonly considered a regular and endemic means of statecraft—with destruction and casualties occurring on a much more limited scale than during the sixteenth- and seventeenth-century Wars of Religion—now revolutionaries hyped the conflict as "the last war," asserting the forces of freedom would triumph over Europe's traditional despots.

Amidst such pressures and treachery, the French cut their ties with the Bourbon monarchy. Faced with further royal duplicity at the Tuileries Palace on August 10, 1792, revolutionaries proceeded to overthrow the French monarchy. No longer able to consider Louis XVI an honest governing partner, the king was stripped of his crown and soon put on trial for treason. Compromises with the forces of old had failed. Revolutionaries came to believe the New Regime would need to look drastically different from the old.

Louis XVI, "Declaration of the King, Addressed to all the French Before His Leaving Paris," June 20, 1791

Louis XVI, just before escaping his capital the night of June 20, 1791, left a lengthy manifesto in his own handwriting justifying his flight and demanding significant changes to the revolutionary compact. He claimed all his actions since the October Days of 1789 had been coerced and, while he had initially gone along for the good of his country, he now found the Revolution's course too troubling not to take action. Louis blamed the

Jacobin Clubs, together with an overactive press and dishonest politicians, for leading the revolution astray—believing royal authority needed to be restored to protect religion, property, personal status, and French glory. From his perspective, the revolution had illegally stripped property and privilege from France's legitimate authorities. Believing the monarchy still retained wide support across France, and witnessing the revolution's continued disorder, he asserted the time had come to rally the people against revolutionary authorities. He failed. After Louis was captured a short distance from France's eastern border, his flight provoked the revolution's greatest crisis yet, as many radicals agitated for establishing a republic.

Insofar as the King could plausibly envision the rebirth of the kingdom's order and happiness by the National Assembly's chosen methods, including by his residence near this assembly in the kingdom's capital, no personal sacrifice has been too great for him. He also did not raise the issue of nullification, despite the absolute loss of his liberty in all he has done since the month of October 1789, in hopes this would be fulfilled. But today, his only recompense for such sacrifices is to see the kingdom's destruction, to see all powers misunderstood, properties violated, personal security endangered, crimes unpunished, and complete anarchy in place of law. Under such conditions, the appearance of authority that sanctions the new Constitution will not be sufficient to repair the evils affecting the kingdom. The King, after solemnly protesting against all actions occurring during his captivity, believes he must set under the eyes of the French and the entire universe an account of his conduct, and that of the government established in the kingdom. . . .

What remains for the King except a vain simulacrum of royalty? He has received twenty-five million for his Civil List,[1] but the splendor of the House he must maintain for the honor and dignity of the Crown of France . . . has absorbed it all. . . .

1. The Assembly, via its committees, continuously exceeds its prescribed limits: it occupies itself with affairs uniquely belonging to the kingdom's executive administration and the judiciary, thereby assuming all powers. Its Research Committee exercises a despotism more barbarous and insupportable than any history ever mentioned.
2. There have been established in almost all cities, and even some towns and villages of the kingdom, associations known as Friends of the Constitution: against the tenor of decrees, they do not suffer anyone unaffiliated with them. They form an immense corporation more dangerous than any existing before. Without being authorized to do so, even when disobeying decrees, they discuss all aspects of government, correspond about everything, make and receive denunciations, publicly post their resolutions, and have achieved such preponderance that all administrative and judicial bodies,

> including the National Assembly itself, almost always obey their orders. . . .

The closer the Assembly comes to its labors' end, the more one sees wise men lose their influence, the more personalities who can only spread difficulty and even impossibility in the government's conduct and inspire mistrust and disfavor augment everyday. . . . The clubs' spirit dominates everyone and vanquishes everything, the thousand calumniating and incendiary newspapers and pamphlets responding to them daily are only their echoes, and manipulate minds whichever way they wish to drive them. . . .

Frenchmen, is this what you waited for when you sent your representatives to the National Assembly? Do you want the anarchy and despotism of clubs to replace the monarchical government under which the nation has prospered for over fourteen hundred years? Do you wish to see outrages heaped upon your King, and see him deprived of his liberty, after he only occupied himself with establishing yours? . . .

Frenchmen, Parisians most of all, inhabitants of a city His Majesty's ancestors pleased themselves with calling the Good City of Paris, do not believe your false friends' suggestions and lies. Return to your king. He is always your father, your best friend. What pleasure would it give him to forget all his personal injuries, and see himself amongst you once a Constitution that he accepts freely is completed, in which our holy religion will be respected, in which the government will be established on stable and useful footing by his actions, in which each person's property and status will not be further troubled, in which the laws will no more be broken with impunity, and whereby liberty will finally be set on firm and unbreakable foundations.

Paris, 20 June 1791. Louis.

Louis XVI and Marie Antoinette's Correspondence with the Revolution's Enemies, May 18, 1790 and March 2, 1792

The royal family turned against the French Revolution and were often not circumspect in hiding their feelings. Considering themselves anointed by god to lead the French people, Louis XVI and Marie Antoinette sought international aid from the most powerful forces in Europe: their fellow monarchs and the Pope. Publicizing the eclipse of traditional authority in France, the royals attempted to convince their fellow sovereigns that the spread of revolutionary ideas and spirit could threaten their own positions. Already in May 1790, Louis XVI wrote to Pope Pius VI, making clear the revolutionaries did not speak for him and that he feared they would destroy true religion in France. Though much of the planning of the Flight to Varennes and Franco-Austrian War was done by subordinates (to give the monarchs plausible deniability), Marie Antoinette made clear in a March 1792 missive both her knowledge of and support for an Austrian invasion to crush the French Revolution. Despite the many displays of the French Revolution's popularity, the royalty continued to assert that a silent majority of their subjects still supported them. The royals played a treasonous double game, continuing in their roles as the French head of state, while trying to subvert the revolution.

Letter of Louis XVI to Pope Pius VI, May 18, 1790

It was not enough that discord spreads fury in my kingdom: the political disputes are joined by religious quarrels. I do not know what infernal spirit wants to submit religion to the principles of innovators, to bizarre ideas and singular reforms. In the assembly, they now agitate the most absurd questions: one could say the disciples of Jansenius and Molina are on the bleachers, and that they pronounce for or against *ultramontaine* opinions.[2] They present a civil constitution for the French clergy: they may render themselves independent of the Holy See, they may accord their election to the people; they may reverse the Gallican Church's antique hierarchy: and to give to this Civil Constitution of the Clergy numerous proselytes, while distancing them from loyal ministers, they want to require an oath.[3] Most Holy Father, this oath could give birth to a schism in the church.

I do not know what premonition more fills me with fear: I see religion debased, its ministers persecuted, the wolf in the henhouse. I have wanted to instruct you, firstly, on the resolution of the Estates General, concerning the project of several hotheads, of several men profoundly perverse, and already very skilled in the art of revolutionizing.[4] I have need of your councils, and can do nothing without consulting you. I will send to you, by M. de M . . . n, a copy of this constitution . . . examine it: your wise advice will guide men; but already the voice of my conscience cries to me that I must not sanction this work of shadows.[5]

Marie Antoinette to the Count of Mercy-Argenteau, March 2, 1792.[6]

It is certainly impossible to believe the ancient order of things can be instantaneously reestablished as they were, but at the same time nothing from this one can remain. Every day, every moment proves that if one wants a monarchical government, the multiplicity of powers, popular elections, and especially the force given to the people must all prolong anarchy, and are consequently the monarchy's total ruin. The nation is effectively divided into different parties, but there is not a single one dominating the others. Whether it be cowardice, indolence or division, even internal, in their opinions, none fail to contest each other. Only via exterior force, when they are sure of being supported, will they have the courage to pronounce their true interests and those of the King. The Emperor's ideas are good, and the declaration's articles seem fitting to me, but it all would have been better six months ago.[7] We have lost much time and they are not wasting a moment here against us. Every day brings new calamities and aggravates evil. The loss of all private fortunes, bankruptcy, costly grain, the impossibility of travelling from one place to another, the total lack of currency and loss of confidence in paper money; finally, the manner in which people insult every day the King's person to their own advantage, whether in writing and speeches, or in all they oblige themselves to say, write, and do, everything announces a coming crisis, and without foreign aid, how can he turn this crisis to his advantage? . . .

I have left out half the things I want to tell you. You desire an accord between us and Vienna; you have the means to make one. You know the King and myself have placed all our confidence in the Baron de Breteuil and Comte de Fersen. They are with you: they know better how to discuss such affairs than me. Talk with them: they know our intentions and position perfectly.

National Assembly, Debates over a War Ultimatum to Austria, January 25, 1792

By early 1792, French revolutionaries believed they could bring freedom to the world by force of arms. After Austria and Prussia contracted an alliance, which many expected the other Crowned Heads of Europe to join, revolutionaries came to believe a final confrontation between the forces of liberty and despotism was essential to create a new world order. While some influential revolutionaries, including Robespierre and Marat, had opposed the war, by January 1792 a widespread consensus emerged that international conflict was necessary. Revolutionaries believed that, with reason and philosophy on their side, military intervention could create a new international order based on freedom and the Rights of Man. As French authorities asserted that their revolution provided a universal model, the rule of kings seemed outmoded. On January 25, the National Assembly discussed, and then passed, an ultimatum on Austria, demanding it renounce all hostile maneuverings against the French nation by March 1. With the counterrevolutionary coalition persisting, France preemptively declared war on April 20, 1792.

M. Daverhoult:[8] Messieurs, your diplomatic committee, applying itself principally to find the veritable meaning of the phrases contained in the Emperor's statement announcing a concert of the different powers for the security and honor of crowns, has set the debate's confines. You have only needed, Messieurs, to occupy yourself regarding the émigrés, insofar as their gatherings, close to the kingdom's frontiers, can incite and encourage our interior enemies' perfidious designs: in concert with you, the king has made the necessary demands of the foreign princes who favor these musters. These diplomatic means ought to be supported by formidable preparations for war . . . we have raised the diplomatic veil covering the intrigues of the different courts: we have calculated their forces, their resources, and their diverse interests . . .

Weak tools of the passions of those surrounding them, constantly misled about their true interests by these greedy men, who profit only from arbitrary authority, all princes have necessarily viewed the French Constitution with horror. Philosophy, a formidable weapon because it draws its force from eternal reason, that existed before thrones and will reign over their debris, that is the enemy against which the princes have formed a defensive league. They are themselves free from this calling's influence, this power that rivals the throne; they ably struggle against the pretentions of the caste that draws its origins from the weakness of princes and the cowardice of peoples. The examples of Sweden and Brabant demonstrate this truth.[9] . . .

This is not about placing a little more or less authority in a prince's hands, but rather about extending the conflict to all other European nations: this is the reform of all abuses, the destruction of all prejudices, this is, in a word, about the holy equality of rights, itself a formidable force that strikes fear in those who govern other men . . .

But, Messieurs, if such are the desires born in the heart of princes, different obstacles appear for executing such a vast design. The first is the courage of twenty-five million free men, portions of which may be vanquished, but all of whom cannot be enslaved. The second is the terror our moral weapons inspire: our Declaration, not of the rights of the French, but of Man, appalls the princes: the first cannon shot fired against France could signal of the wakening of nations, and this possibility would change into certainty, if such a war became prolonged. The worry of seeing the French system extended to their homelands, equally deters peace and open war. . . .

The conventions of Pilnitz, of Padua, of Vienna, the declaration by which, after having recognized Louis XVI's free acceptance of the French Constitution, mentioned the concert between the different powers, the recommendations made by them to the princes leading these circles, to disrupt freedom of the press, and strangle what they call the spirit of innovation. . . . it is not against France, nor against the Constitution, but against philosophy itself that Leopold has formed his offensive league. For a long time his intentions could have been discovered, if your ministers of foreign affairs had demanded from the courts of Vienna and Berlin a clear explanation on the motives of such a bizarre alliance, but it was perhaps in their interest to leave you ignorant, as it suits them better to abandon the friends of liberty . . .

Let us thus leave to philosophy the task of enlightening the universe, and if the blindness of this league of princes advances the hour that has been marked by all eternity to found the only durable empire, that of reason, let us plead for the fate of a suffering humanity, which will only see the glistening light of these beautiful days after an equally terrible storm. . . .

[Decree] The National Assembly, considering that the Emperor, by his circular of November 25, 1791, by the conclusion of a new treaty made between himself and the King of Prussia, July 25, 1791, and presented to the Diet of Regensburg December 6, by his response to the King of the French, on the notification given of his acceptance of the Constitution, dated December 21, 1791, has broken the treaty of May 1, 1756 and sought to excite among diverse powers a concert attacking the nation's sovereignty and security;[10]

Considering that the French nation, after manifesting its resolution not to interfere in any foreign nation's government, has the right to secure for itself a just reciprocity to which it ought not to suffer the slightest attack;

Applauding the firmness with which the King of the French has responded to the office of the Emperor;

After having heard the report of the Diplomatic Committee, decrees the following:

1. The King will be invited, via deputation, to declare to the Emperor that he cannot negotiate with any power except in the French nation's name and in virtue of the powers delegated to him by the Constitution.
2. The King will be invited to demand of the Emperor, that, as head of the House of Austria, he intends to live in peace and good relations with the French nation, while renouncing all treaties and conventions directed against the sovereignty, independence, and security of the nation.
3. The King will be invited to declare to the Emperor, that should he not give the nation, before March 1, full and entire satisfaction on all the points here reported, his silence, as well as all evasive or dilatory responses, will be regarded as a declaration of war.
4. The King will be invited to continue to take the promptest measures for French troops to be ready to campaign once the first order is given.

Duke of Brunswick, *Brunswick Manifesto*, July 25, 1792

Terror developed not just through the heated rhetoric of revolutionaries, but also via their enemies' responses. The counterrevolutionary allied commander the Duke of Brunswick, writing for the Holy Roman Emperor and the King of Prussia, sent what became known as the Brunswick Manifesto, proclaiming that those French who resisted their country's invasion would be subject to military execution and the destruction of their communities if they did not immediately surrender and re-pledge their absolute loyalty to the French monarchy. Brunswick not only threatened French soldiers, but also civilians, with massacre if they did not follow his programme—atrocities recalling the horrors of Europe's Wars of Religion. Louis XVI, alerted of the decree prior to its publication in Paris, gave his tacit approval. As the Revolutionary Wars began, the French expected no quarter, leading to a growing scope and intensification of warfare some historians have described as presaging the "Total War" mobilizations of the twentieth century. Quickly defeated on French soil, the Prussians never engaged in widespread massacres during the Revolutionary Wars, though extensive atrocities against civilians would occur in Spain, Russia, Egypt, Syria, Italy, and elsewhere. Revolutionary temptations for both rhetorical excess and brutality were at least matched by their opponents.

Their Majesties the [Holy Roman] Emperor and the King of Prussia have given me command of the combined armies they have gathered on France's frontiers. I desire to announce to this kingdom's inhabitants the motives determining the two sovereigns' measures and the intentions guiding them.

After having arbitrarily suppressed the rights and possessions of the German princes in Alsace and Lorraine,[11] troubled and overthrown their own good order and legitimate government, exercised against the sacred person of the king and his august family violent attacks that are perpetually renewed from day to day, those who have usurped administrative power have finally dared to declare an unjust war against His Majesty the Emperor, and attacked his provinces situated in the Low Countries. . . .

Convinced that the sane part of the French nation abhors the excesses of a faction that subjects it, and that the greater number of inhabitants wait with patience for the moment of help to declare themselves openly against their oppressors' odious enterprises, His Majesty the Emperor and His Majesty the King of Prussia call and invite them to return without delay to the path of reason, justice, order, and peace. Thus, I, the undersigned General Commander in Chief of these two armies, declare:

1. Forced into the present war by irresistible circumstances, the two allied courts have no other goal but France's happiness, without pretension of enriching themselves by conquests.
2. They do not intend to interfere in the interior government of France, but only want to deliver the king, queen, and royal family from their captivity, and procure to His Very Christian Majesty the security necessary for him to carry out without danger or obstacles the convocations he judges proper, and work to assure the happiness of his subjects, his promises' fulfillment, and the completion of his duties.
3. The combined armies will protect the cities, towns, and villages, and the persons and property of all those who submit themselves to

the king and work for the immediate reestablishment of order and policing across France.

4. National Guardsmen are summoned to pacify the towns and countryside, for the security of French persons and properties, until their Imperial and Royal Majesties' troops arrive, or until otherwise ordered, under pain of being held personally responsible. Conversely, those National Guardsmen who fight against the troops of the two allied courts, and are captured with rifles in their hands, will be treated as enemies and punished as rebels to their king and disturbers of the public peace.
5. The generals, officers, junior officers, and troops of the French line are equally entreated to return to their ancient loyalty, and openly submit themselves to the king, their legitimate sovereign.
6. The officials of the departments, districts, and municipalities will be equally held responsible by their heads and properties for all crimes, conflagrations, assassinations, pillaging, and other acts they let be committed, or that they notoriously did not strive to stop from happening in their territories; meanwhile, they will be retained to provisionally continue in their functions until His Very Christian Majesty, reset at full liberty, makes the final decision, or until it can be otherwise ordered in his name in the interval.
7. The inhabitants of cities, towns, and villages who dare contest the troops of their Imperial and Royal Majesties by firing on them, whether in the field, from the windows, doors, or openings of their houses, will be summarily punished, following the rigors of the right of war, or have their houses demolished or burnt.[12] To the contrary, all the inhabitants of the said cities, towns, and villages who hasten to submit to their king, in opening their doors to their Majesties' troops, will be instantly placed under their safeguard; their persons, their property, their possessions will be under legal protection, and the general security of all and any of them will be provided.
8. The city of Paris and all its inhabitants without distinction, are called upon to submit openly and without delay to the king, to set this prince at full and complete liberty while assuring him, alongside all the royal family, the inviolability and respect to which the right of nature and man oblige subjects towards their sovereigns. Their Imperial and Royal Majesties hold personally responsible for all events, at the price of their heads, for military judgment, without hope of pardon, all members of the National Assembly, of the Department, Districts, Municipality, and National Guard of Paris, judges of the peace, and all others sharing responsibility. The said majesties openly declare, on their faith and word as Emperor and King, that if the Tuileries Palace is forced open or insulted, if the smallest violence, the slightest

outrage is done to Their Majesties the King and Queen, or to the royal family, if they are not immediately granted their security, conservation, and liberty, we will unleash an ever-memorable and exemplary vengeance, turning the city of Paris over to military execution and total destruction, and the rebels guilty of attacks to the torture they merit. Their Imperial and Royal Majesties promise to the contrary to Paris' inhabitants, to employ their good offices to Their Very Christian Majesty to obtain the pardon of their errors and misdeeds and take the most vigorous measures to assure their persons and possessions, if they obey promptly and exactly the injunction above.

Claude-Joseph Rouget de Lisle, *The Marseillaise*, April 1792

Written in Strasbourg, across the Rhine river from the enemy Holy Roman Empire, shortly after the April 1792 Declaration of War by army captain Claude-Joseph Rouget de Lisle, the "Marseillaise," originally titled the "War Chant of the Army of the Rhine," captured the fighting spirit of the French as they embarked on what they considered a fight for freedom against the crowned heads of central Europe. Believing (with good reason) that the Austrians and their allies planned to crush the Revolution and restore the Old Regime, by whatever force necessary, the anthem calls for the French to unite as one. Now, unlike in the limited wars of the Old Regime, "Everyone is a soldier," and responsible for doing their part to defend the homeland. The song quickly became popular across France. Paramilitary revolutionaries from Marseille, marching north to Paris to defend the capital from potential counterrevolutionary attack, sung the song with such regularity and gusto that it became known as "La Marseillaise." Though Lisle would be cashiered from his command for royalism in 1793, the anthem has endured and, despite being outlawed by Napoleon and multiple illiberal French regimes that followed, since 1879 has been France's national anthem. Despite objections about the song's violence, particularly the reference to watering French soil with "impure blood" in the last couplet of the opening verse (though this may refer to commoners mocking the supposed purity of their aristocratic opponents' lineages), the original lyrics have endured.

Come, children of the Fatherland,
The day of glory has arrived!
Against us stands tyranny,
Its bloody banner is raised.

Its bloody banner is raised.
Can you hear in the countryside,

The cry of those ferocious soldiers.
They will come right into your midst,
To slit the throats of your sons and wives!

(refrain) To arms, citizens,
Form your battalions.
March, March!
We will water our fields
With impure blood.

What desires this horde of slaves,
Of traitors and conspiring kings?
For whom are these ignoble restraints,
These irons long prepared?

These irons long prepared?
Frenchmen, they are for us! What outrage,
What fury they excite.
It's us they dare plan
To return to our ancient slavery! (refrain)

What! Foreign cohorts
Will make the law for us?
What! These mercenary phalanxes
Will strike down our proud warriors?

Will strike down our proud warriors?
Great God! With chained hands,
Our heads would bow to their yoke.
Such vile despots would become
The masters of our destinies! (refrain)

Tremble, tyrants and traitors,
The shame of all parties.
Tremble! Your parricidal projects
Will finally receive their recompense!

Will finally receive their recompense!
Everyone is a soldier to fight you,
If they our young heroes fall,
The earth will produce new ones.
Against you, all are ready to fight! (refrain)

Frenchmen, magnanimous warriors
Give or reserve your blows!

Spare these sad victims,
Those who regret arming against us.

Those who regret arming against us,
But not those bloody despots,
These accomplices of Bouillé,[13]
All these tigers who, without pity,
Rip their mother's breast! (refrain)

Sacred love of the Fatherland,
Lead and support our avenging arms.
Liberty, cherished liberty,
Fight with your defenders.

Fight with your defenders.
Under our flags, victory will
Come to your manly accents
While your expiring enemies
Witness your triumph and glory! (refrain)

Grand Telling of the Siege and Taking of the Tuileries Palace, 1792

The insurrection of August 10, 1792 demonstrated to French patriots the worst of what they feared about their opponents. Mobilizing an armed demonstration to the Tuileries Palace, though initially to search the premises for weapons and counterrevolutionaries, the Parisians were lured into combat after the King's Swiss guards made a false truce. The uprising displayed the worst of the revolution—the King's indecisiveness and inability to restrain his followers, the breakdown of trust between factions, the violent treachery of counterrevolutionaries, and the excessive force of revolutionaries who denied them quarter once the battle became a massacre. The event had momentous consequences, leading France to become the largest republic since Ancient Rome. Revolutionaries issued the first proclamation of universal manhood suffrage as they began planning a new National Convention. Written from the insurgents' perspective, likely by radical journalist Jacques-René Hébert, August 10 is here portrayed as a necessary action against a rotten monarchy looking to subvert the revolution and massacre the patriots. Three years into the revolution, many believed the compromises of a constitutional monarchy untenable. A republic seemed necessary to ensure a new order of liberty.

Louis XVI has long declared an open war on the constitution. The people's showing themselves during the uprising of June 20 ought to have had an effect on him, but instead of finally ceding to public opinion, rather than ending the many conspiracies he was always named the head of, he conceived the infernal project of sacrificing those in Paris and throughout France who had constantly defended the people's interests.[14] The proscription list was made. M. Pétion [Mayor of Paris] would have been the first throat slit and his death would give the signal for a new Saint Bartholomew's Day.[15] Those who could escape the assassins' iron would perish by the executioner's hand, which had been arranged to carry out these atrocious acts.

But while despotism conspired, patriotism remained vigilant. The movements at the Tuileries worried everyone. The judgment pronounced by the National Assembly in Lafayette's favor excited general indignation.[16] The next day they discussed the question of removal: the people waited impatiently for the decision, but aristocracy triumphed in the Assembly: instead of discussing removal [of the king], Vaublanc, Dumoulart and their numerous partisans insulted the people with outrageous denunciations.

The people, betrayed by their representatives, arose. The ninth at midnight, the signal was given; alarm bells rang in the Faubourgs St.-Antoine and St.-Marcel and in a great number of sections at the same time: cries rang out of "to arms!" and all the citizens went to their guard units and to the square in front of city hall where the General Council had assembled. [Mayor Jérôme] Pétion was not there: Louis the Faux had called him to the chateau under the pretense of discussing security measures. Alarmed by this order and rightly worrying for the virtuous magistrate's life, groups of citizens marched to the assembly, where already several members woken by the tolling of alarm bells gathered. A decree was obtained, forcing the chateau to release its prey: Pétion appeared at the speaker's rostrum and was restored to his functions and his fellow citizens' esteem.[17]

The conspirators, warned by the general alarm and the cries from all the city's sections, went to the Tuileries to aid the shadowy conspirators: all the Swiss assembled there, grenadiers and marksmen maneuvered in exercises. . . .

During this, all citizens were under arms. The insurrection was universal: the battalions formed, cannons at their head, and marched towards the Tuileries. The Place du Carrousel was soon covered with armed men and artillery. The Marseillais arrived first: each desired combat and seemed disposed to mount a vigorous attack.

The court neglected nothing, on its side, for receiving us. Louis XVI had not slept; during the night they composed a plan of defense; emissaries instructed them in all our movements. Towards six o'clock in the morning, he conducted a review and harangued the grenadiers who carried him home in triumph, shouting "long live the king!" This was the rallying cry. New gold coins were distributed along with plenty of wine to the Swiss manning the cannons.

Louis, after having prepared everything to slit citizens' throats, did not even show the courage of a scoundrel in facing the people when risen and armed, his pride was ruined. He departed with his family towards the National Assembly, cowardly abandoning those devoted to his cause. This terrible spectacle made the same impression on his conspiratorial leadership, who were liable for treason charges if they did not proceed with force.

At 9:30, the doors of the Court of Princes were opened to the people and, being overly confident, we received false protestations of friendship that we reciprocated to the Swiss. They then rained a hail of musket-balls on us; a crowd of our comrades fell at our feet. This treason excited a universal cry of indignation. We rallied; we seized their cannons. In deadly combat, the Marseillais and Bretons were valorous prodigies. The national gendarmerie flew to our aid and fired on the Swiss barracks, where a great number of national guards in uniform were with them. As soon as they ran out, they were fired upon. The chateau was forced open and entered. The carnage became horrible; the apartments, the staircases were covered with our fallen enemies and colored with our own blood. No one was spared. Everywhere was searched. We found Swiss and others hidden in the latrines, in the attic, in the kitchens: some were chased out, others were killed with bayonets; none escaped the public furor and vengeance. . . .

Meanwhile, the traitors in the National Assembly fled and the patriots, emboldened by public opinion, avenged the people by consecrating an authentic oath for liberty and holy equality. Effacing all constitutional provisions, they decreed that all citizens indistinctly, and without recognizing in the future the monstrous title of their line of work, could participate in forming the National Convention to judge the oath-braking king they were suspending.

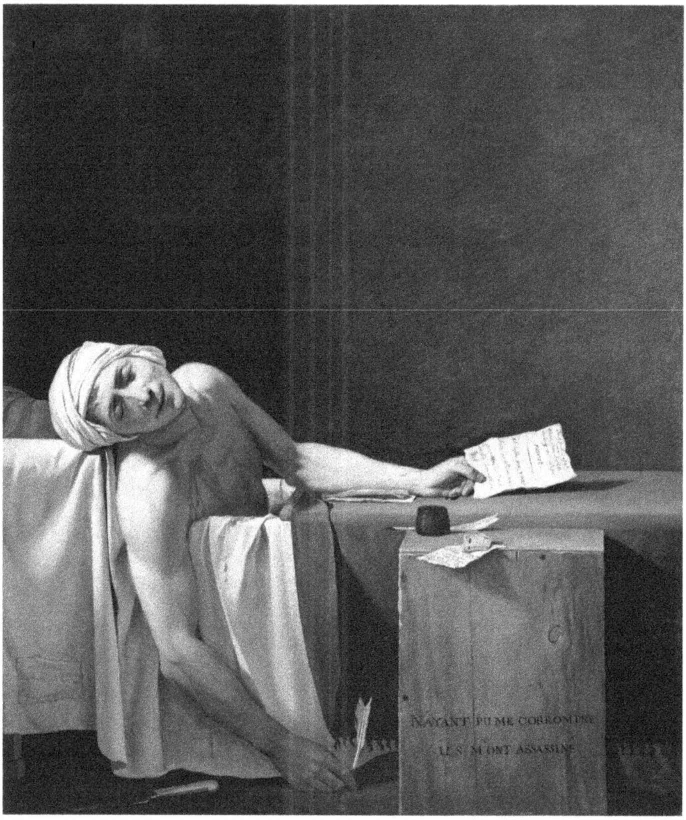

FIGURE 7.1 *Jacques-Louis David,* The Death of Marat. © *Imagno / Getty Images.*

Likely no revolutionary image has become more iconic than Jacques-Louis David's *Death of Marat*. Adapted from traditional pieta images of a dead Jesus, David (Marat's fellow National Convention deputy and radical Jacobin) turns the assassinated journalist into a revolutionary martyr. Marat, a controversial figure when alive who continually asserted that the revolution had not gone far enough to eliminate its enemies, after his July 13, 1793 death became seen as one of the revolution's great heroes. Rather than a menacing bully, Marat here is helpless, slain in his bathtub with a writing quill in his hand. Significantly, Charlotte Corday—the young female assassin from Normandy who travelled to Paris and gained entry to Marat's residence—is not pictured.

7

Debating Terror

Amidst the perils and difficulties of August–September 1792 arose what some historians refer to as the "First Terror." With suspicions of the monarchy proven correct by the treacherous violence of August 10 and the royal family's correspondence with the enemy discovered in the Tuileries Palace thereafter, tolerance for counterrevolutionary opponents receded. As peaceful compromise with aristocrats had failed, revolutionaries spilt blood on an unprecedented scale.

With Austro-Prussian armies menacing Paris—the road to the capital lying open after the fall of Verdun—extreme voices motivated the September Massacres against prisoners in the capital. Between September 2–6, summary justice was dispensed for all in Paris' prisons: roughly half were acquitted and set free, but the other half immolated on the spot. All revolutionary authorities participated, acquiesced, or stayed quiet. The royal family uniquely was spared, though the Queen's favorite the Princess of Lamballe's decapitated head was promenaded before her window. Afterwards, none of the participants were prosecuted. Once the bloodletting ended, however, it did not resume—and indeed, large-scale Parisian popular violence ended for the rest of the revolution.

Needing to mobilize the populace, the National Convention empowered the common people more than any prior regime. Amongst the revolution's continued partisans, fraternity, cooperation, and political activism remained prized. Voting was opened to all adult men (decades before "Jacksonian Democracy" in the United States), while the sections of Paris and municipalities of provincial towns empowered common citizens to help decide local governance. Working-class *sans-culotte* machismo placed significant pressure on authorities—but common activists also sought to highlight fraternity and cooperation with elites.

Temptation built to put the king on trial for his life on treason charges. Yet trying the king unleashed great questions. Ought the revolutionaries to break the Constitution of 1791 that declared the king inviolable? Would executing such a prominent political figure create troubling precedents for the future?

Should the revolution be a force for clemency and humanitarianism, or embrace the use of violence to achieve its extreme goals? While all members of the National Convention voted for Louis' guilt, his immediate execution passed by a single vote. Only reluctantly did revolutionary legislators depart from legality towards a regime of terror.

Revolutionaries increasingly adopted audacious arguments to intimidate the skeptical into compliance. The compromises of moderate enlightened thinking were eclipsed by radical arguments from recent philosophical writing and ancient history. Austere and uncompromising rhetoric proliferated as revolutionaries distanced themselves from the compacts they had made over the preceding years. As their opponents had been unwilling to make real, lasting concessions, revolutionaries now pushed forward harsher, more unbending notions of reason, equality, and virtue.

The king's execution helped alienate many French people already becoming skeptical about the revolution's course. When adherence to the revolution came to demand the wholesale sacrifice of tradition and religion, many refused. In the Vendée region, which had already seen skirmishes over religious issues and the extent of revolutionary authority, a full-scale civil war developed. Elsewhere, many loyally sheltered oath-refusing clergymen or young men refusing the military draft. Local and regional administrators smarted at increasingly stringent orders from Paris. Across many areas, anger against the new order came to exceed antagonisms against the old.

Revolutionaries, in principle, continued to believe in unanimity. In practice, however, they relied on coercion to keep a kaleidoscopic coalition functioning. With their hopes of peaceful coexistence dashed, revolutionaries sought to impose their desired programme by force. Terror—the use of intimidation, threat and violence to achieve political ends—increasingly became part of the revolutionary programme.

Jean-Paul Marat, *The Friend of the People*, No. 679, August 14, 1792

No journalist of the French Revolution caught contemporaries' attention like Jean-Paul Marat. A Swiss doctor, who had served as the Comte d'Artois' physician before the revolution, in September 1789 Marat began publishing *The Friend of the People*, which soon distinguished itself from the many other revolutionary newspapers by its vehemently aggressive language and certainty that revolutionary politics was replete with conspirators and traitors. All too often, Marat wound up being correct—including about early revolutionary leaders like Mirabeau and Lafayette. Most notably, he correctly perceived the royal family's duplicitous intentions. After the revolution of August 10, 1792, Marat sought to exert his influence, endorsing "popular executions" against the revolution's enemies, which would soon occur in the September Massacres. With the capital fearful of annihilation by the Austro-Prussian forces, Marat successfully maneuvered to be elected a deputy for Paris to the new National Convention. A radical Jacobin, who helped provoke the confrontations that overthrew the Girondins, Marat would continue to accumulate influence until his assassination in July 1793.

When public affairs appear the most hopeless, several smacks often suffice to set them right again. Nothing equals the atrociousness of the plot the royal court unleashed the morning of the tenth of this month, but also nothing matches the ministerial cabinet's folly, the patriots' imprudence, and the marvelousness of the fortuitous means by which we escaped the abyss. It is only too obvious that the ex-monarch, a traitor and false oath-taker, had planned to kill the capital's patriots. To set this in execution, the execrable project attempted to draw them under the crosshairs at the Tuileries Chateau, to incite their attack, and bring them under the fire and iron of his counterrevolutionary followers. . . .

Thanks must be rendered to the Tuileries council's delirious spirit, to the counterrevolutionaries' cowardliness, to the commander of the Swiss Guards, to Louis Capet's ineptitude and stupidity, to the conversion of the gendarmes, to the people's audacity, the valor of the federal soldiers and Parisian *Sans-Culotte*[1] guards. Victory has crowned the cause of justice. She has appalled the despot and his servants, consternated the senate's rotten majority, stopped the court's audacious machinations, given consistency to the commune's patriotic deputies, affirmed their authority, reversed the department, courts and justices of the peace prostituted to them, annihilated the counterrevolutionary general staff, dismayed the revolution's enemies, rendered the good citizens liberty, and given the people the means to signal their power, by bringing under the sword of justice the head of the conspirators. But this striking victory's fruits will be soon lost, if the commune's patriotic deputies do not remain in place, and if they do not deploy all their energy until liberty is cemented in place.

Louis Capet is a hostage along with his family: do not permit any of his creatures to approach them, and keep him well-guarded. That is the way to cut all the criminal counterrevolutionary conspiracies' strings. . . .

It is up to the Commune to immediately arm all the capital's good citizens and drill them in carrying weapons, to place Paris in a state of defense against their enemies' blows of despair, if they dare attack. . . .

The Fatherland has been pulled back from the abyss by the effusion of revolutionary enemies' blood, a method I have continuously indicated is the only effective one. If the sword of justice finally strikes the conspirators and the corrupt, you will not hear me speak further of popular executions, a cruel recourse that the law of necessity can only grant to a people reduced to despair, but that the voluntary inaction of the law always justifies.

The Commune's commissars have already set into practice several measures I recommended as indispensable to liberty's triumph, including taking the Capet family as hostages, seizing counterrevolutionary papers, rigorously pursuing public enemies, proscribing monopolizing merchants and money-changers. They also deserve to be recognized for several other beautiful civic acts. They move marvelously. If they continue with the same energy until the constitution is reformed by the National Convention, if the ministers prove themselves to always be good patriots, and if the people carefully surveil them, I will regard public safety as assured.

François de Jourgniac Saint-Méard, *My Agony of Thirty-Eight Hours*, 1792

A royalist military officer and conservative pamphleteer, François de Jourgniac Saint-Méard was arrested by Paris city officials following the insurrection of August 10. In early September, he witnessed the September Massacres, the bloodiest event in Revolutionary Paris. Fearing that counterrevolutionary armies, having just taken Verdun, would soon arrive to take Paris, local authorities (with the non-opposition of the National Convention) began purging the city's prison systems. Some prisoners were murdered immediately, but most were brought before hastily implemented revolutionary tribunals, which either acquitted and released them, or sentenced them to immediate death. About half of those judged were proclaimed "innocent"—including Saint-Méard, after claiming to have had his identity stolen by a newspaper editor—but between 11–1400 died, including 250 priests. Not just political prisoners but prostitutes and thieves were amongst those killed. Saint-Méard provides a vivid first-person account of the massacres, highlighting the vulnerability prisoners—and many others—felt as the killings occurred. The massacres' lawlessness lessened the French Revolution's reputation for human rights, justice, and due process both at home and abroad, and provided a lived experience of terror legislative elites drew upon when they assembled their own revolutionary tribunals the following year.

Sunday, September 2.—Our warden served us dinner sooner than normal; his stunned manner, his haggard eyes presaged to us something sinister.—At two p.m. he came back: we gathered around him, he was deaf to all our questions, and after he, going against ordinary practice, gathered all the knives that we carefully placed in our napkins, he ordered Swiss officer Réding's personal guard to leave.[2]

2:30 p.m.—The horrifying noise the people made was terribly amplified by drums beating the general alarm, by three soundings of the alarm cannon, and by alarm bells tolling from all directions.

In these moments of shock, we saw three carriages pass, escorted by an innumerable crowd of furious men and women, who cried: "To the Force [Prison], to the Force!" They were led to the Abbaye Cloister, where many priests were held.—An instant afterwards, we heard it said that people were coming to massacre all the bishops and other ecclesiastical authorities brought to this place.

Around four o'clock.—The bloodcurdling cries of a man being hacked to death with sabers brought us to the turret window and we saw, outside the prison entryway, the body of a man splayed dead on the pavement; an instant afterwards, they massacred another—and so on.

It is quite impossible to explain the horror of the profound and somber silence reigning during these executions; it was only interrupted by the cries of those being immolated and the swoop of swords onto heads.—The sound of their hitting the earth resounded, reinforced by surrounding cries of "Long live the nation!" a thousand times more shocking for us than the horror of silence.

In the interval from one massacre to the other, we heard said under our windows: "there's no reason for anyone to escape; all must be killed, especially those in the chapel; it's filled with conspirators." They were speaking about us. Of course, we hoped for the best for those shut in the horrid dungeons.

Every most terrible worry tormented us and pulled us into the most dreadful reflections: a moment of silence in the street was broken by noise beginning inside the prison.

Five p.m.—Several voices called loudly for Monsieur Cazotte; an instant afterwards we heard pass on the stairs a crowd of persons who spoke loudly, jangling weapons, amidst the cries of men and women.[3]—They dragged out an old man, followed by his daughter. Once he was beyond the gates, this courageous girl rushed to defend her father. The people, touched by this spectacle, asked for her pardon, and obtained it.

About seven.—We saw two men enter, with bloodied hands clutching swords; they were led by a warden carrying a torch, to find the unfortunate Réding's bed.—In this terrible moment, I took his hand and tried to console him . . .

Midnight.—Ten men, swords in hands, preceded by two wardens who carried torches, entered into our prison, and ordered us to sit at the edge of our beds. After they counted us, they told us to respond one after the other, and swore that if just one of us escaped, everyone would be massacred, without recourse to the tribunal's president.—These words gave us a ray of hope; but we still did not know if we would be heard before being killed.

Monday September 3, 2 a.m.—They forced the prison door after many blows: we thought they smashed the front door to come massacre us in our bedrooms, but we were a bit reassured when we heard said on the staircase that it went to a dungeon where several prisoners were barricaded.—Soon afterwards, we learned they had slit the throats of all found there.

At ten a.m. Father l'Enfant, the King's confessor and Father Chapt-Rastignac ascended the pulpit of the chapel serving as our prison . . . They told us our last hours approached and invited us to humble ourselves to receive their benediction.—An electric, undefinable movement led us all to take a knee, and with hands joined, we received it . . . Half an hour afterwards, these two priests were massacred, and we heard their cries! . . .

Around noon.—Overwhelmed, annihilated by a more than supernatural agitation, absorbed by reflections of which the horror is inexpressible, I threw myself onto a bed and slept profoundly.—I believe I owe my existence to this moment of rest.—I dreamt I would be judged before the most imposing tribunal. They would attentively listen to me, despite the terrible noise of alarm bells and the cries probably heard. My plea finished, they would set me free. . . .

Eight p.m.—The agitation of the people calmed down, and we heard voices cry: "Mercy, mercy for those remaining."—These words gained applause, but weakly. At this moment a ray of hope appeared for us; several believed their deliverance coming, that they had already accomplished their task; but soon, new death cries plunged us back into our agonies.

Eleven p.m. Ten men armed with swords and pistols ordered us to get in line, and took us to the second guard-door, next to those already lined up to be judged by the tribunal. . . .

Around Midnight.—The supernatural noise that had not stopped for thirty-six hours, began to let up; we thought our judges, overly fatigued, would not judge us with their executive power until they took some rest; they busied themselves in arranging beds for us, and made a new proclamation to this effect, which was universally booed.—

Finally, Tuesday, at one a.m . . . . my prison cell door opened and I was called. I stood forward. Three men took me into the horrible courtyard. . . .

By the light of two torches, I saw the terrible tribunal that would grant me life or death. The President, in a grey coat, a saber at his side, pulled himself up from a table, on which could be seen papers, a writing stand, pipes, and several bottles. The table was surrounded with ten men, standing or sitting . . . others slept on the benches. Two men in shirts colored with blood, sword in hand, guarded the door . . .

The President sat down to write, and after they had (apparently) registered the name of the poor man they were carrying off, I heard him say "another."

Soon I was brought before this expeditious and bloody tribunal, in the presence of which there was no good protection . . .

President: "Your name, your profession?"

One of the judges: "You will be lost with the smallest lie."

Saint-Méard: "My name is Jourgniac Saint-Méard; I have served twenty-five years as an officer and I come before your tribunal with the assurance of an innocent man, who consequently does not lie."

President: "Do you know the reason for your arrest?"

Saint-Méard: "Yes, Monsieur President, and I can believe, after the falseness of the denunciations made against me, that the commune's surveillance committee would not have imprisoned me, without the precautions the people's safety required.

"I have been accused of being the editor of an anti-Feuillant newspaper, *The Court and the City*.—This is not true.—That was a man named Gautier, whose signature resembles mine a little, who only out of meanness signed for me . . ."

[After further interrogation, the tribunal decrees:] "We, commissars named by the people to give justice to the traitors detained in the Abbaye Prison, have judged, on September 4, citizen Jourgniac Saint-Méard, a decorated former officer, who has proven the accusations against him false and that he has never entered any plot against the patriots: we proclaim him innocent in the people's presence, who applaud the liberty we have granted him. In good faith we deliver the present certificate, at his request: we invite all citizens to render him assistance."

Georges-Jacques Danton, "Always Audaciousness" speech, September 2, 1792

Possibly among the co-organizers of the September Massacres, radical Jacobin and Minister of Justice Georges-Jacques Danton seized the moment of the mass-killings to make a daring speech before the National Assembly, calling for an unprecedentedly total war against the Crowned Heads then invading France. Word had just arrived of France's most important fortress, Verdun, falling to the enemy Prussians, placing the enemy in position to march directly westwards on Paris. Danton's speech would be remembered (often with its context amidst the Massacres forgotten), for capturing the revolutionary spirit—uncompromising and demanding that with an ever-more audacious spirit the French achieve liberty or death. Danton had passionate followers amongst the Parisian populace: having first achieved renown as a fiery popular orator at the Cordeliers Club, a haven for Left Bank radicals, Danton had risen through the revolutionary ranks, becoming a sectional representative at the Paris Commune. With the Legislative Assembly a lame-duck, waiting for the National Convention elections to conclude, it ruled in cooperation with Paris' Insurrectional Commune (hence Danton's promotion to lead the Justice Ministry). Danton secured election to the Convention as a deputy for Paris. In April 1793, he became the first President of the Committee of Public Safety.

It is very satisfying, Messieurs, for the ministers of a free people to announce to them that the fatherland will be saved.

Everyone rises, everyone is moving, all burn to fight. You know that Verdun is no more; it is in your enemies' hands. You know the garrison has promised to immolate the first who tries to enter. Some of the people are carrying themselves to the frontiers, others are building trenches, and the third, with pikes, defends our interior cities. Paris encourages these great efforts. The Commune solemnly invites citizens to arm themselves and march to defend the fatherland.

It is in this moment, Messieurs, that you can declare the capital has well merited all of France. In this moment, the National Assembly will become a true war council.

We ask that you work with us to direct this sublime movement of the people, by naming commissars who can second these great measures. We ask that whoever refuses to serve in person, or give back their arms, be punished with death. We ask citizens be given instructions to guide their moments. We ask that couriers be sent into all departments to inform them of our decrees.

The alarm bell that's going to sound is not a warning signal; rather, it signals an offensive against the fatherland's enemies. To win, Messieurs, we need audaciousness, more audaciousness, always audaciousness, and France will be saved.

Charles-François Morrison, Proposal of Punishment for the King, November 13, 1792

A moderate deputy from the Vendée Department—that would soon see the worst counterrevolutionary violence in France—Charles-François Morrison, presenting for a National Convention committee, argued in favor of preserving the King's life on November 13, 1792. With Louis now seeming most important as a symbol, Morrison wanted revolutionaries to uphold the rule of law, keeping to what had been guaranteed the king in the Constitution of 1791. Expelling the king from the country, however, likely would have resulted in his joining the counterrevolutionary armies invading France, while many legislators feared he would be sprung from prison by a new counterrevolutionary conspiracy. The committee's argument also minimized the seriousness of the treason charge facing the monarch, which the French Constitution did not strictly adjudicate for conspiracies, emboldening more radical legislators to embrace arguments based on "natural law." Morrison's constitutionality soon appeared un-pragmatic to most Convention legislators amidst a serious revolutionary crisis.

Citizens, since we have to determine a question of the greatest importance, a question essentially related to politics and the principles of distributive justice, we should only decide after the most thorough discussion. . . .

Citizens, I feel my spirit penetrated, like yours, by the strongest indignation, as I consider the crimes, the treachery, the atrocities by which Louis XVI rendered himself guilty. My first impulse, the most natural, without a doubt, is to see this bloody monster pay for his crimes with the cruelest torments. He deserves them all, I know. But at this tribunal, representing a free people, representing a people who only search for their happiness and prosperity in acts of justice, in acts of humanity, of generosity, of charity, because they can only be found there, I must stop myself from hearing any except the councils of reason, to only consult the spirit and dispositions of our laws, to only look out for our fellow citizens' interests, without a doubt the only object for all our deliberations.

Your committee of legislation, of which I have the advantage of being a member, proposes discussing the following questions:

Can the king be judged? What should the charges be? In what manner should he be judged? For myself, citizens, without deviating from the principal object we are discussing at this moment, I present to you a series of questions . . .

Is it in the interest of the Republic that he be judged?

Do we not have the right to take, in his regard, measures for general security?

Finally, what ought these measures to be? . . .

Can Louis XVI be judged? Citizens, I treat this question amidst a people who exercise without constraint their full sovereignty; I have no intention here of contesting their rights, I will always know to respect them: but these rights have limits; limits even more sacred than those of nature itself, which sets them for our happiness, for the happiness of the entire human race . . . to be able to judge him, there must be a positive preexisting law to apply to him.

But no such law exists.

The penal code, which supersedes all previous criminal laws, pronounces the death penalty against those who commit treason against the fatherland.

Louis XVI has evidently committed treason against his fatherland: he has rendered himself guilty of treachery several times; he plotted to place us under the yoke of despotism; he raised much of Europe against us; he sold our positions and the properties of our brothers; he sacrificed our generous defenders; he attempted everywhere to spread anarchy and disorder; he sent French money to arm enemies, who have coalesced against us; he slit the throats of thousands of citizens who committed no other crime towards him than of loving their country and liberty; the blood of these unfortunate victims still burns around this wall; it calls all the French to avenge them. But here we are religiously under the empire of the law: as impartial judges, we coldly consult our Penal Law; well, this Penal Code does not contain any disposition that could be applied to Louis XVI; since the time of his crimes there existed a positive law that carried an exception in his favor; I speak of the Constitution.

I open, citizens, this shapeless and unreasonable work, this work contradictory with the first principles of social order, but which remains necessary since the crimes we groan under have been committed. There are these constitutional articles:

"The person of the King is inviolable and sacred.

"If the king sets himself at the head of an army and directs its forces against the nation, or if he does not oppose by a formal act such an exercise executed in his name, he will be considered to have abdicated the kingdom.

"After a legal or expressed abdication, the King will be considered a citizen, and he can be accused and judged like them for acts subsequent to his abdication." . . .

Citizens, I must here remind you of a very useful truth to propagate, a truth without which we would be already plunged into the horrors of anarchy: this truth is that laws not abrogated by subsequent laws remain in full force, and each citizen is fully obliged to respect them for their happiness and the happiness of everyone. . . .

Louis XVI was going to crush us under the weight of his treacheries; the liberty of which we were the guardians, may have escaped our hands if the throne of Louis XVI existed a moment longer. We needed to overthrow it . . .

Our powers would no longer exist, because they could no longer be exercised in the constitutional order. Louis XVI covered himself in crimes and treacheries; he merited losing his crown a thousand times over, which was the penalty determined by the Constitution. . . .

England let the head of the criminal Charles Stuart fall from the scaffold, and England still finds itself dependent on a King; Rome, on the contrary, more generously, only chased away the Tarquins, and Rome long enjoyed the happiness of being a Republic.[4] . . .

We could keep him captive amongst us; but let's calculate this measure's inconveniences. Louis XVI, in his captivity, could still attract partisans: especially amongst those men who could not rise to revolutionary dignity, who are so weak, so ignorant to love the monarchy and king . . .

In consequence, I call the preliminary question on the project of the committee, and I propose the following decree: . . .

1. Louis XVI is banned in perpetuity from the territory of the French Republic.
2. If, after his expulsion from France, Louis XVI returns to its territory, he will be punished with death. All citizens, in this case, are enjoined to attack him as an enemy, and a bounty of 500,000 pounds will be paid to anyone who, should he attack French territory, slays him dead.
3. The present decree will be sent to the diverse powers of Europe with whom we retain political or commercial relations.

Louis-Antoine de Saint-Just, selections from "One Cannot Reign Innocently" speech, November 13, 1792

At age twenty-five, the youngest member of the National Convention, Louis-Antoine de Saint-Just immediately followed Morrison's call for banishment by offering a radical justification for the king's execution. Louis could not be considered inviolable (per the terms of the Constitution of 1791) because the king had violated the highest dictates of morality and nature. In alluding to the "law of nature," Saint-Just asserted that Louis XVI needed to be tried as an enemy of the human race—who ought to be eliminated for the general good. Realizing the historical fragility of republics, severity, rather than constitutionality, appeared the most necessary to Saint-Just. A published pornographic writer before entering politics, Saint-Just earned a growing reputation as a revolutionary hard-liner, demanding ever-stricter penalties against those he considered to be the revolution's enemies.

The committee's only goal is to persuade you that the king needs to be judged as a simple citizen.[5] As for myself, I will say that the king must be judged as an enemy, that we need less to judge him than combat him. As he no longer exists in the contract uniting the French, his trial's format comes not from the civil law, but from the law of nations.

If mistaking these distinctions, one falls into forms without principles that carry the king to impunity. . . .

The same men who want to judge Louis have a Republic to found; those who attach any importance to the just punishment of a king will never found a Republic. Among us, refined spirits and characters are a great obstacle to liberty; they embellish all errors, and, most often, the truth is only the seduction of our taste. . . .

Citizens, if the Roman people, after six hundred years of virtue and hatred against all kings; if Great Britain, after Cromwell's death, brought kings back to life, despite their energy, ought it not to worry the good citizens amongst us who are friends of liberty to see the hatchet tremble in our hands, and a people from the first day of their liberty respect the memory of their irons? . . .

You search for a law permitting the king's punishment; but, in the form of government we are leaving, if there was an inviolable man, it was him . . . yet between people and king, I no longer know of any natural rapport. It belongs to a nation to stipulate the clauses of the social pact, surrounding its magistrates with a character capable of making them respect all rights and follow each of them . . . The citizens followed this contract; the sovereign did not . . . Thus, Louis' inviolability does not extend above his crimes and the insurrection;[6] or, if one judged him inviolable afterwards, if one pursues this interpretation, it would follow, citizens, that he could not be deposed, and ably oppress us via his authority over the people.

Our pact is a contract between citizens, and not with the government: there is no contract when one is not obligated. Consequently Louis, who was not obligated, cannot be judged civilly; this contract was so oppressive that it obliged the citizens and not the king: such a contract is necessarily null, now nothing is legitimate outside of what finds sanction in morals and in nature. . . .

Outside of these motifs, to not judge Louis as a citizen but to judge him as a rebel, what right could he claim for being judged civilly, according to the agreement we have made with him, since it is clear he has violated the only pact he took towards us, to protect us? What would this last act of tyranny be except pretending to be judged by the laws he destroyed? And, citizens, if we grant him the right to be judged civilly, according to the laws, as a citizen, if we judge him by this title, it would judge the people themselves.

For myself, I do not want any middle ground: this man must reign or die. . . .

One cannot reign innocently: such a notion's folly is too evident. Every king is a rebel and a usurper. Do kings themselves not treat would-be usurpers to their authority likewise? Should we not have a trial due to Cromwell's example? Certainly, Cromwell was no more a usurper than Charles I. Yet, since that people were so cowardly to let themselves be led by tyrants, domination became the first claimant's right, and is no more sacred or legitimate on one head or another. . . .

Citizens, if you desire that Europe admires the justice of your judgment, such are the principles that ought to determine it; those the Committee of Legislation proposes to you are a monumental injustice. The trial format is hypocritical; you will be judged in turn according to your principles. . . .

Louis was another Cataline; the murderer, like the consul of Rome, swore he had saved the fatherland.[7] Louis combatted the people; he is vanquished. He is a barbarian, a foreign prisoner of war. You have seen his perfidious designs; you have seen his army; this traitor was not King of the French, he was the king of some conspirators. He raised troops secretly, kept magistrates in his pocket; he considered citizens his slaves; he secretly proscribed all good men of courage. He is the murderer of the Bastille, of Nancy, of the Champ de Mars, of Tournai, of the Tuileries: what enemy, what traitor could have treated us worse?[8] He needs to be judged promptly; this is the council of wisdom and political sanity; this is a kind of hostage-taking that saves the rogues. They seek to stir pity; they will elicit tears; they will do everything to interest us, even corrupt us. People, if the king is forever absolute, remember that we will never be more worthy of his confidence, and you can accuse us of perfidy.

Legislators pronounce their verdicts in the King's Trial, January 16–17, 1793

The Convention's unanimous 693-0 vote on the King's guilt (absences and abstentions aside) gave way to a bitter divide over the king's fate. Calls by the Girondin faction for an "appeal to the people," in which the King's fate would be decided by popular referendum, failed. With sentencing to be decided by the Convention's vote, each deputy came to the rostrum to pronounce their penalty. Some decided that imprisonment or banishment would be more prudent sentences, worrying about the effects that such bloodshed and extra-legality would have on revolutionary politics. Yet, arguments to deliver an exemplary punishment against the king for having violated the nation's fundamental laws—particularly given the treasonous nature of his offensives—carried the day. Many humanitarians who had previously considered abolishing executions, including Robespierre, asserted that the exigency of the moment demanded swift punishment. A significant majority wanted the death penalty, yet many sought to suspend the sentence until the republic stabilized. Immediate death for the king passed by only a single vote—with 361 of 721 deputies calling for death without qualification.

The question is posed in these terms: What penalty ought to be inflicted on Louis, the former King of the French?

Jean-Baptiste Mailhe:[9] As a natural consequence of the opinion I have already given on the first question [of guilt], I vote for Louis' death. I will make a single observation: if death wins the majority, I think it would be fitting for the National Convention to examine whether it would be politically wise and useful to expedite or delay the execution. This proposition is independent of my vote. I come back to the first question and I vote for death.

Jean-François Delmas:[10] Before mounting the tribune, I consulted my conscience; it reproaches me for nothing. I only know one penalty for conspirators. I vote for death. . . .

Emmanuel Perès de Lagesse:[11] I will in few words explain my advice, which was not predetermined: I will make a free man of him. I believe the tyrant would threaten us more by his death than by continuing his shameful existence. From another perspective, we are a political body, and not a tribunal. We cannot judge without becoming despots. We have the power to take a measure of general security. I conclude as a legislator and statesman that he should be imprisoned until the peace, and then banished.

Jean Julien:[12] If there was a moment since the National Convention's opening when we have taken all precautions, imposed silence on all passions, it is in this case where we are called to pronounce on a citizen's life. I close my eyes to the happy or unhappy future awaiting us; I can only consult my conscience, thereby giving the sad and sorrowful verdict I must render. I thus declare, on my conscience, that Louis merits death and I vote for that penalty.

Jean-Marie Calés:[13] I vote for death, and all I regret is to not be able to pronounce it for all tyrants.

Antoine Estadens:[14] I vote for imprisonment until the peace and banishment at that time. . . .

Julien Mazade:[15] I declare I do not believe it in my power to judge him. I vote, as a legislator, for perpetual imprisonment.

Louis Bon de Montaut:[16] Opening the penal code, I read that the penalty against traitors and conspirators is death. Louis is guilty of conspiring. I read also, in the Declaration of the Rights of Man, that the law must be equal for all, whether it protects or punishes. I condemn the tyrant to death. . . .

Joseph Cappin:[17] I do not believe any society has the right to condemn a person to death, if not for the public interest. The death of Louis does not seem useful to me . . . I vote for imprisonment until the securing of liberty and banishment at that point. . . .

Pierre-Victurien Vergniaud:[18] I have voted for the decree or judgment rendered by the National Convention to be submitted to the people's sanction. In my opinion, the principles and political considerations of the largest interest become the Convention's duty. The National Convention has decided the matter otherwise. I obey: my conscience is clear. Now it is necessary to decide the penalty to inflict on Louis. I declared yesterday that I consider him guilty of conspiracy against liberty and national security. It is not permitted for me today to hesitate on this penalty. The law speaks: it calls for death, but in pronouncing this terrible word, worrying about my country's fate, about the dangers menacing liberty itself, above all the blood that could be spilt, I pronounce the same view as Mailhe . . .

Jacques-Paul Duplantier: Though voting against the appeal to the people, I could not hide the inconvenience of a definitive judgment. Nevertheless, I have consulted my conscience and the law. I vote for death, with Mailhe's amendment. . . .

Pierre-Joseph Cambon:[19] The view of all the French is perfectly well known: they want to destroy all privileges and the punishment of everyone resisting the establishment of the regime of equality . . . today I have one of the privileged to judge, convicted of treason against the fatherland. The law is positive, his crime is notorious. I would believe myself guilty of violating national justice if I supported deportation. I vote for death. . . .

Pierre Castilhon:[20] If I only consulted Louis' crimes and the penalty they merit, I would not hesitate to pronounce death, but fear of seeing his odious blood mix with those of a people I cherish makes me vote for imprisonment and banishment at the peace.

Jean-Denis Lajuinais:[21] As a man, I would vote for Louis' death, but as a legislator, considering only the health of the state and liberty's interest, I known no better means of conserving and defending them against tyranny, than by keeping the former king alive. . . . I vote for imprisonment until the peace, and banishment afterwards, under pain of death if he returns to France. . . .

Charles-François Duval:[22] As an organ of the law, I pronounce death. . . .

Louis Lepage:[23] Nature has set in my hand an invincible horror at the spilling of blood. I think a man has no right to condemn another man to death: I ask the tyrant be detained throughout the war and banished at the peace. . . .

Jean-Etienne Bar:[24] Louis merits death. . . .

François Poultier:[25] Death within 24 hours. . . .

Maximillien Robespierre:[26] I do not long love speeches on obvious questions . . .

The sentiment that led me to ask, in vain, that the Constituent Assembly abolish the death penalty, is the same forcing me today to demand it be applied to the tyrant of my fatherland, and to royalty itself in his person. I do not know how to predict or imagine future tyrants; I can only strike those I declare convicted, with this assembly's near-unanimity, and whom the people have charged me to judge with you. Real or chimerical factions cannot be, in my eyes, reasons to spare him, because I am convinced that the means of destroying factions is not to multiply them, but to crush them under the weight of reason and national interest. I council you not to preserve the king, to oppose those factions to which his death could give rise, but to strike him down, and then raise the edifice of general happiness over the ruin of all the anti-popular parties. I will look no more, like many others, to find ways of saving the former king by the menacing efforts of the despots of Europe, because I hate them all, and my intention is not to let the people's representatives capitulate to them. I know that the only means of defeating them is to elevate the French character to the heights of republican principles, and to exercise on kings and the slaves of kings the power of fierce and free spirits upon those insolent and servile. . . . I do not know how to oppose empty, senseless words and unintelligible distinctions to certain principles and imperious obligations. I vote for death.

Georges-Jacques Danton:[27] I am not of that group of statesmen who violate the rule not to collaborate with tyrants, who ignore that one only strikes tyrants in the head, who ignore that one ought not to negotiate with those of Europe except through the force of our arms. I vote for the tyrant's death.

Marchioness de Bonchamps, selections from *Memoirs of the Vendée*, published 1815

The French Revolution produced domestic counterrevolutionaries as passionate as the revolutionaries themselves. In the Vendée department, south of Brittany where the Loire River meets the Atlantic Ocean, after years of scattered guerilla uprisings, in March 1793 a massive uprising occurred, fighting in the name of the Bourbon monarchy and Catholic faith. The French Revolutionary leadership brutally suppressed the uprising, killing perhaps 200,000 people, both insurgents and civilians—perhaps a quarter of the Vendée's population. Nevertheless, periodic uprisings in the area continued to occur across the rest of the revolution and much of the nineteenth century. The Marchioness de Bonchamps, a surviving local noble whose husband help lead the uprising, published her memories of the initial insurrection in 1815 as the Bourbons returned to power. While a romanticized account, it captures the powerful reactions the French Revolution inspired amongst those disagreeing with its core principles. The uprising has had a long, heroic legacy among French conservatives.

The terrible news of the king's assassination ended M. de Bonchamps' cautiousness. When he heard of this horrible catastrophe, my husband was beset with such profound grief and vehement indignation, that he became dangerously ill, and for a few days I trembled for his life. Then, the National Convention ordered three hundred thousand men drafted. The decree desolated the peasantry of our district, that part of the Vendée known as the Bocage. The uprising it produced here was almost unanimous at two places, fairly far apart—at Challans, in Bas-Poitou, and Saint-Florent, on the Loire's banks. The uprising, far from being a revolt, was the most legitimate defense the people could make to the most tyrannical persecution. This people, faithful to their religion, and to their ancient race of kings, only took arms to avenge the murdered and resist barbarous men, stained with blood, who in their sacrilegious and regicidal fury had just immolated the most virtuous monarch, while simultaneously overturning throne and altar.

At the news of our canton's uprising, the Convention commanded those troops sent into the Vendée to exterminate men, women, children, even animals and vegetation. Such was the unheard-of rage with which the Vendeeans' resistance to the decree levying troops had inspired the assembly. The military draft was scheduled for March 10, at Saint-Florent: all the young men went there, determined not to submit. They were harangued, and insulted with expressions of contempt, alongside the most horrible threats. A piece of artillery was even pointed against them and fired. The young men, enraged, furiously threw themselves at the gun and seized it. They scattered all before them; the district hall the Republicans had occupied was pillaged and their papers burnt. Taking the treasury, the conquerors distributed the money amongst themselves, which added to the rejoicings of this first victory. They had beaten the gendarmerie, taken two culverins and some muskets, but had no leaders. When the intoxication of their first success subsided, they fearfully considered that the republicans would soon return with new forces and that, animated with the thirst of vengeance, they had only to expect a merciless rage and the most atrocious cruelties from them.

They knew only an experienced leader could save them and naturally looked to my husband. . . . I shall never forget what he told me before assuming command: "Arm yourself with courage, redouble your patience and fortitude—you shall need them. We must not deceive ourselves. We must not aim at worldly rewards: they would be beneath the purity of our motives and the sanctity of our cause. We must not even seek human glory; civil wars do not give that. We shall see our houses burnt, we shall be plundered, persecuted, entrapped, calumniated, and perhaps sacrificed. Let us thank God that he has granted us this conviction, since our faith, redoubling our actions' merit, will enable us to anticipate the joy of that heavenly hope, which unshaken constancy in danger, and true heroism in defeat, can bestow. Finally, let us elevate our souls and all our thoughts towards heaven, for it is there we shall find a guide that cannot lead us astray, a strength nothing can shake, and an infinite reward for this moment's labors." . . .

The Bishop of Agra, before battle, at the head of several other priests, clothed in their canonical garb, harangued the soldiers in these words: "Ancient and faithful race of the servants of our kings, pious defenders of the throne and altar, children of the Vendée, fight on and triumph: God himself commands you."[28]

The whole army replied with enthusiasm that they would obey. They kept their word. This noble harangue became a prophecy. . . .

Around this time there was extraordinary activity in the cottages of the Vendée, and in the villages and small towns of which the peasants had made themselves masters. Arms were rudely fabricated; herdsmen turned warriors made their peaceful huts into workshops, where the iron rung under the heavy blows of the hammer. Instruments of husbandry, intended for the tranquil cultivation of the soil, became transformed into murderous arms. Originally for growing human food, they now carried death and destruction into the fields they fertilized. However, agriculture was not abandoned: cultivation was entrusted to women and children. If fortune did not favor the men's bravery, the women immediately abandoned their labors to fly to their assistance, protect their retreat, even to fight with them to repel the enemy. During the battles, the air resounded with the repeated cries of "Long live religion! Long live the King! Long live the Bourbons!" . . . In an engagement where the Vendeeans were sure to be overwhelmed by numbers, they cried aloud, "let us march to Heaven," penetrating the enemy battalions, happy to rush into martyrdom. . . .

FIGURE 8.1 *Lesueur Brothers,* Patriotic Women's Club. © *DEA / G. DAGLI ORTI / Getty Images.*

French Revolutionary women refused to accept that the Rights of Man belonged to men alone. Although voting and office-holding remained confined to male suffrage, women found ways of making their voices heard in politics—mobilizing protests, attending National Assembly and Jacobin Club sessions, and in some cases even founding their own political clubs. Here, in one of the Leseur Brothers' famous prints, we see women engaged in political behavior much as men would be—reading and discussing the latest revolutionary news. More distinctively, a middle-class woman offers her jewelry as a "patriotic donation" to the nation (a tactic women repeatedly used to gain admission as petitioners to revolutionary assemblies). While women continued to be constrained by male prejudice and traditionalist interpretations of gender roles, they nevertheless found many ways to participate in the revolution.

8

A Cultural Revolution

The French Revolution was no mere political event, but a cultural revolution questioning the very bases of society. As commoners won legal equality with nobles, women examined their own subservient role in society—dictated by custom but often enforced by law. If taking the principle of equality seriously, as revolutionaries claimed, why could equality not extend to gender roles? The ideas the French Revolution unleashed could not be restrained to the relatively limited functions many National Assemblymen wanted them to serve—virtually all groups considering themselves oppressed sought to turn such emancipatory concepts to their own advantage. The principles of human rights unleashed in 1789 were too all-encompassing to be easily limited or controlled.

No revolutionary changes appeared more fundamental or shocking than those related to gender issues and the family. Though many men, when pressed on the legitimacy of male dominance, tried to attribute "natural" differences to biology, women activists continued pressing for full inclusion into French political life. Women founded or contributed to many political clubs, wrote pamphlets and books, and took to the streets in large numbers. Even though many male politicians and activists responded with disdain, others carefully considered their grievances, and French Revolutionary feminism helped create the template for modern women's rights movements.

While female voting and office-holding remained unachieved, major social reforms passed by the early first republic. Approving divorce laws upended the traditional nature of marriage, allowing partners to escape what had typically been perpetual legal bonds. The French pursuit of happiness led them to alter what had previously been considered the bedrock of the social order. Gender equality also entered inheritance law—instead of estates going to the eldest surviving male, now all "natural children" (including those born out of wedlock) received equal shares. Fairness and inclusion, instead of Old Regime exclusion and hierarchy, were the virtues and hallmarks of revolutionary social policy.

Much as gender discrimination was increasingly contested, revolutionaries newly celebrated working-class culture as social prejudices fell. Whereas previously high status and privilege dominated, now almost everyone emphasized their *sans-culotte* bona fides, speaking in the popular vernacular and emphasizing popular wisdom. Solidarity with common workers appeared essential for a radical regime claiming to speak for all the people—and newly subject to election via universal manhood suffrage, the un-propertied included. Exclusion appeared an aristocratic vice.

Amidst the French Revolution's dizzying changes, the last could be first and the first could be last. Yesterday's aristocrat became today's exile or arrestee, while pushing the revolution's radical potential for a time appeared the quickest route to political advancement and promotion. Humble *sans-culotte* origins became a sign of virtuousness and authenticity. Even where French Revolutionary reforms remained unachieved, and most redistribution of resources and power wound up going to middle-class men, the audacity of the era's examples would echo across future generations, into modern movements for women's and workers' rights.

Olympe de Gouges, *Declaration of the Rights of Woman*, 1791

The French Revolution helped inspire modern feminism, with radical activists asking for the first time why women were not being accorded the same "natural" rights as men. Olympe de Gouges, a playwright, longtime Paris salon participant, recent revolutionary club member, and author of an abolitionist drama set in the Caribbean, in 1791 published an unprecedentedly radical broadside, re-writing the Declaration of the Rights of Man and Citizen from a female perspective, while mocking male revolutionaries for overlooking female potential. Much as commoners faced systematic discrimination in France before 1789, so did women remain oppressed under the new order of supposed liberty and equality. A regenerated France could also include revolutionized notions of marriage and the family. Women's political participation became a growing issue as the Revolution progressed, though no male governing bodies seriously considered granting them suffrage. Women would not vote in France until 1945. Gouges, moreover, proved a poor coalition-builder, dedicating her work to Marie Antoinette (who had no interest in the Rights of Man, much less applying them to females), and by the First Republic allied herself with the Girondin faction. She would be executed for her political writings soon after the former queen in November 1793.

Dedicated to the Queen.

Little can be accomplished with the language one speaks to Kings. I will not employ the adulation of courtesans to render homage to you with this unique production. My goal, Madame, is to speak to you frankly. I have not waited to thus express myself for the era of liberty: I have risen with the same energy in a time when the blindness of despots punishes such noble audaciousness.

Since all the empire accuses you and declares you responsible for its calamities, only I, in a time of trouble and storms, have dared to take your defense. I have never been able to persuade myself that a princess, raised amidst grandeur, has the lowliest vices. . . .

If you were less educated, Madame, I might worry that your private interests would not encompass those of your sex. You love glory: consider, Madame, that the greatest crimes achieve immortality as the greatest virtues; but what difference is fame in the splendor of history! The one is ceaselessly taken for an example, while the other is the eternal execration of the human race.

Working for the restoration of morals is never a crime, to give to your sex consistency despite its susceptibilities. This work is not the work of a day, unfortunately so for the new regime. This revolution will only occur when all women realize their deplorable condition and the rights they have lost in society. Madame, please support such a beautiful cause. Defend this unfortunate sex, and you will soon have half the kingdom's support, and at least a third of the other.

Here, Madame, are the undertakings you need to employ to your credit. Believe me, Madame, our life is a small thing, especially for a Queen, when this life is not embellished by the love of peoples and the eternal charms of charity. . . .

Here, Madame, are my principles. In speaking to you of my fatherland, I lose view of this dedication's goal. Every good citizen sacrifices their glory and interests when they have no interest except that of their county.

I am with the most profound respect,
Madame,
Your very humble and obedient servant,
De Gouges.

THE RIGHTS OF WOMAN.

Men, are you capable of being just? This is a woman asking you the question; you will not deny her that right. Tell me, what has given you the sovereign right to oppress my sex? Your strength? Your talents? Observe the creator in his wisdom; examine nature in all its grandeur, which you seem to want to emulate, and give me, if you can, the reason for this tyrannical empire. Go look in the animal kingdom, consult the elements, study plants, take a glance at all the varieties of organic matter, and examine the evidence I offer you. Search, research, and distinguish, if you can, the sexes' roles in nature. Everywhere you find them mixed, everywhere they cooperate as a harmonious ensemble in this immortal masterpiece.

Man alone is presented as an exception to this principle. Bifurcated, blinded, bloated on the sciences and degenerated, in this century of enlightenment and wisdom, by the crassest ignorance, they want to command like a despot a sex possessing all the same intellectual facilities. They pretend to make a revolution and reclaim the rights of equality without saying anything more about them.

DECLARATION OF THE RIGHTS OF WOMAN AND CITIZEN

To be decreed by the National Assembly in its last sessions, or in the next legislature's.

PREAMBULE

Representatives of the nation: mothers, daughters, sisters ask to be represented in the National Assembly. Considering that ignorance, forgetting, or contempt of the rights of woman are the sole cause of public ills and the corruption of governments, they have resolved to expose in a solemn declaration the natural, inalienable, and sacred rights of woman. To such an end, this declaration incessantly summons all members of the social body, reminding them ceaselessly of their rights and duties, so female and male power can always work together towards the goals of all political institutions. Thereby, female citizens' grievances will become more respected. They will be founded from this point forward on simple and incontestable principles, always supporting the constitution, good morals, and the happiness of all.

In consequence, the sex superior in beauty as in courage and maternal suffering, recognizes and declares, in the presence and under the auspices of the Supreme Being, the following rights of Woman and Citizen.

I. Woman is born free and remains equal to man in rights. Social distinctions can only be founded on communal utility.

II. The goal of all political association is the conservation of natural and imprescriptible rights of Woman and Man: these rights are liberty, property, security, and especially resistance to oppression.

III. The principle of all sovereignty resides essentially in the Nation, which is only the reunion of Woman and Man: no body, no individual, can exercise authority not emanating from it explicitly.

IV. Liberty and justice must render everything relating to them; thus, the exercise of the natural rights of woman has no limits except the perpetual tyranny with which man opposes them; these limits must be reformed by the laws of nature and reason.

V. The laws of nature and reason forbid all actions harmful to society: everything not forbidden by wise and divine laws cannot be avoided, and no one can be constrained to do what they do not allow.

VI. The law must be the expression of the general will; all male and female citizens must come together personally, or by their representatives, in its formation; it must be the same for everyone: all female citizens and all male citizens, equal in their eyes, must be equally admissible to all dignities, places, and public employments, according to their capacities, and without other distinction than their virtues and talents.

VII. No woman can be exempted; she shall be accused, arrested, and detained in the cases determined by law. Women, like men, will obey the law rigorously.

VIII. The law must only establish penalties strictly and evidently necessary, and none can be punished except in virtue of a law established and promulgated prior to the crime and legally applied to women.

IX. Any woman must be declared guilty, following every rigor of the law.

X. None ought to worry about making their opinions known, even fundamental ones. Women have the right to mount the scaffold; she should equally have the right to mount the speaker's rostrum, so long as her actions do not trouble the public order established by law.

XI. The free communication of thoughts and opinions is one of the most precious rights of woman, since this liberty assures the legitimacy of fathers towards their children. Every female citizen can thus freely say, I am the mother of a child that comes from you, without barbaric prejudice stopping the truth being known, while having to respond to the abuse of this liberty in the cases determined by law.

XII. The guarantee of the rights of woman and citizen constitutes a major utility; this guarantee needs to be instituted for everyone's advantage, not for the private use of those for whom it is currently confided.

XIII. For the support of public forces, and for administrative expenses, women and men's contributions are equal; women take part in all kinds of work, in all unpleasant tasks; she ought thus to have an equal part in the distribution of positions, jobs, public functions, dignities, and industries.

XIV. Female and male citizens have the right to determine for themselves, or via their representatives, the level of public contributions. Female citizens cannot agree to them except by being granted an equal share, not only in fortune but also in public administration, and in determining the quotas, means of payment, collection, and duration of taxes.

XV. The great mass of women, taxed like men, have the right to demand accountability from all public agents and their administration.

XVI. All societies where guaranteed rights are not assured, nor the determined powers separated, have no constitution. The constitution is null, if the majority of individuals composing nation have not cooperated in its writing.

XVII. Property belongs to each sex, whether married or separated; it is a sacred and inviolable right for both. No one can reasonably be deprived of nature's patrimony unless public necessity, legally demonstrated, requires it, and under the condition of a just and preceding indemnity.

POSTAMBULE

Woman, rise up! The alarm bell of reason is ringing across the universe; you must recognize your rights. The powerful empire of nature can no longer be surrounded with prejudices, or fanaticism, or superstition, or lies. The flame of truth has dissipated all the clouds of stupidity and usurpation. . . . O women! Women, when will you cease to be blind? What advantages have you gained in the revolution? More wanton cruelty and clearer disdain. Over centuries of corruption you have only reigned through the weakness of men. Your empire is destroyed. What remains? The conviction of man's injustices. . . .

Women have done more bad than good. Constraint and duplicity have been their lot. What force has taken, ruse has rendered them. They have employed all the resources of their charms and the most irreproachable amongst them does not resist using such methods. Poison, daggers, all have been employed; they possess a command of crime as they do of virtue. . . .

Under the old regime, everyone was vicious, everyone was guilty . . . can reason conceal that every other road to fortune is closed to women when men buy them, like a slave on the coasts of Africa? . . .

FORM FOR A SOCIAL CONTRACT BETWEEN MAN AND WOMAN

We ___ and ___, possessing our own wills, unite ourselves for the length of our life, and for the duration of our mutual inclinations, under the following conditions: We understand and want to share our fortunes together, in reserving the right to separate them in favor of our children, from whatever bed they come from, and that all indistinctly have the right to use the name of the fathers and mothers they avow, and we will follow the law that punishes the denial of one's proper blood. We oblige ourselves equally, in case of separation, to divide our fortune and deduct the portion for our children indicated by law; and, in a perfect union, lasting until death, will leave half the property for their children; and if one dies without children, the next inheritor, at least if the dying has not disposed of the half of their common goods to those they judge proper.

Pauline Léon, from *Address to the National Assembly by the Female Citizens of the Capital*, March 6, 1792

Some Parisian women, rather than following traditional gender limitations, asked to do all that men did—including for military defense. On March 6, 1792, twenty-three-year-old Parisian chocolate-maker Pauline Leon presented a petition sighed by over three hundred women, asking to form their own paramilitary regiments to help defend the city. Recalling the October Days of 1789, when Parisian women had led the march on Versailles, carrying pikes and hauling cannons, Leon asked both for weapons and training in military maneuvers. While still couching her request in as an extension of traditional gender roles, Leon highlighted women's need to defend themselves and their families in a time of military precarity. Though the National Assembly did not accept her offer, Leon remained a dedicated activist. In May 1793, she co-founded the Society of Republican Revolutionary Women, granting women a greater voice than the Jacobins or other assemblies allowed. Women remained banned from serving in France's armed forces—though in numerous cases, individuals defied the ban to enlist as men anyway.

Legislators,

Patriotic women present themselves to you, reclaiming every individual's right to defend their life and liberty.

All seems to announce a sudden violent shock: our fathers, our spouses, and our brothers may be victims of our enemies' furor. Can you forbid us the pleasure of avenging them, or of dying at their sides? We are citizens and cannot be indifferent to the fatherland's fate.

You predecessors have deposited the Constitution as much in our hands as in yours. Well! How can we best conserve this trust, if we do not have arms with which to defend it from its enemies' attacks?

Yes, Messieurs, we need these arms. We come to ask you to procure them for us. Our weak strength is not an obstacle: courage and intrepidity will overcome it. Love of the fatherland and hatred of tyrants will easily allow us to brave all dangers. Do not think our design is to abandon our caring duties, always dear to our hearts, of our family and our house, to run and encounter the enemy.

No, Messieurs: we want only to defend ourselves; you cannot refuse us this. Society cannot take away this right that nature gives us, at least if one does not pretend the Declaration of Rights has no application for women, and that she ought to let her throat be cut like a lamb, without having the right to self-defense. Now, what do you think the tyrants would like to do to us? No, no—they remember October 5 and 6, 1789 . . . Do you know our hidden enemies' number and force? Will they engage us in only one battle? Our lives, are they dearer than theirs? And our children, are they not orphaned by the loss of their fathers, as by that of their mothers? Why not thus employ, for laying the aristocracy and despotism low, all the resources of civic spirit and the purest zeal, that zeal cold men consider fanaticism and exaggeration, but which is only the natural result of a heart burning with love for the public good? . . .

This is what we hope to obtain from your justice and equity:

1. To procure us pikes, pistols, and swords (even guns for those with the strength to use them). We will submit to the police regulations.
2. To muster us on holidays and Sundays on the Field of the Federation, or other available places, to exercise in the maneuvering of said arms.
3. To name, for commanding us, members of the former French Guards, always in conformity with the rules the wisdom of Monsieur Mayor prescribes for the good order and public tranquility.

Signed, Léon, daughter, &c.
[over three hundred signatures]

Petition to legalize divorce from Department of Paris, February 13, 1792

Asserting freedom could not end at the doorstep, French Revolutionaries sought to extend liberty and equality into family relations. Realizing the extent to which patriarchal families could oppress subordinate members, on February 13, 1792, a joint deputation of men and women from the Paris region presented a petition before the National Assembly, proposing a divorce law to prevent "despotism" at home. The proposal was sent to the Legislation Committee and on September 20, the Assembly's last day, France's first modern divorce law passed. With the separation of civil law from religious authorities (who previously determined marriages and rare annulments), divorce in France gained an unprecedented lassitude. While a blow to Catholic teachings on marriage, equality became too important a guiding principle to be confined only to narrow political questions. Modern divorce law began with the French Revolution.

Letter from several male and female citizens of the Department of Paris soliciting from the Assembly provisional laws on divorce and the status of family sons, daughters and women in all the kingdom, and set limits to paternal and conjugal despotism.

Messieurs,

The Legislative Assembly, ceaselessly detoured from its works by artificial maneuvering, is forced to suspend ruling definitively on the necessary laws for determining the status of sons and daughters, who are more dependent and servile than ever. The state of marriage also merits scrupulous and vigilant attention. This question is felt, but not examined under its real conditions, both civil and political. Consider, Messieurs, how so much despotism exists at home that we cannot consider ourselves a race of free men. Generations yet to be born, familiarized with worry, as with capricious actions, will not be valorized nor made reasonable. Consider that foreign nations will not believe that we are establishing the reign of liberty and equality, if paternal and marital power retains the character of despotism and if the majority of the human species remains subordinated, contradictorily to our principles, to the arbitrary will of those whom feudalism accorded the titles of lord and master.

We believe it useful to render a provisional law protecting women and children from the tyranny of wicked fathers and husbands, a law that eliminates a state prison regime inside the home, that admonishes fathers and husbands to respect the rights of equality and rights of nature that give woman her proper dignity.

Léonard Robin, *Instruction on the Law that Determines the Causes, the Method and the Effects of Divorce, passed on September 20, 1792*, February 6, 1793

A deputy for Paris in the first National Assembly and thereafter a judge in a Parisian court, Léonard Robin addressed the National Convention in February 1793 on the need to specify the full latitude to be given in divorce cases. While the right to divorce had passed the previous September, the law had subsequently been left for judicial interpretation—some justices granting far more expansive purviews for unhappy couples than others. Robin sought a maximalist interpretation: with liberty considered the new order's foundation, being trapped in an unhappy marriage appeared a form of slavery. This could occur not only in cases of shocking cruelty, but from incompatibility: petty tyrannies to Robin appeared just as corrosive. Divorce could serve as a liberation, with individuals then free to pursue happiness elsewhere.

Instructions on the Law Determining the Causes, Methods, and Effects of Divorce.

In individual liberty, divorce has its true foundation.

Personhood itself, all the partners' affections, are engaged by marriage. It is evident that they will lose their liberty and become reciprocal slaves to each other if their engagement is irrevocable and their union indissoluble.

For too long this slavery, the most onerous of all, when disgust, discord, and hatred establish themselves in the household, has appeared consecrated by religious solemnities.

Civil law has finally declared that it no longer recognizes religious vows; it pronounces that it only considers marriage a civil contract.

The Constitution implicitly introduced the institution of divorce in France; and the Legislative Assembly, in decreeing this, only enunciated a constitutional principle.

This principle is founded on spouses' inalienable liberty. It means that, not only can the spouses break their marriage by divorce through a common accord, but that one can also demand and pronounce a divorce, without the consent and against the will of the other. Otherwise, a spouse's refusal to consent to divorce would suffice for one to hold the other in the bounds of a most terrible slavery. . . .

There cannot be, moreover, a stronger and more just cause for divorce than true incompatibility, than a lasting antipathy that manifests itself between spouses; and often this incompatibility affects the affections, habits, continual little acts, and petty arguments insensible for everyone except the spouse suffering them. Even worse, they hold secret vices, sometimes criminal, of which one or the other spouse has only too cruel of knowledge, but which they cannot prove, and which their delicateness, or perhaps duty, prevents them from uncovering.

Divorce thus, as founded on spouses' inalienable liberty, can take place in three ways:

1. By spouses' mutual consent.
2. By one spouse's demand, for the simple cause of incompatibility of humor or character, without other motives and without other allegation of acts.
3. By one spouse's demand, for the causes determined or acts specifically indicated by the law.

Mary Wollstonecraft, selections from *A Vindication of the Rights of Woman*, 1792

A forerunner of modern feminist thinking, Mary Wollstonecraft's *Vindication* makes a passionate case for female intellectual equality—arguing that only male neglect and condescension has prevented women from attaining the same intellectual achievements. With her title adapted from the most popular British radical pamphlets of the era, Thomas Paine's *Rights of Man* and James Mackintosh's *Vindicae Gallicae* (both published in 1791), Wollstonecraft hoped to make gender equality part of the international movement for more equal rights. Responding to pseudoscientific theories that considered women mentally inferior beings—particularly those of Jean-Jacques Rousseau, whose book *Emile* deeply influenced Enlightened child-rearing—Wollstonecraft instead argues that they are conditioned for a life of subservience that prevents them from realizing their full capabilities. As a former governess herself, Wollstonecraft asserts female children's potential, until they are forced down a path of comparative ignorance. Fascinated by the possibilities of French-style liberation, after publication Wollstonecraft moved to Paris, where she spent much of the next three years, before returning to London and marrying the early anarchist William Godwin. She died giving birth to the author of *Frankenstein*, the future Mary Shelley.

After considering the historic page, and viewing the present world with anxious solicitude, the most melancholy emotions of sorrowful indignation have depressed my spirits, and I have signed when obliged to confess, that either nature has made a great difference between man and man, or that the civilization which has hitherto taken place in the world has been very partial. I have turned over various books written on the subject of education, and patiently observed the conduct of parents and the management of schools; but what has been the result?—a profound conviction that the neglected education of my fellow creatures is the main source of the misery I deplore, and that women, in particular, are rendered weak and wretched by a number of concurring causes, originating from one hasty conclusion. The conduct and manners of women, in fact, show clearly that their minds are not in a healthy state; for, like the flowers planted too rich a soil, strength and usefulness are sacrificed to beauty; and the flaunting leaves, after having pleased a fastidious eye, fade, disregarded on the stalk, disregarded, long before the season when they ought to have arrived at maturity.—One cause of this barren blooming I attribute to a false system of education, gathered from the books on the subject by men, who, considering females rather as women than human creatures, have been more concerned to make them alluring mistresses than rational wives; and this understanding of the sex has been so bubbled by this specious homage, that the civilized women of the present century, with a few exceptions, are only anxious to inspire love, when they ought to cherish a nobler ambition, and by their abilities and virtues exact respect.

I shall first consider women in the grand light of human creatures who, in common with men, are placed on this earth to unfold their faculties; and afterwards I shall more particularly point out their peculiar designation. . . .

My own sex, I hope, will excuse me, if I treat them like rational creatures, instead of flattering their *fascinating* graces and viewing them as if they were in a state of perpetual childhood, unable to stand alone. I earnestly wish to point out in what true dignity and human happiness consists—I wish to persuade women to endeavour to acquire strength, both of mind and body, and to convince them that the soft phrases,

"susceptibility of heart"
"delicacy of sentiment," and
"refinement of taste"

are almost synonymous with epithets of weakness, and that those beings who are only the objects of pity and the kind of love, which has been termed its sister, will soon become objects of contempt. . . .

I wish to show that elegance is inferior to virtue, that the first object of laudable ambition is to obtain a character as a *human being*, regardless of the distinction of sex, and that secondary views should be brought to this simple touchstone. . . .

Men, in general, seem to employ their reason to justify prejudices, which they have imbibed, they cannot trace how, rather than to root them out. The mind must be strong that resolutely forms its own principles; for a kind of intellectual cowardice prevails which makes men shrink from the task, or only do it by halves . . .

To account for, and excuse the tyranny of man, many ingenious arguments have been brought forward to prove, that the two sexes, in the acquirement of virtue, ought to aim at attaining a very different character: or, to speak explicitly, women are not allowed to have sufficient strength of mind to acquire what really deserves the name of virtue. . . .

If then women are not a swarm of ephemeron triflers, why should they be kept in ignorance under specious name of "innocence"? . . .

I have, probably, had more opportunity to observe girls in their infancy than J. J. Rousseau—I can recollect my own feelings, and I have looked steadily around me; and far from coinciding with him in opinion respecting the first dawn of the female character, I will venture to affirm, that a girl, whose spirits have not been damped by inactivity, or innocence tainted by false shame, will always be a romp, and the doll will never excite attention unless confinement allows her no alternative. Girls and boys, in short, would play harmless together if the difference between the sexes was not inculcated long before nature makes any difference. —I will go further, and affirm, as an indisputable fact, that most of the women in the circle of my observation, who have acted like rational creatures, or shown any vigour of intellect, have accidentally been allowed to run wild . . .

That woman is naturally weak, or degraded by a concurrence of circumstances, is, I think, clear. But this position I shall simply contrast with a conclusion, which I have frequently heard fall from sensible men in favour of an aristocracy:

> that the mass of mankind cannot be any thing, or the obsequious slaves who patiently allow themselves to be penned up, would feel their own consequence, and spurn their chains. Men, they further observe, submit every where to oppression, when they have only to lift up their heads to throw off the yoke; yet, instead of asserting their birthright, they quietly lick the dust and say "Let us eat and drink, for tomorrow we die."
>
> . . .

A wild wish has just flown from my heart to my head, and I won't stifle it although it may arouse a horse laugh. Except in cases where love animates the behaviour, I do earnestly wish to see the distinction of sex confounded in society—that is, I wish things could be managed in such a way that it was usually not clear whether a given person was male or female. . . .

Would men but generously snap our chains, and be content with rational fellowship instead of slavish obedience, they would find us more observant daughters, more affectionate sisters, more faithful wives, more reasonable mothers—in a word, better citizens. We should then love them with true affection, because we would learn to respect ourselves; and the peace of mind of a worthy man would not be interrupted by the idle vanity of his wife, and his babes wouldn't be sent to nestle in a strange bosom because they never found a home in their mother's. . . .

Moralists have unanimously agreed, that unless virtue be nursed by liberty, it will never attain due strength—and what they say of man I extend to mankind, insisting that in all cases morals must be fixed on immutable principles; and that the being cannot be termed rational or virtuous, who obeys any authority, but that of reason. . . .

From the tyranny of man, I firmly believe, the greater number of female follies proceed; and the cunning, which I allow makes at present a part of their character, I likewise have repeatedly endeavoured to prove, is produced by oppression. . . .

Let woman share the rights and she will emulate the virtues of man; for she must grow more perfect when emancipated, or justify the authority that chains such a weak being to her duty.

Rosalie Julien, selected letters from a Convention deputy's wife and mother, September 2 and December 28, 1792

Though no woman was elected to the National Convention (or other revolutionary legislatures), many nevertheless became passionately interested in politics. Groups of radical women commonly sat in the visitor galleries of the Convention and Jacobin Clubs, often applauding or booing, and sometimes offering their own impromptu remarks. Many politicians' wives gained significant influence, arranging dinners and salon-style discussion groups, gathering information, or otherwise working behind the scenes to further their spouses' causes and careers. Rosalie Julien, the wife and mother of Convention deputies, wrote a series of politically passionate letters to each while they were away from the capital on missions for the government. Julien did not flinch at even the revolution's most notorious excesses—justifying the thousands killed in the September massacres of 1792, excusing the proscription of Girondin deputies in July 1793, and supporting arrests and guillotinings during the Terror. Her son, Marc-Antoine Julien, became one of the most fearsome government agents, helping lead the repression of the Vendée revolt in Western France. Though forced by gender constraints to funnel her political ambitions through her husband and son, Julien demonstrates the ecstatic commitment many women came to feel for the revolutionary programme.

September 2, 1792, to her husband.

When wanting a certain outcome, a way to achieve it must be found: there is no barbarous humanity. The people have risen. The people, terrible in their fury, avenge the crimes of three years of the most cowardly treasons. Oh, my friend! I take refuge in your arms, to cry a torrent of tears, but I cry to you first: France is saved! These tears, I shed them for the fate of our unhappy brother patriots, fallen under the Prussians' iron. Verdun is besieged and cannot hold out more than two days. The joy of ferocious aristocrats contrasts with our profound affliction. Listen, tremble: the warning cannon sounded around noon; the alarm bell rang, the general alarm reverberated. People responded, coming into the streets. All was in the most violent crisis: the municipality's moving proclamation fixed the people's attention and touched their hearts: "Fly to the aid of your brothers! To arms, to arms!" Many quickly joined. Finally, four thousand men departed that evening to throw themselves against the Prussians, whether at Verdun or closer, if they advance. The martial furor that seized all Parisians is a wonder; fathers of families, *bourgeois*, troops, *sans-culottes*, all types. The people said: "we are leaving our women, our children at home, amidst our enemies, let us purge them from the land of liberty." My friend, I place, with a trembling hand, a veil over the crimes the people have been forced to commit against all those whom, for three years, they have been the sad victim. The dark plots discovered everywhere carry into the light the most awful examples, and certainly show the fate that stalks and menaces patriots. If they do not kill, they will die! Atrocious necessity, fateful work of our enemies! Heads cut, priests massacred . . . I cannot recite them all to you, however enlightened by my reason that cries to me: the Prussians and the kings have done a thousand times worse.

December 28, 1792, to her son.

My heart is saddened from all the tempests swirling around our heads in these disastrous days. Before discussing the matter at hand, I will tell you that as much as my body is cured, my spirit grows sick. I blame apathy and egoism for my sadness; they form a double rampart against my sensibility. Today, I sense recovery, but I doubt I have really improved; as I feel consumed with worries and civic-mindedness, that to me are a real proof of health. . . . .

The National Convention is more agitated than the ocean's greatest furies. You cannot expect anything one way or the other. The majority, seduced by all the Brissotin and Rolandin artifices, for three months has been the toy of this cabal. The true patriots, unshakable in principles and strong in conscience, are so vigorous that I still see victory hanging over their head. The problem is that they are misunderstood almost as if in the tower of Babel, and the exaggeration of supposing them to be a party with leaders is quite great; now they are isolated and must scrupulously and tactfully carry on, since the evildoers are coalesced, assembled, armed, engaging the credulous to incite terror in Paris. Your papa had maintained here the eye of a lynx of philosophy and the most perfect judicious spirit.[1]

Selections from *Père Duchesne* newspaper Number 253, 1793

As the Revolution advanced and the audience for newspapers expanded, some writers sought to speak directly to the common people. Jacques-René Hébert developed the character of Père Duchesne, an artisan speaking like a common Parisian (profanity included). Though Hébert earned a law degree from the College of Alençon, he had left the legal profession and spent most of the 1780s working as a hairdresser and would-be playwright in Paris. Founding the *Père Duchesne* newspaper in 1790, by the early First Republic Hébert became known as the "voice of the *sans-culottes*," denouncing the revolution's perceived enemies with abandon. In this selection from 1793, Hébert inflames common grievances against merchants and speculators, blaming them for the economic problems facing the revolutionary capital. His sharp tongue, however, brought the enmity of Robespierre—whom

Hébert had denounced for being too moderate—which led to Hébert's guillotining in March 1794.

Great Anger of Father Duchesne,

Against financial rogues, money grabbers, monopolizers, hoarders, who worship their strongbox while exciting disorder and pillage to conduct a counterrevolution. His good advice to all those with something to risk, to put their heads together in a bonnet with the *Sans-Culottes*, who protect their properties and will defend them. . . . .

Nothing better proves liberty's value than some people's efforts to rape it. Yeah, fuck it, if our revolution would not bring the people's happiness, the crowned brigands would not bother to try to snatch it from us. Is it not incredible to see all Europe on fire, supposedly to avenge a single man? Hey! What was this guy but an infamous drunk![2] When he was at the height of his glory and power, he was despised, even by his fellow emperors, kings, princes, and archdukes, for whom he counted for nothing in all their political bullshit; they counted him as a zero, while he sat on the first throne of the universe . . .

The Austrian tigress was seen in all the courts as France's most contemptible prostitute. She was loudly accused of cavorting who-knows-where with valets, and all were embarrassed to determine which practitioner performed her monstrous abortions. Hunchbacked and gangrened, they came out her door three deep. Everyone talks of the debaucheries, villainies, and buggery in the royal menagerie. Never has Sodom braved such thunder as in the bordellos of the Trianon and Bagatelle.[3] An honest woman cannot say the name Antoinette without blushing. . . .

If the Austrians and the Prussians could enter Paris, they would not stab fewer of the rich than the poor, and the fat merchants of the rue St. Honoré who pass themselves off for the toughest Jacobins, despite their moderatism and cold Feuillantism, would be sacked and pillaged.[4] . . .

None of you would bat an eye, hoarders and monopolizers of Paris; you would not have any other choice except to humbly embrace sans-culottism; with that, you have nothing to worry about and your properties will be assured. The patriots only ask that you do not harm them; but a pox on you, motherfuckers, if you continue plotting against the Republic, making foodstuffs disappear by hoarding them! Imagine you are between two fires: on one side or the other you are certain to perish, if you do not play the game well with good money.

Despite you, motherfuckers, despite all the tigers unchained against France, despite the gold of England, the republican constitution will be accepted . . .

The Constitution will rally everyone together. But to strangle all our enemies at home and abroad at the same time, we cannot have nobles heading our armies, we cannot have pillaging in Paris. Good laws are needed against expensive foodstuffs and monopolization, and to give prompt aid for the poor. Public instruction is as fucking necessary as bread, right?

"What is a *Sans-Culotte*?" 1793

While common workingmen had been in the vanguard of revolutionary popular protest and politics from the beginning, by 1792 they increasingly referred to themselves as *sans-culottes*. Originally a term of disdain for manual laborers—white silk stockings could not be worn by those walking through the open-sewer streets or fields, as they would quickly become splattered with dung or mud—now *sans-culottes* were considered the embodiment of the people. Whereas many middle-class revolutionaries under the old regime had added the aristocratic "de" participles to their names (including Robespierre and Danton), now many asserted they were true *sans-culottes* themselves. As they sought to make a revolution for the people, working-class dress, culture and language became more common amongst the revolutionary leadership. This anonymous pamphlet describes the energetic salt-of-the-earth rank and file of those devoted to the *sans-culotte* revolutionary vision.

It means a being who goes always on foot, who does not have millions as you all would like to have, possessing no castles, no valets to serve him, and who lodges himself simply with his wife and children, if he has them, on the fourth or fifth floor.[5] He is useful, he knows how to labor in the field, forge, saw, file, cover a roof, make shoes, and bleed until the last drop of his blood for the health of the Republic.

As he works, you can be sure to not encounter his figure either in the cafés or gambling dens where conspiracies form, or at the theater. In the evening, he presents himself to his section,[6] without a powdered wig, cologne or fine leather boots in the hope of being remarked upon by the female citizens in the galleries, but to push for good measures with all his force. As to the rest, a *sans-culotte* always has his sword to split the ears of all the evil-doers. Sometimes, he marches with his pike, but at the first sound of the drum, you will see him leave for the Vendée, for the Army of the Alps, or the Army of the North.

FIGURE 9.1 Tragic End of Louis XVI. © *Roger Viollet / Getty Images.*

A woodblock print, designed for quick reproduction and sale, *The Tragic End of Louis XVI* shows the king's severed head being presented by the executioner to the crowd of National Guardsmen and onlookers at Revolution Square (today Place de la Concorde). Civilians raise their hands to cheer. Some may have purchased this print to show their approbation of the revolutionaries' elimination of a traitorous king. Others, as the "Tragic" title implies, may have bought it to venerate the martyred king—during an era in which the Catholic Church also increasingly fell under attack. Revolutionary violence offered no clear outcomes or interpretations, heightening the political stakes and instability as the early French Republic progressed.

9

Executing Terror

The terror advanced in part because many of the French believed a near-utopia to be close at hand. If only the revolution's selfish and irrational opponents could be suppressed, seemingly a new order of equality and opportunity could flourish. As cultural revolutions overturned virtually every aspect of French life—leveling the social hierarchy, outlawing Catholicism, and removing suspect officials—an exhilarating sense of possibility and terrifying fear simultaneously beset many.

The new regime promised formal human rights unmatched in human history. The revised 1793 Declaration of the Rights of Man and Citizen gave French people freedoms unparalleled anywhere else in the world, broadening the principles of equality and making "insurrection the most sacred of duties" if their guaranteed freedoms were ignored. The early First Republic instituted universal manhood suffrage, in some cases even paying workers substitute wages so they could join in political deliberations. In many respects, the regime sought to empower common men—helping turn "democracy" from an epithet into the foundation for modern government.

By late 1793, however, those at the center of the revolutionary process could see conspirators almost everywhere. In part, this resulted from how many real conspiracies the revolutionaries had dealt with over the short years of the revolution. Mirabeau, the great orator of 1789, had been in the pay of the royal court. Louis XVI had consistently betrayed the revolution despite his oaths and protestations to the contrary. Leading revolutionary generals, including Lafayette, had defected to the enemy Austrians. Yet, this healthy skepticism about individuals' motivations turned into political intolerance towards broad groups of dedicated revolutionaries—none believed in political parties or a "loyal opposition," while many considered it virtuous to denounce even those closest to them if they showed signs of departing from the (often arbitrarily defined) political consensus.

Notions of "virtue" drawn from Greco-Roman antiquity proved particularly influential—demanding rigid consistency and punishing those unwilling to sacrifice revolutionary comrades and close friends. Believing conspirators had fatally undermined the ancient republics, revolutionaries idolized Brutus and other dedicated republicans willing to lay down their lives to defend the public good. Jacobin Clubs undertook reviews of all their members—seeking to purge and "purify" their membership. Politicians were denounced as potential Catilines,[1] while ambitious generals appeared potential Caesars. Those whose fidelity came to appear suspect were cast out of the body politic, sometimes at the cost of their lives.

Under the supposed reign of reason, revolutionaries increasingly pared back judicial protections as the terror proceeded. "Revolutionary Tribunals" had been established by the National Convention in March 1793, limiting judicial protections for defendants in the name of protecting the revolution from their conspiracies. Proponents argued that if the Convention refused such a measure, subversion would be rife, or else the populace would take measures into their own hands via more massacres. September 1793's Law of Suspects broadened revolutionary authorities' rights of arrest. By June 1794, the "Prairial Laws" permitted group trials of suspects—while requiring only "moral proofs," rather than actual evidence, for conviction. Justice and compassion receded, as revolutionaries continued to feel compelled to extend their use of terror.

Maximillien Robespierre is the figure most closely associated with the Terror, yet is seen by some historians as a tragic figure. An Enlightened humanitarian before the revolution, Robespierre rose in influence as the "Incorruptible," unwilling to bend his core principles—even as his desire to abolish the death penalty became superseded by his drive to eliminate those he believed to be conspiring against the French Republic. Yet, stereotypes of Robespierre as a dictator are largely misplaced—he remained only one of twelve members of the central Committee of Public Safety (which itself remained formally equal with another twelve-man Committee of General Security). Robespierre's influence only existed to the extent the National Convention shared his vision—which, by the revolutionary "hot month" of Thermidor in July 1794, they would not.

The terror created unfortunate new models that revolutionaries around the world have been all too ready to employ since—trying to force others into compliance through violence and intimidation, rather than relying on reasoned persuasion. Survivors invented "terrorism" as a political term just after the French Revolution's great terror to describe what had happened. Though a cautionary tale about the excesses of political passion, many revolutionary enthusiasts still believe the terror was a necessary defense against France's many enemies.

Declaration of the Rights of Man and Citizen, 1793

No text remained inalterable during the French Revolution—even the *Declaration of the Rights of Man and Citizen*. For the Constitution of

1793, the National Convention (with a strong hand from Robespierre) re-wrote the declaration, purging its compromises with monarchy and strengthening many key provisions. Adopted in June 1793, not long after Parisian *sans-culottes* had helped radical Jacobins purge the Convention of liberal Girondin leaders, the compact extended the rights of equality, declaring "communal happiness" the goal of government. Meanwhile, the new declaration heightened political liberty, assuring all citizens' petitioning rights and access to political deliberations. To guarantee these freedoms, the right of resistance was expanded: insurrection became "the most holy of duties" when the constitution's key precepts were violated—killing a would-be dictator became enshrined in law. The radical *Declaration* never went into effect, however, as revolutionaries suspended its implementation in fall 1793, arguing such extensive liberties could not be guaranteed in wartime.

The French people, convinced that contempt and forgetting of the natural rights of man are the sole causes of the world's misfortune, have resolved to expose, in a solemn declaration, these sacred and inalienable rights, so all citizens can continually compare the acts of government with the goal of all social institutions, not letting themselves ever oppress and debase by tyranny; to the end that the people have always before their eyes the bases of liberty and happiness, while the magistrate has the rules for his duties, and the legislator, the object of his mission.

In consequence, they proclaim, in the presence of the Supreme Being, the following Declaration of the Rights of Man and Citizen.

1. The goal of society is communal happiness.

   Government is instituted for guaranteeing to man the pleasure of his natural and imprescriptible rights.
2. These rights are equality, liberty, security, property.
3. All men are equal by nature and before the law.
4. The law is the free and solemn expression of the general will; it is the same for all, when it protects and when it punishes; it can only ordain what is just and useful to society; it can only forbid what is harmful.
5. All citizens are equally admissible to public employment. Free people have no other preference in their elections than virtues and talents.
6. Liberty is the power belonging to man to do everything not bothering the rights of others. It takes nature for its principle, justice for its regulations, and the law for its safeguard. Its moral limit is this maxim: do not do unto another what you would not want done unto you.
7. The right to manifest one's thoughts and opinions in the press or in any other manner, the right to assemble peacefully, the free exercise of cults, cannot be forbidden.

The necessity of enunciating these rights supposes the presence or recent memory of despotism.

8. Security consists in the protection society accords to each of its members, to conserve their person, rights, and properties.
9. The law must protect both public and individual liberty against the oppression of those who govern.
10. No one ought to be accused, arrested, or detained, except in cases determined by the law, and according to the forms it prescribes. Every citizen called or seized by legal authority must obey instantly. He renders himself guilty by resistance.
11. Every act exercised against a man, outside the cases and without the forms the law determines, is arbitrary and tyrannical. Those against whom one tries to do so by violence, has the right to repulse them by force.
12. Those who solicit, expedite, sign, execute, or allow the execution of arbitrary acts are guilty and must be punished.
13. Every man must be presumed innocent until declared guilty. If it is judged necessary to arrest him, all excessive rigor used for his capture must be severely reprimanded by law.
14. No one ought to be judged and punished without being heard or legally summoned in accordance with a law promulgated before the crime.

    A law punishing offenses committed before they were stated would be tyranny. Retroactive measures passing into law would be a crime.
15. The law ought to only discern the penalties strictly and evidently necessary. The penalties ought to be proportionate to the crime and useful to society.
16. The right of property belongs to every citizen to enjoy and dispose of their possessions, their revenues, the fruit of their labor, and their industry at their pleasure.
17. No genre of work, culture, or commerce can be forbidden to citizens' industry.
18. Every man can offer his services and time, but cannot sell himself or be sold.[2] His person is not alienable property. The law does not recognize domesticity.[3] It can only exist by a mutual engagement of caring and recognition, between the man who works and he who employs him.
19. No one can be deprived of the smallest portion of their property without their consent, if legally proven public necessity does not demand it, and under the condition of a just and predetermined indemnity.

20. No taxes can be established except for the general utility. All citizens have the right to give their opinions on contributions, to oversee their implementation, and render accounts of them.
21. Public aid is a sacred debt. Society needs to give sustenance to unfortunate citizens, whether by finding work for them or by assuring the means of existence to those out of work.
22. Instruction is everyone's duty. Society must do all in its power to favor the progress of public reason, and place instruction within all citizens' reach.
23. The social guarantee consists in everyone working to assure to all others the enjoyment and conservation of their rights. This guarantee rests upon national sovereignty.
24. It cannot exist, if the limits of public functions are not clearly determined by law, and if all functionaries' responsibility is not assured.
25. Sovereignty resides in the people. It is one and indivisible, imprescriptible, and inalienable.
26. No portion of the people can exercise the entire people's power; but each section of the sovereign, assembled, must be able to enjoy the right of expressing their will with full liberty.
27. Every individual who usurps sovereignty must immediately be put to death by free men.
28. A people always have the right to revisit, reform, and change their constitution. One generation cannot subjugate future generations to its laws.
29. Each citizen has an equal right to participate in the law's formation and the nomination of its representatives and agents.
30. Public functions are essentially temporary. They cannot be considered as distinctions, nor as rewards, but rather as duties.
31. The crimes of the people's representatives and agents must never go unpunished. No one has the right to pretend they are more inviolable than other citizens.
32. The right to present petitions to the holders of public authority cannot in any case be forbidden, suspended, or limited.
33. Resistance to oppression is the consequence of the other rights of man.
34. There is oppression against the social body when any of its members are oppressed. There is oppression against each member when the social body is oppressed.
35. When the government violates the people's rights, insurrection is for the people, and for each portion of the people, the most sacred of rights and the most indispensable of duties.

Ça Ira, 1790 and 1793 versions

No song's evolution captures the changing tenor of the French Revolution better than *Ça ira* [*It'll Be Alright*]. The original version written in 1790 (supposedly by a soldier turned street-singer, set to an already popular melody) echoes the optimism of the Revolution's most peaceful year, asserting that despite the continued uncertainty, compromise and reconciliation could triumph. By 1793, however, a new version of the song with imaginatively violent new lyrics gained popularity, especially with *sans-culottes* seeking to intimidate their opponents. Turning away from conciliation, the new lyrics promised exemplary and terrible punishment against those who persisted in violating revolutionary principles.

1790 version:

Ah! It'll be alright, it's alright, it's alright
The people today repeat over and over,
Ah! It'll be alright, it's alright, it's alright
Despite the mutinies, it'll all work out![4]

Our confused enemies shall stay that way,
And we will sing "Hallelujah!"
Ah! It'll be alright, it's alright, it's alright
When Bolieau talked about the clergy[5]

Like a prophet, he saw this coming.
By singing my little song,
With pleasure people will say:
Ah! It'll be alright, it's alright, it's alright

Following the Gospel's maxims,
Legislators will accomplish everything.
Those who raise themselves up will be brought down,
Those who humble themselves will be raised up.
The true catechism will instruct us,
And terrible fanaticism will be snuffed out.
Every French person shall train
At being obedient to the law.
Ah! It'll be alright, it's alright, it's alright.

Pierrette and Margot sing bar songs,
Let's rejoice, good times are coming!
The French people used to keep quiet,
The aristocrat says, "I'm guilty!"
The clergy regrets the wealth it has,

By justice, the nation will get it.
Thanks to the prudent Lafayette,
Everyone will calm down.

Ah! It'll be alright, it's alright, it's alright
By the torches of the august assembly,
Ah! It'll be alright, it's alright, it's alright
The armed people will always watch out for themselves.
We will know what's true and false,
Citizens will support us for good.

Ah! It'll be alright, it's alright, it's alright
When the aristocrat protests,
The good citizen will laugh in his face,
Without it troubling his soul,
And will always be stronger for it.

The little and the great are soldiers in spirit,
In a time of war none shall betray.
All good Frenchmen shall courageously fight,
If he sees something wrong, he shall speak up.
Lafayette says, "Follow me if you will!"
Without fear of fire or flame,
The French will always win!

1793 version:

Ah! It'll be alright, it's alright, it's alright
Hang the aristocrats from the lamp-post!
Ah! It'll be alright, it's alright, it's alright
The aristocrats, we'll string them there!
If we don't hang them,
We'll break them.
If we don't break them,
We'll burn them.

Ah! It'll be alright, it's alright, it's alright
Hang the aristocrats from the lamp-post!
Ah! It'll be alright, it's alright, it's alright
The aristocrats, we'll string them there!
We'll have no more nobles or priests.

Ah! It'll be alright, it's alright, it's alright
Equality shall reign everywhere,
The Austrian slave will follow,

Ah! It'll be alright, it's alright, it's alright
And their infernal clique
Shall go straight to the devil.

Ah! It'll be alright, it's alright, it's alright
Hang the aristocrats from the lamp-post!
Ah! It'll be alright, it's alright, it's alright
The aristocrats, we'll string them there!
And when we've hung them all,
We'll ram a shovel up their ass!

Law of Suspects, September 17, 1793

As the legal machinery of the Terror consolidated, France's National Convention passed the Law of Suspects in mid-September 1793. The legislation's original intent was to provide a more precise definition of a "suspect," but the final measure allowed anyone deemed a "counterrevolutionary," and unable to produce a "civic certificate" from revolutionaries showing their public virtue, to be arrested by authorities. Despite their earlier emphasis on creating a new legal order based on the Rights of Man, under difficult conditions revolutionary legislators abolished judicial protections to accelerate arrests with impunity. With the law's application largely left at the discretion of increasingly zealous committeemen and administrators, and the penalty for treason being death, the Law of Suspects allowed violent repression to accelerate. The National Convention never did declare "terror the order of the day," as Parisian militants asked them to on September 5. Yet, alongside the suspension of the Constitution of 1793 on October 10, the Law of Suspects is often seen as the integral event in creating the atmosphere many historians refer to as the "Reign of Terror."

The National Convention, after having heard the Legislation Committee's report on how to execute its law of August 12 last, decrees the following:[6]

I. Immediately after this decree's publication, all suspect men still at liberty in the Republic's territory will be placed under arrest.

II. Suspect men are considered to be: 1. Those who, whether by their conduct, relationships, speech, or writings, have become partisans of tyranny or federalism, and enemies of liberty; 2. Those who cannot justify, in the manner prescribed by the law of 21 March last, their means of existence or the discharge of their civic duties; 3. Those who have been denied civic certificates; 4. The public functionaries suspended or deprived of their functions by the

National Convention or its commissars, and not reintegrated, notably those who have been or ought to be deprived by virtue of the law of 14 August last; 5. Those who were nobles, including the husbands, wives, fathers, mothers, sons or daughters, brothers or sisters, and agents of emigrants, who have not constantly shown their attachment to the revolution; 6. Those who emigrated between July 1, 1789 and the publication of the law of April 8, 1792, whether they returned to France in the delay fixed by this law, or previously.

III. The surveillance committees established after the law of March 21 last, or those they substituted for, whether it be by the decrees the representatives of the people sent to the armies and departments, or by virtue of the National Convention's particular decrees, are charged to prepare, each in his district, the list of suspect men, to discern against them the arrest charges, and fix the seals on their papers. The commanders of the public force to whom these charges will be sent, will be required to execute them immediately, on pain of removal.

IV. The committee cannot order any individual's arrest without at least seven members being present, via the absolute majority of voices.

V. The individuals arrested as suspects will then be taken to the area jail: if there is no facility, they will be under guarded house arrest.

VI. In the next eight days, they will be transferred into national houses that the administration of each department will have, soon after receiving the present decree, to design and prepare to this effect.

VII. The detained will be able to transfer into these houses the absolutely necessary furniture; they will remain guarded until the peace.

VIII. The cost of the guard will be charged to the detained, or split between them equally; this guard will be preferentially entrusted to men with children and the parents of citizens who are marching or will march to the frontiers. The salary is fixed for each guardsman, at the equivalent of a day and a half of work.

IX. The surveillance committees will send to the National Convention's Committee of General Security without delay the status of the persons arrested, with the reasons for their arrest and the papers seized from them.

X. The civil and criminal tribunals will be able to, if there is space, hold under arrest as suspect men, and send to the jailhouses above described, the defendants of charges even of the sort where it will be declared there is no room for accusation, or who will be acquitted of accusations carried against them.

Camille Desmoulins, selections from *The Old Cordelier*, Frimaire—Nivôse Year II (December 1793–January 1794)

Camille Desmoulins by late 1793 possessed one of the most impressive revolutionary résumés: he played a central role in inciting the Bastille insurrection in July 1789, and thereafter wrote and published several of the revolution's most influential newspapers, including *Revolutions of France and Brabant*. He participated in the August 10, 1792 uprising that overthrew the monarchy and gained election to the National Convention as a representative for Paris (despite being from Picardy). Moreover, he became an influential Jacobin Club member, closely allying with his former schoolmate Maximillien Robespierre. Yet, by December 1793, Desmoulins turned against the Committee of Public Safety leadership to argue in a new newspaper, the *Old Cordelier* (its name conjuring the early days of the suppressed faction headed by Hébert) that the revolution was violating its foundational principles of liberty. Desmoulins did not sway the regime into changing course, but nevertheless appeared too popular to be detained immediately. Only months later would Desmoulins be arrested, tried as an "indulgent" alongside his ally Georges-Jacques Danton, and after a quick conviction guillotined.

No. 1, 15 Frimaire Year II

I know that, in handling great affairs, one typically departs from the austere rules of morality. This is sad, but inevitable. The needs of state and the perversity of the human heart render such conduct necessary, and make such necessities the first maxim of politics. If a man in office advised by saying all he thought, all he knew, he would expose his country to certain ruin. What good citizens do not fear the movements and intemperance of my pen? I have a hand filled with truths, and will guard myself against fully telling them, but will let enough escape to save France and the one, indivisible Republic.

My colleagues have all been so occupied and swept along by the torrent of affairs, some in committees, others on missions, that they have lacked time for reading, I almost say for thinking. I, who have not had any mission, any committee on which I have had anything to do; who, amidst this excess of work from my Montagnard colleagues, to consolidate the Republic, have composed, almost by myself (if they allow me the expression), their committee of speakers and thinkers. I promised them, a year ago, to present this committee's report, to offer them the lessons of history, the only master, whatever one says about it, on the art of governing, and give them the advice of Tacitus and Machiavelli, the greatest politicians who ever lived.[7] . . . A year ago, with good reason, we mocked the pretended liberty of the English, who lacked an unlimited liberty of the press; and now what man of good faith can thus avoid comparing France and England today! See with what audacity the *Morning Chronicle* attacks Pitt and the war strategy?[8] What journalist, in France, dares stand up against our committees' blunders, and those of the generals, the Jacobins, the ministers, and the Commune, as the opposition stands up to the British ministry? And myself, a Frenchmen, Camille Desmoulins, I shall not be as free as an English journalist! This thought makes me indignant. They say we are in revolution, and that it is necessary to suspend press liberty during the revolution. Is England, is all of Europe not also in a state of revolution? Are the principles of press liberty less sacred in Paris than in London, where Pitt must have such a great fear of light?

No. IV, 30 Frimaire Year II

. . . everyone justifies themselves by this phrase: "We all know that the present state is not one of liberty; but be patient, you will be free one day."

Those people apparently think liberty, like childhood, needs to pass through tears and tantrums to arrive at maturity. It is contrary to liberty's nature that, to experience it, one must only desire it. A people are free from the moment they want to be (we remember this is Lafayette's phrasing); they regained the fullness of all their rights from July 14 onwards.[9] Liberty knows neither childhood nor decrepitude. She has only one age, that of force and vigor. Those wanting to kill her for the republic would be as stupid as the Vendée fanatics, who kill for the fruits of a paradise they will never know.

No. 5, 15 Nivôse Year II

The ship of the republic sails, as I've said, between two reefs, moderatism and exaggeration. I started my newspaper by a profession of political faith that needed to disarm calumny: I said, with Danton, that "outraging the revolution had less peril and was worth more than saying too little," that, on the vessel's route, it was better to approach the rocks of exaggeration than the sands of moderation. . . .

I cannot hold my tongue, whatever danger there may be of having to fight with a Revolutionary Tribunal jury, denunciation by denunciation. . . .

I conspired for your liberty . . . on 12 July [1789], with a pistol in my hand, I called the nation to arms and to liberty . . . .

I have not ceased to conspire thereafter, with Danton and Robespierre, against tyrants. I conspired in *Free France*, in the articles of the *Parisian Lantern*, in *Revolutions of France and of Brabant*, in the *Tribune of the*

Patriots. My eight volumes attest to my conspiracies against aristocrats of all kinds, royalists, Feuillants, Brissotins, Federalists. . . .

The society [of Jacobins] is now ready to judge between my denunciators and myself. My friends know I remain the same as in 1789; that I have not had a thought since then that was not for the affirmation of liberty, for prosperity, for the French people's happiness, for the maintenance of the one and indivisible republic. Hey! What other interest could I have displayed in the newspaper I write, except zeal for the public good? Why would I have brought against myself such all-powerful hatred, and called onto my head implacable resentments? . . . I will maintain republican audaciousness until my death against all despots; and I do not ignore Machiavelli's maxim, that "there is no worse tyranny than that of petty tyrants."

They will despair at trying to intimidate me by terrors and rumors of my arrest that they spread for me to hear! . . .

Despite the factious, let the Mountain remain one and indivisible, like the republic! Do not debase, in the third session, national representation. Liberty of opinion or death! Let us occupy ourselves, my colleagues, not in defending our life like sick men, but in defending liberty and principles, like republicans! . . .

No. 6, 10 Nivôse Year II

I believe a representative is no more infallible than inviolable. If public safety requires, in a revolutionary moment, restraining press liberty for citizens, I believe a legislator should never be denied the right of giving his opinion. I believe he must be permitted to error; it is in consideration of his errors that the French people have such a great number of representatives, so some can correct the others. I believe that, without this indefinite liberty of opinion, National Assemblies will not endure . . .

Maximillien Robespierre, selections from "Virtue and Terror" speech, 18 Pluviôse Year II (February 6, 1794)

Both the idealism and shortcomings of Maximillien Robespierre's thinking may be best encapsulated in his famed "Virtue and Terror" speech. Though never holding actual dictatorial powers, the austere politician known as "The Incorruptible" came to exercise substantial influence by early 1794 over his fellow Committee of Public Safety members and Convention deputies. Robespierre's speech paints a rosy picture of what a completed revolution might look like—featuring the greatest extent of democracy ever seen in a large republic. However, his vision of democracy required a virtuous public, with citizens faithfully working together towards a common good. Since the prevalence of counterrevolutionaries in France seemed to prevent this from happening, Robespierre reasoned that terror was necessary to purge the republic of counterrevolutionaries and consolidate a virtuous citizenry. If terror had previously been associated with despotic government, Robespierre sought to use terror to enable freedom. The beauty of his virtuous ideals made violence appear an acceptable price for accomplishing them.

Report on the Principles of Moral Politics that Ought to Guide the National Convention in the Republic's internal Administration, Made in the Name of the Committee of Public Safety, 18 Pluviôse, Year II.

Citizen Representatives of the People,

We declared, some time ago, the principles of our foreign policy: today we will develop the principles of our interior policy.

After hazardously proceeding for a long time, carried by the movement of contradictory factions, the French people's representatives have finally established their character and government. A sudden change in the nation's fortune announces to Europe the regeneration occurring in national representation. But up to the moment I speak, it must be said that we have been mostly guided, in such stormy circumstances, by the love of good and what we felt the country needed rather than by an exact theory or precise rules of conduct, which we have not had the leisure to trace.

It is time to clearly mark the goal, and how soon we will get there: it is time for us to take account of the obstacles keeping us from it, and the means we must take to get there . . .

What is the goal we seek? The peaceable pleasure of liberty and equality: the reign of eternal justice, with which the laws have been engraved, not on marble and rocks, but in the hearts of all men, even in the slave who forgets them and the tyrant who denies them.

We want an order in which all base and cruel passions are enchained, and all charitable and generous passions are aroused by the laws, where ambition becomes the desire to merit glory and serve the fatherland, where distinctions are only born from equality itself, where the citizen must submit to the magistrate, the magistrate to the people, and the people to justice, where the fatherland assures each individual's well-being, and each person takes pride in the fatherland's prosperity and glory, where all spirits grow with the continual communication of republican sentiments, and all want to merit the esteem of a great people. . . .

We want, in a word, to fulfill nature's wishes, accomplish humanity's destiny, take hold of philosophy's promises, and absolve providence of crime and tyranny's long reign. France, once prominent amongst the enslaved countries, now eclipses the glory of all the free people that ever existed, becoming the model of nations, the fright of oppressors, the consolation of the oppressed . . . in sealing our work with our blood, we can see at least the aurora of universal happiness . . . .

What nature of government can realize these marvels? Only democratic or republican government: these two words are synonyms, despite the abuses of vulgar language . . . Democracy is not a state where the people, continually assembled, regulate by themselves all public affairs, and even less that where a hundred thousand factions of the people, by isolated, precipitous, and contradictory measures, decide the entire society's fate: such a government has never existed, and cannot exist, except for delivering the people to despotism.

Democracy is a state where the sovereign people, guided by laws that are their labor, do for themselves all that they can do well, and give to delegates all they cannot.

It is thus in the principles of democratic government that you must search for the rules of your political conduct. But, to found and consolidate democracy amongst us, to arrive at the peaceful reign of constitutional laws, liberty's war against tyranny must end, and we must happily traverse the revolution's storms: such is the goal of the revolutionary system you have regularized. You must thus continue regulating your conduct according to the tempestuous circumstances in which the republic finds itself, and your administrative plans must reflect the revolutionary government's spirit, combined with the generous principles of democracy.

Now, what is the fundamental principle of a democratic or popular government, which is to say the essential spirit that supports it and makes it move? It is virtue . . . this virtue is nothing except love of the fatherland and its laws. . . .

The French are the world's first people to have established real democracy, in calling all men to equality, and the full rights of citizens; this, in my opinion, is the real reason why all the tyrants leaguing against the Republic will be defeated. . . .

If the spirit of popular government in peace is virtue, the spirit of popular government in revolution is simultaneously virtue and terror: virtue, without which terror is horrible, and terror, without which virtue is powerless. Terror is nothing other than prompt, severe, inflexible justice. It is thus an emanation of virtue. It is less a singular principle than a consequence of the general principle of democracy applied to the fatherland's most pressing needs. They say terror is the spirit of despotic government. Does ours thus resemble despotism? Yes, as the sword that shines in the hands of the heroes of liberty resembles that arming tyranny's drones. . . . Revolutionary government is the despotism of liberty against tyranny. . . .

Social protections are only due to peaceful citizens: there are no citizens in the Republic except republicans. The royalists, the conspirators are for her only foreigners and typically enemies. In this terrible war supporting liberty against tyranny, could we be divided? Are our domestic enemies not the allies of those abroad? The assassins who break apart the fatherland in its interior, the intriguers buying the consciences of the people's representatives, the traitors selling themselves, the mercenary libelers bribed to dishonor the people's cause, to kill political virtue, to fan the flame of civil discords, and to prepare the political counterrevolution by moral counterrevolution; are all these men less guilty or less dangerous than the tyrants they serve? All those interposing their parricidal softness between these scoundrels and the avenging sword of national justice resemble those throwing themselves between the satellites of tyrants and our soldiers' bayonets. . . .

What is the remedy for all these evils? We know none except the development of the republic's general spirit, virtue. Democracy perishes by two excesses: the aristocracy of those who govern, or the people's contempt for the authorities they have established themselves. . . .

The twin task of moderates and false revolutionaries is to perpetually tear us between these two rocks.

But the people's representatives can avoid both of these as long as the government is just and wise. With such character, it is sure to have the people's confidence.

It is quite true that the goal of all our enemies is to dissolve the Convention; it is true that the tyrant of Great Britain and his allies promise to their Parliament and subjects to take away your energy and the public confidence you have earned. . . .

But let us reassure ourselves: here is the sanctuary of truth: here the founders of the Republic reside, the avengers of humanity and destroyers of tyrants.

Here, to destroy an abuse, it is sufficient to identify it.

Proceedings of the Revolutionary Tribunal, 14 Germinal Year II (April 3, 1794)

The sessions of the Revolutionary Tribunal, in which many legal protections were lessened to allow for speedy trials, were partially reported in the government newspaper, the *Moniteur universel*. In this most famous of revolutionary trials, "Indulgents" who dared speak out against the escalating use of Terror—Camille Desmoulins and Georges Danton, who had respectively led some of the revolution's most audacious acts—were prosecuted alongside twelve other alleged conspirators, for (improbably) having secretly worked to help reestablish monarchy in France. Although the accused were allowed to make a defense, the *Moniteur* only printed the April 3 arraignment. While allowing the accused to posture as martyrs, with Desmoulins comparing himself to Jesus, the Revolutionary Tribunals did not allow the public access to its evidence—or often, lack thereof. Support for the radical government of the Year II began to hollow as their persecutions of reputed figures grew.

The accused legislators appeared before the tribunal, in the Hall of Liberty Section, during the session of the thirteenth, with the five individuals charged with complicity in the same conspiracies. Here are the names, ages and occupations of the fourteen accused, who, after the decree and charge of the Public Accuser, are accused of complicity with Orléans, Dumouriez and other enemies of the public to have engaged in conspiracy intending to reestablish monarchy, destroy national representation, republican government, etc.[10]

P.-F. Fabre d'Eglantine, aged thirty-nine years, native of Carcassonne, man of letters, deputy to the Convention, rue l'Evéque.

J. Delaunay, aged thirty-six years, native of Angers, former lawyer, deputy to the Convention, boulevard Montmartre.

F. Chabot, aged thirty-three years, native of Saint-Geniez, Aveyron Department, former Capucin monk, deputy to the Convention, rue d'Anjou, faubourg St. Honoré.

B. Camille Desmoulins, aged thirty-three years, native of Guise, Asine Department, man of letters, deputy to the Convention, rue du Théâtre-Français.

J.-F. Lacroix, aged forty years, native of Pont-Audemer, Eure Department, former lawyer, deputy to the Convention, rue Lazare.

P. Philippeaux, aged thirty-two years, native of Ferrière, Oise Department, former lawyer, deputy to the Convention, rue de l'Echelle.

Claude Basire, aged twenty-nine years, native of Dijon, archivist of the former Burgundian Estates, deputy to the Convention, rue Pierre-Montmartre.

M.J. Hérault de Séchelles, aged thirty-four years, native of Paris, general lawyer to the former Parliament of Paris, member of the Appeals Court, deputy to the Convention, rue Basse-du-Rempart.

G.-J. Danton, aged thirty-four years, native of Arcis-sur-Aube, former lawyer, deputy to the Convention, rue de Marat.

M.-R. Sahuguet d'Espagnac, aged forty-one years, native of Pry, Corrèze Department, former clergyman, rue de l'Université.

Sigishmond-Junius Frey, aged thirty-six years, born and become tobacco tax collector in Brübo, in Moravia, supplier to the army, who lives off his rents, rue d'Anjou, faubourg Honoré.

A.-M. Gusman, aged forty-one years, native of Grenada in Spain, naturalized French in 1781, who lives off his rents; his parents enjoy all qualifications in Spain.

E. Frey, aged twenty-seven years, native of Brünn, in Moravia, brother of Junius Frey, who lives off his revenues, rue d'Anjou.

C.-F. Diedericksen, aged forty-one years, native of Luchembourg, in Holstein, lawyer in the court of Denmark, in France since 1792, staying at the Carrousel.

Fabre d'Egalantine occupied the distinguished place, the chair. He appeared to be suffering.

Camille Desmoulins, having seen Renaudin amongst the jurors, asked for his recusal; but the tribunal decided this request was not conforming to law, because it needed to be made twenty-four hours beforehand in writing, and thus could not be admitted.[11]

The same Camille, asked about his age, responded: “I am the same age as the *sans-culotte* Jesus, thirty-three years old.”

Danton, asked about his name and residence, responded: “My residence will soon be in nothingness, as to my name, you will find it in the pantheon of history.”

Hérault de Séchelles, asked about his name and profession before the revolution, responded: “I am Marie-Jean, names of little importance, even among the saints. I sit in this room, where I was detested by the legislators.” Hérault asked Simon, a presently-detained legislator, be his official defender.

In the midst of the act of accusation, Lacroix, Camille Desmoulins, and others testified their shock at finding themselves side by side with rogues. They asked for access to Saint-Just’s report. The tribunal acceded to this demand.

It appears that the counter-poison worked effectively on Chabot; the voice of this accused man is not altered at all.[12]

Decree Establishing the Worship of the Supreme Being, 18 Floréal Year II (May 7, 1794)

The French Revolution’s euphoric spirit led its most passionate adherents to believe a new nature-based faith could replace religion itself. As the Revolution’s split with the Catholic Church became total, and Dechristianization advanced, legislators sought to create positive expressions to substitute for the old creed. On May 7, 1794, the National Convention formally established a Cult of the Supreme Being, legislating ways to worship reason and nature. More deist than atheist in nature, accepting a form of god and the soul’s immortality, revolutionaries attempted to create a purified faith, purged of the superstition and irrationality they believed to mar Catholicism and other established creeds. The Cult of the Supreme Being failed to establish spiritual bonds with most French people, however, and would increasingly be disregarded. Making only one day in ten a religious holiday under the new Revolutionary Calendar, instead of one day in seven, did not help win popular support. Many French people resented the new imposed faith, with some continuing to practice Catholicism underground, while many others no longer bothered with religious observance.

I. The French people recognize the existence of the Supreme Being and the immortality of the soul.

II. They recognize that the cult worthy of the Supreme Being is the practice of man’s duties.

III. They set among the most important of these duties the detestation of bad faith and tyranny, by punishing tyrants and traitors, by caring for the unfortunate, respecting the weak, defending the oppressed, doing unto others all the good one can, and not being unjust towards anyone.

IV. Festivals will be organized to recall man to thoughts of the divine and the dignity of his being.

V. They will take their names from our Revolution's most glorious events, from the virtues most dear and useful to man, and from nature's greatest gifts.

VI. The French Republic will celebrate every year the festivals of July 14, 1789, August 10, 1792, January 21, 1793 and May 31, 1793.

VII. We will celebrate on Decadis the following festivals:[13]

To the Supreme Being and Nature
To the Human Race
To the French People
To Humanity's Benefactors
To Liberty's Martyrs
To Liberty and Equality
To the Republic
To the Liberty of the Earth
To the Love of the Fatherland
To the Hatred of Tyrants and Traitors
To Truth
To Justice
To Modesty
To Glory and Immortality
To Friendship
To Frugality
To Courage
To Good Faith
To Heroism
To Disinterestedness
To Stoicism
To Love
To Conjugal Love
To Paternal Love
To Maternal Tenderness
To Filial Piety
To Childhood

To Youth
To Virile Age
To Old Age
To Misfortune
To Agriculture
To Industry
To Our Forefathers
To Posterity
To Happiness

VIII. The Committees of Public Safety and Public Instruction are charged to present a plan for organizing these festivals.

IX. The National Convention calls all talents worthy of serving humanity's cause to the honor of working towards its establishment with hymns and civic chants, and by all methods that can contribute to their embellishment and utility.

X. The Committee of Public Safety will distinguish those works appearing the most proper to fulfill this object and compensate their authors.

XI. Freedom of religion is maintained, conforming to the decree of 18 Frimaire.

XII. Every gathering that is aristocratic and contrary to public order will be suppressed.

XIII. In case of trouble, when one cult of whatever nature is the perpetrator or object, those who have excited it by fanatical predictions or counterrevolutionary insinuations, or provoke it by unjust and gratuitous violence, will be equally punished according to the law's rigors.

XIV. A specific report will be made on the details of the present decree.

XV. There will be celebrated, next 2 Prairial, a Festival to the Supreme Being. David is charged with presenting a plan for it to the National Convention.

Legislators' Denunciations of Robespierre, 9 Thermidor Year II (July 27, 1794)

The radical Jacobin phase of the French Revolution came to a crashing end on 9 Thermidor Year II. The day before, Robespierre, returning from a prolonged absence likely caused by mental illness, claimed to have discovered new conspirators within the Convention itself. When his close collaborator Saint-Just rose the next day to deliver a likely follow-up speech, he was shouted down by a legislature refusing to accept further purges. Robespierre's colleagues turned on him, declaring the "Incorruptible" had perverted the revolution instead of purifying it. While many of the denunciators were deeply implicated in the Reign of Terror themselves—Jean-Baptiste Tallien was a member of the Committee of General Security and had committed atrocities in the provinces as a Representative on Mission, while Jacques Billaud-Varenne served on the Committee of Public Safety—they now proclaimed that the revolution had gone too far. Robespierrists soon fled the Convention's hall and unsuccessfully called for the Sections of Paris to revolt. The Convention retained the army's loyalty, which that evening captured the Robespierrists at Paris' City Hall. Robespierre, his brother, Saint-Just, and other allies were executed the following day, bringing the revolution's most radical phase to an end.

Saint-Just climbed to the rostrum: he started a speech in the same vein as the one Robespierre read the day before. He promised he belonged to no party, no faction . . .

He was interrupted by [Jean-Baptiste] Tallien, who asked to speak on a point of order.

Tallien: "The orator began by saying he is not the member of any faction. I say the same thing. I only belong to myself, to liberty. For this, I will make truth heard. No good citizen can hold back his tears on the sad path the public good has taken. Everywhere, we see only division. Yesterday, a member of the government isolated himself from it, pronouncing a speech in his private name; today another does the same thing. They come to attack and aggravate the fatherland's troubles, to lead it into the abyss. I demand the curtain be drawn back entirely. (Three rounds of lively applause followed).

[Jacques] Billaud-Varenne: "Yesterday, the Jacobin Society filled with apostate men, none of whom had a membership card. Yesterday, they made plans to slit the National Convention's throats. (This raised tremors of horror). Yesterday, I saw men vomiting forth the most atrocious infamies against those who never deviated from the revolution.

"I see on the Mountain one of these men who menaced the people's representatives. Here he is." (From all sides people cried, 'Arrest him!' 'Arrest him!'—The individual was seized and carried from the room amidst the liveliest applause).

"The moment to tell the truth has arrived . . . .I am shocked to see Saint-Just at the tribunal after what happened. He assured to the two committees to submit his speech to them before reading it at the Convention, and even to discard it if they found it dangerous. . . ."

Billaud-Varenne: "I myself demand that all these men explain themselves before this assembly. One gains strength when justice, probity, and the people's rights are concerned. You shake with horror when you realize the situation, when you know armed force is confided in parricidal hands . . . ."

"When Robespierre told you he distanced himself from the committee because he was oppressed there, he took care not to tell you everything. He did not tell you it was because, having swayed the committee for six months, he encountered resistance there at the moment when, alone, he wanted the decree of 22 Prairial approved.[14] This decree, in the impure hands he chose, became disastrous for patriots (Murmurs of indignation continued). Realize, citizens, that yesterday the Revolutionary Tribunal's president proposed to the Jacobins to chase from the Convention all impure men, that is to say all those who they wanted to sacrifice; but the people are there and patriots are willing to die to save liberty. ("Yes, yes!" cried all the members—Lively applause).

"I repeat, we will all die with honor, I do not believe there is now a single representative here who would survive under a tyrant. ("No, no!" cried everyone from all sides; "death to tyrants!" Applause continued). The men who ceaselessly spoke of justice and virtue in the Convention or at the Jacobins are those who did the contrary when they could, and here's proof. A Committee of Public Safety secretary stole 114,000 pounds. I called for his arrest. Robespierre, who ceaselessly spoke of justice and virtue, was the only person who prevented it. (New wave of indignation).

"There are, citizens, a thousand other acts I could cite—but he accuses us! What? Isolated men, unknown to all, who pass their nights and days at the Committee of Public Safety, who organize victories, these men could be the conspirators! Those who only abandoned Hébert when it was no longer possible to support him are virtuous men! The first time I denounced Danton to the committee, Robespierre rose like a furious man, saying he saw my intentions, that I wanted to sacrifice the best patriots. All this makes me see the abyss opening under our feet. We must not hesitate to bury our cadavers or to triumph over traitors.

"They want to mutilate and destroy the Convention. This intention was so real that they organized espionage against the people's representatives they want to decapitate. It is terrible to speak of justice and virtue when they defy them and we can only exhale when they are stopped or contradicted."

(Robespierre rose to the tribune)

A Great Number of Voices: "Down, down with the traitor!"

Tallien: "I demand the veil be removed. I now see with pleasure that it is, with the conspirators unmasked. They will soon be annihilated and liberty will triumph (lively applause). All announces that the enemy of national representation will fall under the blows. We give to our newborn republic proof of our republican loyalty. I imposed silence on myself until now because I knew, that a man who approached becoming France's tyrant had a proscription list. I do not want to make recriminations, but I saw the Jacobins' session yesterday; I trembled for the fatherland. I saw the new Cromwell's army forming and I armed myself with a dagger to stab his breast if the National Convention did not have the courage to decree his arrest (Lively applause).[15] . . . .

"I call to your attention the speech pronounced yesterday at the Convention and repeated at the Jacobins. Therein I encounter the tyrant, there I find conspiracy, it's in this speech that, with truth, justice and the Convention, I want to find arms to strike down this man whose virtue and patriotism were so vaunted, but who during the memorable epoch of August 10 [1792], did not reappear for three days after the revolution. This man who, before joining the Committee of Public Safety, was the defender of the oppressed; who, rather than keeping his post, abandoned it for four *décades*[16] [forty days] . . ."

(Robespierre interrupted with his cries. Violent murmurs rose against him).

Louchet: "I request an arrest decree against Robespierre."

Lozeau: "Robespierre has constantly been a dominator; I request an accusatory decree based on this alone."

Robespierre the younger: "I am as guilty as my brother; I share his virtues. I request an accusatory decree against myself."

(Robespierre addressed the President and members of the Assembly on the toughest terms).

Charles Duval: "President, since when can one man be master of the Convention?"

Lozeau: "A voice-vote on arresting the two brothers!"

Billaud-Varenne: "I have positive evidence Robespierre cannot deny. I now cite the request he made to the committee to disarm citizens."

Robespierre: "I say they were criminals!" (Murmurs).

Billaud-Varenne: "I said they reproached the committee for wanting to disarm the citizenry. Well, it was only he who took this stance. . . ."

Several Members: "A voice-vote on arrest!"

This was decreed unanimously.

All members rose and filled the room with the cries of "Long live liberty! Long live the republic!"

FIGURE 10.1 *George Cruikshank,* The Radical's Arms. © *Wikimedia Commons (public domain).*

As accounts of the French Revolution diffused across the Atlantic basin, people reacted very differently. Though British proponents of Parliamentary Reform and abolishing the slave trade reacted to the revolution's early advancements with glee, others saw the specter of social breakdown and mass violence as the French sought to rapidly alter their government. From 1792 onwards, conservative social movements sought to shut down British clubs and publications sympathetic to the revolution, while sponsoring propaganda to discredit the revolutionaries. Such depictions became a British tradition: George Cruikshank, here interpreting French events as an orgy of blood and fire, drew two disfigured revolutionaries dancing with drinks and a reddened knife in their hands, beneath a used guillotine topped with bloody axes. The world (specifically, both sides of the Atlantic basin) is in flames behind them. Besides the newspapers at their feet, whose radical rhetoric likely spurred them on, lie discarded symbols—the paraphernalia of church and king most prominently. This image was likely designed to elicit disgust from viewers, though future radicals and revolutionaries found much to appreciate in such French audacity.

10

International Reverberations

"The Revolution" (as eighteenth-century contemporaries most often called it) not only overthrew regimes in France, but shook governments around much of the Atlantic basin. French Revolutionaries believed they were developing universal principles that could be applied to all peoples: local traditions and superstitions appeared as breakable elsewhere as in France.

The French Revolution itself would not have taken the form it did without the radical changes occurring around the Atlantic basin over the previous quarter-century. The American Revolution made a large-scale republic appear newly possible in the modern world, founding a regime based upon stated rights and popular input. British and Irish Parliamentary Reform movements brought attention to the virtues and potential of mixed government. Dutch and Belgian rebels fought against absolutist domination. Abolishing the slave trade, and perhaps in time Atlantic slavery itself, went from appearing impossible to perhaps imminent. People developed a growing cognizance and acceptance of change—increasingly questioning their societies and exploitative practices.

The revolution in France gave reformers and insurgents elsewhere new hope. Rather than carefully honing arguments from precedent and tradition, French Revolutionaries dared to institute new principles. This greatly angered reactionaries like British Member of Parliament Edmund Burke, who abandoned his earlier liberalism to denounce French changes, but empowered those agreeing with famed pamphleteer Thomas Paine, who by 1791 called for the rot in the British system to be excised, in favor of new experiments in democracy. This argument would not be conclusively resolved in either side's favor: indeed, they helped create the basic debate between liberalism and conservatism that remains the bedrock of modern politics.

Particularly as revolutionaries turned to wars of liberation across the 1790s, they promoted an aggressive universalism. Seeing the advancements of their own regime, many (particularly those affiliated with the Jacobin Clubs) came to believe they would be greeted as liberators as they battled the "slave armies" of kings they regarded as despots. Granting citizenship to exemplary foreign liberals and even electing figures like Paine and German Anacharsis Cloots to sit in the National Convention, French revolutionaries strove towards an ideal of universal peace and enlightened progress—even as their new regime created near-endless war and spread modern nationalism.

The French Revolution also upended popular politics in the early United States. Indeed, the American War of Independence was only regularly called the "American Revolution" after the French Revolution changed people's ideas about the potential extent of political change. Although the United States Constitution made no provision for political parties, debates between urban merchant interests and rural agricultural concerns led to the development of antagonistic factions. With the support of newly arrived French ambassador Edmond-Charles Genêt, a series of Jacobin-inspired Democratic-Republican Clubs arose across the new nation. By 1795, merchant-favoring Federalists (often wearing black cockades as European counterrevolutionaries did) squared off in elections against a nationally organized Democratic-Republican Party. Federalists were often derided as "aristocrats," while supporters of Jefferson and Madison's party continued being called "Jacobins" across the 1790s. Jefferson's victory over the Federalist Adams has been described as the Revolution of 1800.

From 1789 until the present day, the French Revolution has continued to inspire movements for revolution and reform around the globe. Whereas American Independence developed many of its justifications from British tradition and precedence, French Revolutionaries believed it was possible to create a new reality—even in ways national traditions had not anticipated. If French Revolutionaries could jump from absolutist despotism to freedom, what could other peoples not accomplish? Future French dissidents, British reformers, German nationalists, Soviet revolutionaries, Chinese radicals, Latin American freedom fighters, South African dissidents, and a host of others would steep themselves in French Revolutionary history and tradition, considering the events of those years a tantalizing (if incomplete) blueprint for change.

Camille Desmoulins, *Revolutions of France and Brabant* Newspaper, October 1789

In the first issue of his new newspaper, *Revolutions of France and Brabant*, journalist Camille Desmoulins set out to track not just political events in France, but also over France's northeastern border in southern Belgium, where the Brabantine Revolution in October 1789 overthrew the Austrian Habsburg rule of enlightened despot Joseph II in favor of a federation known as the United States of Belgium. Given the quick collapse of French absolutist rule, many revolutionaries believed other unpopular and unrepresentative governments in continental Europe could fall quickly as well. Nevertheless, the French National Assembly, exercising caution in foreign affairs while rebuilding French institutions, did not recognize the United Belgian States. The Austrians invaded the rebel provinces in autumn 1790 and quickly reconquered the territory. As when the Dutch Revolt of 1787 was crushed by invading Prussians, France remained in too dire of political straits to engage in foreign adventurism. The Old Regime triumphed over fresh revolutionary spirit. While revolts for liberty were widespread across the Atlantic basin during the era, the French Revolutionary model did not prove to be easily exportable elsewhere.

High amongst accounts of the revolution in Brabant is the *Manifesto of the Brabançon People*, of 14 October 1789, signed H.C.N. Vandernoot, plenipotentiary agent of the Brabançon people.

After having explained in the preamble that nations whose sovereign violated their sworn pact rightfully return to primitive independence, the manifesto reminds us that Joseph II had violated Articles 3 and 5 of his agreement, the so-called "Joyous Entry," by demolishing the fortifications of cities and castles, without the Estates General's approval, as well as Article 28, in suppressing monasteries "arbitrarily and despite the nation's repeated complaints," and disposing with ecclesiastical properties: he reproaches the Emperor with having attacked the Belgian Constitution, in suppressing the committee sent by the Estates, in establishing royal governors, despite the provinces' invincible resistance. . . . Finally, by the ordinance of June 17, the emperor eliminated the Council of Brabant; he revoked and annulled all the province's privileges. He did not see that he could not free himself without simultaneously freeing his people, because it is the same bond that unites them.[1]

For all these reasons, "seeing the immutable perseverance of the emperor to tyrannize the Belgian people, and reduce them to slavery in contempt of the inaugural pact, we have declared Joseph II, Duke of Brabant, stripped of his sovereignty, &c. &c. &c."

The Brabançon people can avoid developing all these excellent rationales: it suffices for them to say, "I suffered under Joseph II's domination, because such was my pleasure." These few words are sufficient justification to him. Yet, the emperor has no good rebuttal to this question: what right do you have to be my sovereign, when I do not want you to be? Conqueror and tyrant are synonymous words. . . .

Have no doubt, the French will not remain spectators in bloody designs made against the noble emulation of their example that has inspired you. Already our soldiers go *en masse* to join your republican legions. If love of my country keeps me amongst my fellow citizens, and stops me from going far from the cradle of liberty born with difficulty in France, where so many serpents try to strangle it, at least I will inspire my fellow citizens by reciting your exploits. The eyes of France are turned towards you. . . .

It is known that still four thousand imperial soldiers commanded by the Major-General Schroeder, furious about their failure at Ternout, in their retreat have satisfied their rage in the suburbs on the women and children. The Brabançons will not put down their arms, they will be free. These are the English cruelties in Germantown; this is the barbarousness of General Grey, stabbing four hundred sleeping Americans in a village, which freed America.[2] There are atrocities one should not pardon, after which one cannot return the sword to the sheath. . . .

They say Portugal is awaking from its slumber over the rights of man.

There are also movements in Madrid. People demand the Cortès.[3] Insurrection has already broken out in Catalonia. I have already predicted it in free France. Philosophy and the spirit of liberty cannot be prevented from crossing the Alps and seas, and I do not despair of seeing the cockade on the Holy Father, the Great Turk, the King of Prussia, the Czarina, and even Joseph II.[4] . . .

What's more, letters assure that patriots appear in the mountains of Savoy, that they speak of a constitution in a Turin café, and that several of our Savoyards, who have returned to their lands since the insurrection of the servants against them, have there reported, in their pages, the flame of philosophy.[5]

Edmund Burke, selections from *Reflections on the Revolution in France*. 1790

No nation appeared better prepared to consider French Revolutionary principles than Great Britain, which had long debated expanding the confines of liberty. Edmund Burke, a British Member of Parliament since 1765, had been a steadfast defender of liberal causes both at home and abroad, supporting American grievances prior to their Revolutionary War, and moderate movements for Parliamentary Reform, religious civil rights for Protestant Dissenters and Catholics, and Irish political autonomy. Early in the French Revolution, a young French revolutionary wrote to Burke, expecting his support. Burke, however, decided to throw his political weight against the French Revolution, and those looking to import its principles and practices into Britain, in this fall 1790 political treatise. Burke denounced revolutionaries' attempt to institute a wholesale new order of things, believing liberty could only result from political traditions and a well-ordered social hierarchy. Revolutionaries to him were destroying a venerable order through violence and impractical philosophy, with little concept of what a workable new order would be. Concurrently, Burke sought to mobilize his fellow Britons against French innovations, calling for loyalist support of British traditions of liberty and order. It is chiefly as a result of this work that Burke is considered the principal founding father of modern political conservatism.

They [French Revolutionaries] have found their punishment in their success. Laws overturned; tribunals subverted; industry without vigour; commerce expiring; the revenue unpaid, yet the people impoverished; a church pillaged, and a state not relieved; civil and military anarchy made the constitution of the kingdom; every thing human and divine sacrificed to the idol of public credit, and national bankruptcy the consequence; and to crown all, the paper securities of new, precarious, tottering power, the discredited paper securities of impoverished fraud, and beggared rapine, held out as a currency for the support of an empire, in lieu of . . . the principle of property, whose creatures and representatives they are, was systematically subverted.

Were all these dreadful things necessary? Were they the inevitable results of the desperate struggle of determined patriots, compelled to wade through blood and tumult, to the quiet shore of a tranquil and prosperous liberty? No! nothing like it. The fresh ruins of France, which shock our feelings wherever we can turn our eyes, are not the devastation of civil war; they are the sad but instructive monuments of rash and ignorant counsel in time of profound peace. . . .

The power . . . of the house of commons, when least diminished, is as a drop of water in the ocean, compared to that residing in a settled majority of your National Assembly. That Assembly, since the destruction of the orders, has no fundamental law, no strict convention, no respected usage to restrain it. Instead of finding themselves obliged to conform to a fixed constitution, they have a power to make a constitution which shall conform to their designs. Nothing in heaven or upon earth can serve as a control on them. What ought to be the heads, the hearts, the dispositions, that are qualified, or that dare, not only to make laws under a fixed constitution, but at one heat to strike out a totally new constitution for a great kingdom, and in every part of it, from the monarch on the throne to the vestry of a parish? But—"Fools rush in where angels fear to tread." In such a state of unbounded power, for undefined and undefinable purposes, the evil of a moral and almost physical inaptitude of the man to the function must be the greatest we can conceive to happen in the management of human affairs. . . .

I see that your example is held out to sham us. I know that we are supposed a dull sluggish race, rendered passive by finding our situation tolerable; and prevented by a mediocrity of freedom from ever attaining to its full perfection. Your leaders in France began by affecting to admire, almost to adore, the British constitution; but as they advanced they came to look upon it with a sovereign contempt. . . .

But as the liberties and the restrictions vary with times and circumstances, and admit of infinite modifications, they cannot be settled upon any abstract rule; and nothing is so foolish as to discuss them upon that principle. . . . What is the use of discussing a man's abstract right to food or to medicine? The question is upon the method of procuring and administering them. In that deliberation I shall always advise to call in the aid of the farmer and the physician, rather than the professor of metaphysics. . . .

The science of constructing a commonwealth, or renovating it, or reforming it, is, like every other experimental science, not to be taught à priori. Nor is it a short experience that can instruct us in that practical science; because the real effects of moral causes are not always immediate; but that which in the first instance is prejudicial may be excellent in its remoter operation; and its excellence may arise even from the ill effects it produces in the beginning. . . .

The nature of man is intricate; the objects of society are of the greatest possible complexity; and therefore no simple disposition or direction of power can be suitable either to man's nature, or to the quality of his affairs. . . . The pretended rights of these theorists are all extremes; and in proportion as they are metaphysically true, they are morally and politically false. . . . Hypocrisy, of course, delights in the most sublime speculations; for, never intending to go beyond speculation, it costs nothing to have it magnificent. . . .

But now all is to be changed. All the pleasing illusions, which made power gentle, and obedience liberal, which harmonized the different shades of life, and which, by a bland assimilation, incorporated into politics the sentiments which beautify and soften private society, are to be dissolved by this new conquering empire of light and reason. All the decent drapery of life is to be rudely torn off. All the superadded ideas, furnished from the wardrobe of a moral imagination, which the heart owns, and the understanding ratifies, as necessary to cover the defects of our naked shivering nature, and to raise it to dignity in our own estimation, are to be exploded as a ridiculous, absurd, and antiquated fashion. . . .

When antient opinions and rules of life are taken away, the loss cannot possibly be estimated. From that moment we have no compass to govern us; nor can we know distinctly to what port we steer. . . .

Formerly your affairs were your own concern only. We felt for them as men; but we kept aloof from them, because we were not citizens of France. But when we see the model held up to ourselves, we must feel as Englishmen, and feeling, we must provide as Englishmen. Your affairs, in spite of us, are made a part of our interest; so far at least as to keep at a distance your panacea, or your plague. If it be a panacea, we do not want it. We know the consequences of unnecessary physic. If it be a plague, it is such a plague, that the precautions of the most severe quarantine ought to be established against it. . . .

Have these gentlemen never heard, in the whole circle of the worlds of theory and practice, of any thing between the despotism of the monarch and the despotism of the multitude? Have they never heard of a monarchy directed by laws, controlled and balanced by the great hereditary wealth and hereditary dignity of a nation; and both again controlled by a judicious check from the reason and feeling of the people at large acting by a suitable and permanent organ? Is it then impossible that a man may be found who, without criminal ill intention, or pitiable absurdity, shall prefer such a mixed and tempered government to either of the extremes; and who may repute that nation to be destitute of all wisdom and of all virtue, which, having in its choice to obtain such a government with ease, or rather to confirm it when actually possessed, thought proper to commit a thousand crimes, and to subject their country to a thousand evils, in order to avoid it? Is it then a truth so universally acknowledged, that a pure democracy is the only tolerable form into which human society can be thrown, that a man is not permitted to hesitate about its merits, without the suspicion of being a friend to tyranny, that is, of being a foe to mankind? . . .

I know how easy a topic it is to dwell on the faults of departed greatness. By a revolution in the state, the fawning sycophant of yesterday is converted into the austere critic of the present hour. But steady independant minds, when they have an object of so serious a concern to mankind as government, under their contemplation, will disdain to assume the part of satirists and declaimers. They will judge of human institutions as they do of human characters. They will sort out the good from the evil, which is mixed in mortal institutions as it is in mortal men. . . .

Rage and phrenzy will pull down more in half an hour, than prudence, deliberation, and foresight can build up in an hundred years. . . .

But am I so unreasonable as to see nothing at all that deserves commendation in the indefatigable labours of this assembly? I do not deny that among an infinite number of acts of violence and folly, some good may have been done. They who destroy every thing certainly will remove some grievance. They who make every thing new, have a chance that they may establish something beneficial. To give them credit for what they have done in virtue of the authority they have usurped, or which can excuse them in the crimes by which that authority has been acquired, it must appear, that the same things could not have been accomplished without producing such a revolution. Most assuredly they might; because almost every one of the regulations made by them, which is not very equivocal, was either in the cession of the king, voluntarily made at the meeting of the states, or in the concurrent instructions to the orders. Some usages have been abolished on just grounds; but they were such that if they had stood as they were to all eternity, they would little detract from the happiness and prosperity of any state. The improvements of the national assembly are superficial; their errors, fundamental.

Thomas Paine, selections from the *Rights of Man*, 1791–2

Explicitly responding to Burke's *Reflections*, pamphleteer Thomas Paine—already famous for *Common Sense* and other pamphlets supporting American independence—took up his pen in support of the French Revolution.

Published in two parts in 1791–2, Paine declared the new era of liberty to represent the natural state of humankind, believing despotism's reign would cease across Europe and, soon, the world. Confronting a British political system largely based on tradition, Paine called for a sharp break with the past and the embrace of reason. He encouraged the British to embark on a new era of liberty and join an alliance with America and France to make the world free. Paine's work sold over 200,000 copies (an unprecedented number for a political pamphlet), and emboldened radical clubs to challenge the British political establishment. In September 1792, despite knowing no French, he was elected to France's National Convention, where he served as a member of its Constitutional Committee, before falling afoul of the Jacobins. Though imprisoned in 1794, he survived the terror, but would die penniless after alienating mainstream Anglo-American opinion with his militantly deistic *Age of Reason* challenging the Bible's veracity.

There never did, there never will, and there never can, exist a Parliament, or any description of men, or any generation of men, in any country, possessed of the right or the power of binding and controlling posterity to the "end of time," or of commanding for ever how the world shall be governed, or who shall govern it; and therefore all such clauses, acts or declarations by which the makers of them attempt to do what they have neither the right nor the power to do, nor the power to execute, are in themselves null and void. Every age and generation must be as free to act for itself in all cases as the age and generations which preceded it. The vanity and presumption of governing beyond the grave is the most ridiculous and insolent of all tyrannies. Man has no property in man; neither has any generation a property in the generations which are to follow. . . . Mr. Burke is contending for the authority of the dead over the rights and freedom of the living . . . if antiquity is to be authority, a thousand such authorities may be produced, successively contradicting each other . . .

Every history of the creation, and every traditionary account, whether from the lettered or unlettered world, however they may vary in their opinion or belief of certain particulars, all agree in establishing one point, the unity of man; by which I mean that men are all of one degree, and consequently that all men are born equal, and with equal natural right . . .

It has been thought a considerable advance towards establishing the principles of Freedom to say that Government is a compact between those who govern and those who are governed; but this cannot be true, because it is putting the effect before the cause; for as man must have existed before governments existed, there necessarily was a time when governments did not exist, and consequently there could originally exist no governors to form such a compact with.

The fact therefore must be that the individuals themselves, each in his own personal and sovereign right, entered into a compact with each other to produce a government: and this is the only mode in which governments have a right to arise, and the only principle on which they have a right to exist. . . .

Much is to be learned from the French Constitution. Conquest and tyranny transplanted themselves with William the Conqueror from Normandy into England, and the country is yet disfigured with the marks. May, then, the example of all France contribute to regenerate the freedom which a province of it destroyed! . . .

The President of the National Assembly does not ask the King to grant to the Assembly liberty of speech, as is the case with the English House of Commons. The constitutional dignity of the National Assembly cannot debase itself. Speech is, in the first place, one of the natural rights of man always retained; and with respect to the National Assembly the use of it is their duty, and the nation is their authority. They were elected by the greatest body of men exercising the right of election the European world ever saw. . . .

The opinions of men with respect to government are changing fast in all countries. The Revolutions of America and France have thrown a beam of light over the world, which reaches into man. The enormous expense of governments has provoked people to think, by making them feel; and when once the veil begins to rend, it admits not of repair. Ignorance is of a peculiar nature: once dispelled, it is impossible to re-establish it. It is not originally a thing of itself, but is only the absence of knowledge; and though man may be kept ignorant, he cannot be made ignorant. The mind, in discovering truth, acts in the same manner as it acts through the eye in discovering objects; when once any object has been seen, it is impossible to put the mind back to the same condition it was in before it saw it. Those who talk of a counter-revolution in France, show how little they understand of man. . . .

From the Revolutions of America and France, and the symptoms that have appeared in other countries, it is evident that the opinion of the world is changing with respect to systems of Government, and that revolutions are not within the compass of political calculations. The progress of time and circumstances, which men assign to the accomplishment of great changes, is too mechanical to measure the force of the mind, and the rapidity of reflection, by which revolutions are generated: All the old governments have received a shock from those that already appear, and which were once more improbable, and are a greater subject of wonder, than a general revolution in Europe would be now. . . .

What were formerly called Revolutions, were little more than a change of persons, or an alteration of local circumstances. They rose and fell like things of course, and had nothing in their existence or their fate that could influence beyond the spot that produced them. But what we now see in the world, from the Revolutions of America and France, are a renovation of the natural order of things, a system of principles as universal as truth and the existence of man, and combining moral with political happiness and national prosperity. . . .

From what we now see, nothing of reform in the political world ought to be held improbable. It is an age of Revolutions, in which everything may be looked for. The intrigue of Courts, by which the system of war is kept up, may provoke a confederation of Nations to abolish it: and an European Congress to patronise the progress of free Government, and promote the civilisation of Nations with each other, is an event nearer in probability, than once were the revolutions and alliance of France and America . . .

What Archimedes said of the mechanical powers, may be applied to Reason and Liberty. "Had we," said he, "a place to stand upon, we might raise the world." . . .

As revolutions have begun (and as the probability is always greater against a thing beginning, than of proceeding after it has begun), it is natural to expect that other revolutions will follow. The amazing and still increasing expenses with which old governments are conducted, the numerous wars they engage in or provoke, the embarrassments they throw in the way of universal civilisation and commerce, and the oppression and usurpation acted at home, have wearied out the patience, and exhausted the property of the world. In such a situation, and with such examples already existing, revolutions are to be looked for. They are become subjects of universal conversation, and may be considered as the Order of the day. . . .

If universal peace, civilisation, and commerce are ever to be the happy lot of man, it cannot be accomplished but by a revolution in the system of governments . . .

Some gentlemen have affected to call the principles upon which this work and the former part of Rights of Man are founded, "a new-fangled doctrine." The question is not whether those principles are new or old, but whether they are right or wrong.

James Watt, Jr. and Thomas Cooper. "Speech of the Delegates of the Manchester Constitutional Society Pronounced before the Paris Jacobin Club," April 13, 1792

Whilst Paris' Jacobin Club had been founded after receiving an encouraging letter from the London Revolution Society in late 1789, by spring 1792 radical Britons looked to France for inspiration as they attempted to form more radical reform societies. Manchester and other growing industrial cities underrepresented in the British Parliament proved particularly receptive to such ideas. Thomas Cooper, a writer and scientist, and James Watt Jr., son of the steam engine's developer, arrived in Paris a week before France's declaration of war against Austria to present a vision of international fraternity and freedom. Just a week before the Franco-Austrian war began, the British activists projected hopes of a future pact between France and a liberalized Britain. The French Revolution brought movements for modern democratic representation to Britain for the first time—as radicals ceased to base their arguments on British precedent and instead demanded universal rights of man. Though the British radical societies would be suppressed by a larger conservative reaction, subsequent movements to expand suffrage (slowly, from less than 1% of males to the full adult population) took inspiration from these activists. The British government incited war against the French in early 1793, thwarting hopes for an alliance between free peoples in favor of twenty-two more years of war between the two nations.

Brothers and Friends,

We feel a deep satisfaction in communicating to you the dispatch in which our brothers of the Constitutional Society of Manchester came to nominate their deputies to the patriotic societies of France.

At the present moment, when a concert of Europe's despotic powers forms to destroy the cause of liberty and annihilate the rights of man, we hope to bring you pleasure in informing you that there are men everywhere (even amongst the peoples where the intrigues of kings and courtesans have too often made them appear enemies) who take a lively interest in your cause, the cause not only of the French, but of the human race.

The light that you are coming to shine on the true principles of politics and the natural rights of man (light which still only reaches England scattered through the clouds of civil ignorance) must make us feel that the time has come to abolish all national prejudice and embrace as brothers all free men, from whatever country they come from. For too long the machinations of despots, always opposed to nature, have taught men to mutually regard each other as enemies.

Considering the Jacobin Club not only as the Friends of the French Constitution, but also under the still more respectable title of the friends of man, we ask, in the name of the Constitutional Society of Manchester, for communication and friendly correspondence with them, if not as a beginning, then at least as the continuation of this general federation between the patriotic societies of Europe, of which the object will be the fraternal union of all men.

Our society will find itself happy to join its efforts to yours to spread the important principles of universal liberty, which alone can establish the empire of peace and happiness of men on a solid and unbreakable basis.

We congratulate the Jacobin Club on the involuntary homage that they have rendered one of the despotic courts of Europe, in indicating them as the most determined enemy of arbitrary power. Follow, Messieurs, the course of your philanthropic works, and continue to merit the execration of tyrants and the benedictions of humans.

French National Assembly Bestows Citizenship on Exemplary Foreigners (Paine, Wilberforce, Washington and Hamilton Included), August 26, 1792

Seeking to encourage international efforts for liberty, France's second National Assembly, less than a month before the National Convention began, bestowed French citizenship on foreign nationals at the forefront of international movements for freedom. While French knowledge of the figures in question appears partial (misspelling several names and referring to the Anglophile Alexander Hamilton as "Jean"), they nevertheless sought to place the French Revolution within a broader movement towards more enlightened government, while encouraging causes for greater liberty elsewhere. The list is eclectic: several British parliamentary reformers and abolitionists, three American politicians, an Italian general fighting for France, a Polish general who fought in the American Revolution, three German writers, a Dutch philosopher, and a Swiss journalist. Yet, to French revolutionaries, they possessed an essential similarity as fellow friends of freedom, justice, and the rights of man. Enlightened reason connected their efforts despite local particularities. Despite the counterrevolutionary hordes the French armies were then combatting, hope remained that activists abroad could convince other peoples to see the light and embrace revolutionary thinking.

The National Assembly, considering that those men who by their writings and courage have served the Cause of Liberty and prepared the freeing of peoples cannot be regarded as strangers by a nation whose enlightenment and courage have rendered them free,

Considering that if five years living in France suffices for a foreigner to obtain the title of French Citizen, this title is more justly deserved by those who, whatever soil they inhabit, have devoted their arms and watchfulness to defending the cause of peoples against the despotism of kings, banning prejudices from the earth, and pulling back the limits of human knowledge,

Considering that if it is not permitted to hope that all men will not one day form before the law as before Nature a single family, a single association, the friends of liberty and universal fraternity ought not to be less dear to a nation proclaiming their renunciation of all conquests and their desire to fraternize with all peoples,

Considering, finally, that at the moment where a National Convention will fix France's destiny, and prepare perhaps that of the human race, it falls to a generous and free people to gather all enlightenment and give the right to contribute to this great act of reason and to those men who by their sentiments, their writings and their courage have so eminently distinguished themselves.

We bestow the title of French Citizen to Doctor Joseph Priestley, Thomas Payne, Jérémie Bentham, William Wilberforce, Thomas Clarkson, Jacques Mackintosh, David Williams, N. Gorani, Anacharsis Cloots, Corneille Paw, Joachim-Henry Campe, N. Pestalozzi, George Washington, Jean Hamilton, N. Maddison, H. Klopstock, and Thadée Kociusko.

Regulations of the Democratic-Republican Society of Philadelphia, 1793

Political organizing in the French Revolutionary era led to more lasting political changes in the United States than France. America's 1787 Constitution made no provisions for political parties, which the Founding Fathers initially abhorred. The split in George Washington's cabinet between Treasury Secretary Hamilton and Secretary of State Jefferson, however, led to the development of opposing factions—spreading into Congress, and then amongst the populace. The Democratic Society was organized in Philadelphia in conscious imitation of France's Jacobin Clubs. French revolutionary ambassador Edmond-Charles Genet attended their founding meeting and, after Philadelphians suggested naming the society the Sons of Liberty, Genet instead proposed a name speaking to the group's core principle: "the Democratic Club." It was from a revolutionary Frenchman that the Democratic Party took its name.

Principles, Articles and Regulations, Agreed upon, Drawn and Adopted, May 30, 1793.

The Rights of Man, the genuine objects of Society, and the legitimate principles of Government, have been clearly developed by the successive Revolutions of America and France. Those events have withdrawn the veil which concealed the dignity and the happiness of the human race, and have taught us, no longer dazzled with adventitious splendor, or awed by antiquated usurpation, to erect the Temple of LIBERTY on the ruins of *Palaces* and *Thrones*.

At this propitious period, when the nature of Freedom and Equality is thus practically displayed, and when their value, (best understood by those, who have paid the price of acquiring them) is universally acknowledged, the patriotic mind will naturally be solicitous, by every proper precaution, to preserve and perpetuate the Blessings which Providence hath bestowed upon our Country: for, in reviewing the history of Nations, we find occasion to lament, that the vigilance of the People has been too easily absorbed in victory; and that the prize which has been achieved by the wisdom and valor of one generation, has too often been lost by the ignorance and supineness of another.

With a view, therefore, to cultivate the just knowledge of rational liberty, to facilitate the enjoyment and exercise of our civil Rights, and to transmit, unimpaired, to posterity, the glorious inheritance of a *free Republican Government*, the DEMOCRATIC SOCIETY of Pennsylvania is constituted and established. Unfettered by *religious* or *national* distinctions, unbiased by party and unmoved by ambition, this Institution embraces the interest and invites the support of every virtuous citizen. The public good is indeed its sole object, and we think that the best means are pursued for obtaining it, when we recognize the following, as the fundamental principles of our association.

I. THAT the people have the inherent and exclusive right and power of making and altering forms of Government; and that for regulating and protecting our social interests, a REPUBLICAN GOVERNMENT is the most natural and beneficial form, which the wisdom of Man has devised.

II. THAT the Republican Constitutions of the UNITED STATES and of the STATE of PENNSYLVANIA, being framed and established by the People, it is our duty as good citizens, to support them. And in order to effectually do so, it is likewise the duty of every Freeman to regard with attention, and to discuss without fear, the conduct of public Servants, in every department of Government.

Theobald Wolfe Tone, selections from *Memoirs*, published 1826

The French Revolution sparked a new era of political contestation in Ireland. While the British-dependent kingdom in 1783 had gained new Parliamentary autonomy, the Irish political system remained closed to all but a small Anglo-Protestant elite. The revolution led by Catholics in France motivated their Irish co-religionists to push for political rights, initially through reformist social movement organizing in the early 1790s under an inclusive association known as the United Irishmen and then—after the moderate movement's repression once war was declared with France in early 1793—an underground secret society movement. Theobald Wolfe Tone, a Dublin lawyer, became one of the movement's most prominent voices, effective organizers, and able diplomats. Once the organization radicalized, Wolfe Tone travelled to Paris seeking military aid for an uprising, spent time in exile in Philadelphia, then returned to the continent to join French forces in an Irish invasion, which landed in October 1798. Their attempts to spark a unified Irish uprising failed, however, and Wolfe Tone died in British captivity. Two summers before, in Paris, he wrote his memoirs, describing how the French Revolution helped embolden the Irish to demand freedom.

The French revolution had now been above a twelvemonth in its progress; at its commencement, as the first emotions are generally honest, every one was in its favor; but, after some time, the probable consequences to monarchy and aristocracy began to be foreseen, and the partizans of both to retrench considerably in their admiration: at length, Mr. Burke's famous invective appeared; and this in due season produced Paine's reply, which he called "Rights of Man." This controversy, and the gigantic event which gave it, changed in an instant the politics of Ireland. Two years before, the nation was in lethargy. The puny efforts of the Whig Club, miserable and defective as their system was, were the only appearance of any thing like exertion, and he was looked on as extravagant who thought of a Parliamentary reform, against which, by the by, all parties equally set their face. . . . But the rapid succession of events, and, above all, the explosion which had taken place in France, and blown into the elements a despotism rooted for fourteen centuries, had thoroughly aroused all Europe; and the eyes of every man, in every quarter, were turned anxiously on the French National Assembly. In England, Burke had the triumph completely to decide the public; fascinated by an eloquent publication, which flattered so many of their prejudices, and animated by their unconquerable hatred of France, which no change of circumstances could alter, the whole English nation, it may be said, retracted from their first decision in favour of the glorious and successful efforts of the French people; they sickened at the prospect of the approaching liberty and happiness of that mighty nation; they calculated, as merchants, the probable effects which the energy of regenerated France might have on their commerce; they rejoiced when they saw the combination of despots formed to restore the ancient system, and perhaps to dismember the monarchy; and they waited with impatience for an occasion, which happily for mankind they soon found, when they might, with some appearance of decency, engage in person in the infamous contest.

But matters were very different in Ireland, an oppressed, insulted, and plundered nation. As we well knew, experimentally, what it was to be enslaved, we sympathized most sincerely with the French people, and watched their progress to freedom with the utmost anxiety; we had not, like England, a prejudice rooted in our very nature against France. As the revolution advanced, and as events expanded themselves, the public spirit of Ireland rose with a rapid acceleration. The fears and animosities of the aristocracy rose in the same, or a still higher proportion. In a little time the French Revolution became the test of every man's political creed, and the nation was fairly divided into two great parties, the Aristocrats and the Democrats, (epithets borrowed from France,) who have ever since been measuring each other's strength, and carrying on a kind of smothered war, which the course of events, it is highly probable, may soon call into energy and action. . . .

[in 1792] It was determined by the people of Belfast to commemorate this year the anniversary of the taking of the Bastille with great ceremony.

For this purpose they planned a review of the volunteers of the town and neighborhood, to be followed by a grand procession, with emblematical devices, etc. They also determined to avail themselves of this opportunity to bring forward the Catholic question in force, and, inconsequence, they resolved to publish two addresses, one to the people of France, and one to the people of Ireland . . . a grand assembly took place on the 14th July. After the review, the volunteers and inhabitants, to the number of about 6,000, assembled in the Linen-Hall, and voted the address to the French people unanimously. The address to the people of Ireland followed, and as it was directly and unequivocally in favor of the Catholic claims, we expected some opposition, but were soon relieved from our anxiety, for the address passed, I may say, unanimously: . . . Suffice it to say, that the hospitality shown by the people of Belfast to the Catholics, on this occasion, and the personal acquaintance with the parties formed, riveted the bonds of their recent union, and produced in the sequel the most beneficial and powerful effects.

Excerpts from Tone's journal:

14 [July 1792]. *Era of the French Revolution!* Knocked up early by Neilson; get on my regimentals, and go breakfast with the Catholics. McKenna arrived. Drums beating, colors flying, and all the honors of war. Brigade formed, and march off by ten; 700 men, and make a tolerable appearance. . . . The review tolerably well. Some companies filled by little squads of six or eight men, who come in of their own motion, without officers. . . .

March into town at three. Meet Haslit and Neilson: take the word "Catholic" out, and put in the word "Irishmen" of every religious denomination. Procession. Meeting at the Linen Hall, astonishing full. Question moved by the Draper. Before the debate goes on five minutes, satisfied that we have it hollow . . . . More and more satisfied that their moderation is nonsense and stuff. Carry the question . . . The business is now fairly settled in Belfast and the neighbourhood. Huzza! Huzza! Dinner at Donegal Arms. Every body as happy as a king . . . Huzza! God bless every body! Stanislaus Augustus! George Washington! *Beau-jour*. Who would have thought it this morning? Huzza! Generally drunk—Broke my glass thumping the table. Home, God knows how or when. Huzza! . . .

16 [July 1792] . . . Dinner; McTier in the chair. Chequered at the head of the table, a Dissenter and a Catholic.[6] Delightful! The four flags, America, France, Poland, Ireland, but *no England*. Bravo! . . .

14th [August 1792]. The county Down getting better every day on the Catholic question. . . . The Belfast men get warm with wine and patriotism. . . . The Catholics offer to find soldiers, if Belfast will provide officers. . . . Something will come out of all this. . . . Huzza! Generally drunk. Vive la nation! D—n the Empress of Russia! Success to the Polish arms, with three times three. Huzza! Generally *very* drunk. Bed. . . .

15th. Waken drunk. Breakfast with Neilson, the Jacobin, &c. More volunteer companies springing up like mushrooms, nobody knows why. . . . This country will never be well until the Catholics are educated at home, and their clergy elective. Dinner at Tanner's: all well. The Rev. T. Birch, of *Botany Bay*, tells us that he is just returned from a meeting of eighteen Dissenting clergymen from different parts of Ulster, and had the pleasure to find them *all* well-disposed to Catholic liberty: he has no doubt but the cause is spreading most rapidly. He thinks, what I fear is true, that the Catholic clergymen are bad friends to liberty. The priest of Saintfield preached against United Irishmen, and exhorted his people not to join such clubs . . .

19. *Sunday*. Go to mass; foolish enough; too much trumpery. The king of France dethroned!! Very glad of it, for now the people have fair play. What will the army do! God send they may stand by the nation. Every thing depends upon the line they take. Our success depends on things which some of us are such fools as not to see. . . . Dr. Moody, the Dissenting minister, says grace; bravo! All very good; toasts excellent. United Irishmen mentioned again, and the idea meets universal approbation; hope it may do; wonderful to see how rapidly the Catholic mind is rising, even in this Tory town, which is one of the worst spots in Ireland; . . .

Anacharsis Cloots, extract from *Constitutional Bases for the Republic of the Human Race*, 1793

Though himself a wealthy German noble, the Baron de Cloots—better known by his revolutionary name of Anacharsis Cloots, taken from an ancient Greek Cynic philosopher—became the most enthusiastic proponent of French universalism. Declaring himself the "orator of mankind" (as well as the "personal enemy of Jesus Christ"), he received honorary French citizenship and gained election to the National Convention. A prominent Jacobin, he believed the French Revolution set an example the other peoples of the world would soon follow. In his *Constitutional Bases*, Cloots sets the stage for a transition of France's National Convention into a universal convention for all the world, in which peoples could live in peace under a single government. In so doing, he became perhaps the first modern proponent of a global government, promoting a universal model of human rights even more explicitly than either 1789 or 1793's Declaration of the Rights of Man and Citizen. As the French Revolutionary War intensified, however, revolutionaries became increasingly fearful of foreign agents. Drawing Robespierre's enmity, Cloots was expelled from the Jacobin Club and then arrested and guillotined under thin pretenses in March 1794.

Our constituents have given us an urgent and succinct mandate: Legislators, we want a constitution marrying permanent happiness with permanent liberty.

To respond to the wishes of France, Europe, and the world, we will labor in the vast fields of genius, while our fellow citizens labor in fertile fields, while they fill the workshops of industry. We will destroy error, while our brothers in arms battle the erroneous.

All peoples ask to become French departments.[7] We do not know how to respond to this fraternal solicitation except after having presented the values and developed principles that essentially conserve the liberty we have conquered with so much effort and glory. The Roman people studied to perpetuate slavery in the universe; the French people occupy themselves with perpetuating universal liberty. We are going to sound out the terrain, examine the foundations, measure the first effects of our political constitution. We will calculate its solidity and dimensions before receiving the many guests arriving from all over. I fool myself badly if there will not be a place for all the world.

It is not always a question of conquering liberty, but always a question of conserving it. The conquest is easy, the conservation is difficult. Instead of four revolutionary years, our political convulsions would not have lasted four months, if a good constitution had been raised over the Bastille's ruins. . . .

We will now set the first stone of our constitutional pyramid on the unbreakable rock of the sovereignty of the human race. . . .

It is in consulting nature that I discover a political system of which the simplicity will be perfectly seized by anyone desiring full independence, all the happiness of which humans are susceptible. An individual does not know how to be free alone; a small number of individuals do not know how to stay free for long. We are not free, if foreign barriers stop us at ten or twenty leagues from our manor; if our security is compromised by invasions; if our repose is troubled, our revenue taken by military forces; if our commerce is interrupted by hostilities; if our industry is closed in the tight circle of this or that country. We are not free, if a single moral obstacle stops our physical movement over a single point of the globe. The rights of man extend to the totality of men. A corporation calling itself sovereign gravely injures humanity, it is in open revolt against good sense and happiness, it cuts the channel of universal prosperity. Its constitution, lacking a basis, will be contradictory, banal, and failing. . . .

The attributes of a fantastical divinity really belong to political divinity. I say, and repeat, that the human race is God; aristocrats are the atheists. It's the regenerated human race that I have in view, when I speak of the People-God of which France is the cradle and the rallying point. Sovereignty resides essentially in the entire human race; it is one, indivisible, imprescriptible, immutable, inalienable, imperishable, unlimited, absolute, without limits and all-powerful . . . How can one have the impiety to refuse a demand founded on eternal principles, on invariable reason? Clear waters pool at the first point of contact, enlightened peoples unite at the first recognition of eternal laws. Newton united all philosophers by his discovery in physics; I unite all men by my political discovery. Every free people will recognize my principle, in evaluating the inestimable advantages of sovereign unity: now, if all the peoples declare the same truth, the same rights, a single nation will naturally result, of which the peace will never be troubled by jealous neighbors, nor by turbulent factions. Lies carry discord from one pole to the other; truth will carry concord from one hemisphere to the other. . . .

Regarding the formation of government, there is not a single Frenchman who does not reject with indignation the American regime. The united sovereign people do not know how to admit the English balancing, or accept the most limited veto. A precipitous decree's effects are still preferable to the English veto: what ruins an aristocratic senate saves a national assembly. The invasion of powers is impossible in a great biennial assembly in which the sovereign oversees all actions. The French only sound the alarm bells to bring down the Bastille and the Tuileries. In England, where the people's rights are not recognized, where a man treats the inhabitants as his subjects, or three powers dispute over the morsels of sovereignty, it appears necessary to oppose the counterweight of the royal veto to all the high chamber's maneuvers. It has created a ridiculous scaffolding to support an edifice lacking foundation. But in France, our excellent constitutional bases permit us to adopt pure forms to achieve the constitution of the universe. . . .

I propose thus to the Convention of the French, as much as to the other Conventions of the World, to decree or preliminarily declare the attractive principle of indivisible sovereignty, the supreme and unique will of the human race. This truth, recognized by all men, will produce their union. Let us set this foundation today, and our subsequent works will be imperishable: we will count on one more great uprising in the annals of the world's regeneration. The first year of the French Republic is the first year of the Universal Republic.

Here are the three articles, three results of profound meditation, which I submit to the wisdom of my colleagues.

DRAFT OF DECREE

The National Convention, wanting to end the errors, the inconveniences, the contradictory pretentions of the corporations and the individuals who call themselves sovereigns, solemnly declare under the auspices of the Rights of Man:

I. There is no other sovereign than the human race.

II. Every individual, every community recognizing this luminous and immutable principle will receive the rights of our fraternal association, in the republic of Men, of First Cousins, of Universals.

III. When lacking contiguousness or maritime communication, we will wait for the propagation of truth to admit these communes, these distant slaves.

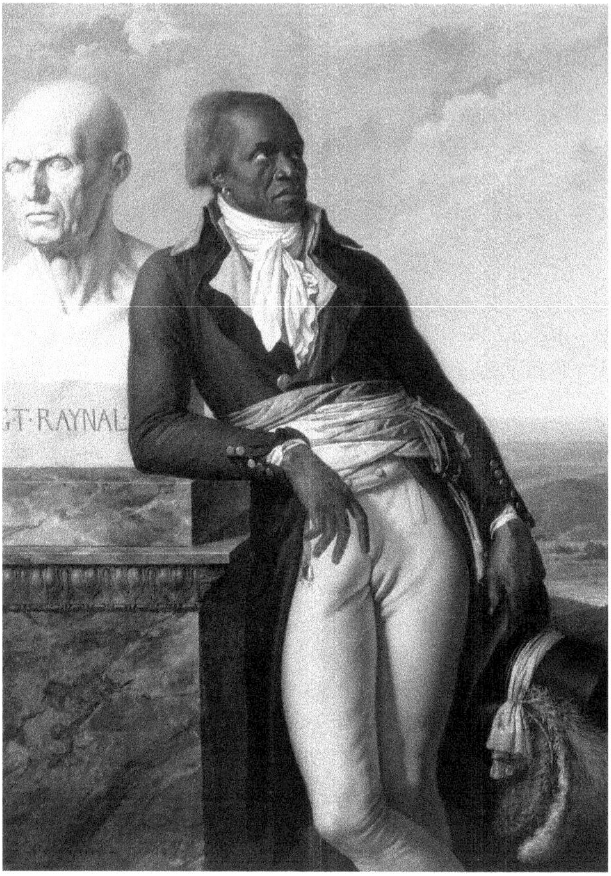

FIGURE 11.1 *Anne-Louis Girodet de Roucy-Trioson,* Jean-Baptiste Belley, *1797.* *© Photo Josse / Leemage / Getty Images.*

The French Revolution's striving for universal rights led to racial revolutions unparalleled in the eighteenth-century Atlantic World. While no blacks would sit in the United States Congress until after the Civil War, nor the British Parliament until 1987, the National Convention featured men of color from the colonies. Jean-Baptiste Belley had been born a slave, bought his freedom, fought in the American War of Independence, and joined with the French forces in the multi-sided civil war unleashed by the slave rebellion that became the Haitian Revolution. Though French revolutionaries had been torn between pragmatism and principle over the question of slavery, the Convention ratified the abolition of slavery in February 1794 after the colonial revolt worsened. In this 1797 portrait, Belley is painted leaning on the bust of early abolitionist the Abbé Raynal (see Chapter 1), suggesting radical enlightenment principles had directly influenced the upheaval in the colonies.

11

The Haitian Revolution

Not coincidentally, the only successful slave revolt in recorded human history began amidst the French Revolution. The principles of the French Revolution, particularly the Declaration of the Rights of Man and Citizen's assertion that "all men are born and remain equal in rights," destabilized French colonial politics, creating near-civil war between groups of free men that emboldened the slaves to rise. The French Revolution opened new possibilities for liberation and equality, but the oppressed in the colonies still needed to fight against their French overlords for their own freedom.

Elections for the Estates General emboldened Free Men of Color (of African and mixed-race descent, the majority of the free population) to seek political equality with colonial whites. White planters, however, met secretly to elect representatives, while lower-class white mobs harassed and attacked mixed-race assemblies. Free Men of Color in France organized as well—sending their own delegates to France to be seated in the Estates. Particularly after word of the early events of 1789 arrived—followed by heated debates over free-black colonial rights—all were uncertain how their revolutionary parent-state would respond to their claims, opening a power vacuum in the colony even more profound than that in France itself.

Concurrently in France, the abolitionist Society of the Friends of the Blacks sought significant colonial changes. Building from recent American and British efforts to end the Atlantic slave trade, the Paris-centered organization founded in 1788 advocated for the end of France's international trade, while improving life for colonial blacks. Many soon-to-be prominent Jacobin leaders got their first club experience in the abolitionist group. Even as French merchants (organizing their own lobbying network called the Club Massiac) successfully blocked proposals to abolish the slave trade, French Revolutionary instability led many to predict that colonial slavery might be the next unjust privilege to fall.

The accelerating breakdown in colonial authority—which soon split along regional as well as racial lines—gave slaves the latitude necessary to rise. By mid-1791, near-civil war conditions existed between Saint-

Domingue's governor and regional assemblies. Planters (not unlike their trading partners in the American South) believed the revolution ought to principally benefit them, bringing self-government for white colonial elites. Incensed at their conduct, mixed-race radical Vincent Ogé returned to the colony in early 1791 and raised an armed band, but failed to spark a general uprising. Turned over to white authorities, he was brutally executed. Many prognosticated, however, that his uprising would not be the last. Possibility, fear, and opportunity coalesced.

Slaves, who constituted over 90% of the colonial population, had been politically ignored by all sides throughout the revolutionary controversies. In August 1791, a conspiracy spread across the colony's Northern Plain. After an animal sacrifice, slaves rose and overwhelmed plantations, massacring whites, burning crops and destroying sugar refineries. Within days, 50–100,000 slaves rebelled and over 450 plantations burned. Vast fires of sugarcane—the exploitative cash-crop behind the colonial economy—blotted out the sun for days.

Haitian slaves' war for freedom was long and complex. Initially, slave rebel leaders attempted to negotiate their own freedom, along with humanitarian reforms (abolishing whipping and seeking an extra day of rest per week) for the insurrection's rank-and-file. With slavery an entrenched institution in the rebels' native African societies, universal freedom was a foreign concept. With the revolt successfully resisting oppression, by early 1793, the British navy invaded the southern coast, while the Spanish invaded over their land-border from Santo-Domingo (today the Dominican Republic). By October 1793, French authorities' position became so embattled that commissioner Léger-Félicité Santhonax took the audacious step of declaring all Saint-Domingue's free, attempting to win back their loyalty. The following February, France's National Convention abolished slavery throughout the French Empire—becoming the first nation in the world to explicitly do so.

The new order that solidified in Haiti ran through dictatorship instead of democracy. For several years, the French agreed to work through slave rebel leader Toussaint Louverture to reestablish order in the colony. Once Napoleon came to power, however, he attempted to reinstall the planters in their old positions of dominance, re-instituting slavery and sending armed forces to subdue the island. Free black forces (with the aid of malaria) nevertheless subdued the French troops, however. Haiti became an independent nation in 1804, but fell under the dictatorship of General Jean-Jacques Dessalines. Surrounded by powers unwilling to encourage an African-American nation, Haiti rapidly fell from being the richest colony in the eighteenth-century Atlantic, to being its poorest nation since. While the Haitian example stretches our understanding of the Age of Revolutions as a "Democratic Revolution," the overthrow of a colonial slave society may have been the greatest social revolution of an audacious era. Over the nineteenth century, in part because of the Haitian rebels' fearsome example, slave systems were abolished across the Americas.

Julien Raimond, selections from *Observations on the Origin and Progress of White Colonials' Prejudice Against Free Men of Color*. 1791

The "free men of color," as numerous as the whites of France's Caribbean islands and oftentimes slave-owners themselves, in the early revolution battled for their rights as fiercely as any French person. Planters in early 1789 called their own assemblies to select Estates General representatives for the colony of Saint-Domingue (the future Haiti)—excluding free blacks or those of mixed racial parentage, regardless of their economic standing, not to mention the slaves that constituted over ninety percent of the population. Julien Raimond, of mixed-race parentage, came from a slave-owning family, and at the revolution's outbreak was tending to investments in Paris. He joined the Society of the Friends of the Blacks, helping advocate for the abolition of the slave trade and humanitarian reform of the slave system (though not yet countenancing the abolition of slavery itself). After the planters' political offensive, the Friends of the Blacks took up the free men of color's political cause as well. Raimond's account demonstrates how the revolution's radical egalitarianism could not be confined to European France, but instead overtook and destabilized the French colonies—in the process, laying groundwork for later civil rights and anti-colonial movements worldwide.

For a long time a great question has agitated our colonies: should free men of color have the rights of active citizens in the colonies?

The white planters, who are aristocrats, the colonial nobility, want to deny these invaluable rights to the free mulattoes, whom they detest and want to degrade. To reach their goal, they have artificially conflated the cause of the free men of color with that of the slaves; and this calculated confusion has quite embroiled ideas about the true state of the free men of color. Until now, most National Assembly members did not clearly understand the status of these free men of color who are both free and property owners.

It is thus essential to enlighten them, and to explain here whom the free men of color were originally, how they have kept going, and finally, what their role is now.

A mulatto is the offspring of a white man with a black woman.

When people say "men of color" or "mixed-bloods," they mean the offspring of mulattoes together or of mulattoes with whites, and their different progeny. . . .

When the colonies were established, at the moment when Africans were introduced to cultivate them, there were almost no European women . . . These first whites lived with [African] women as in a state of marriage; they had children. Some of them, touched by these women's tenderness, and filled with paternal love, married their slaves. In freeing them, they legitimated the fruit of their passions or habits. When they died, they usually left to these children their cultivated lands. . . ..

Once the colony became further developed, and the government began paying them more attention, there were more white women sent to increase the white population . . .

The peace of 1749 brought to the islands a great number of white families which soon developed resentments and prejudices that the old whites also started showing against the free men of color, particularly as their fortunes increased. . . .[1]

Thus, prejudice grew to the ultimate extent. Now the daughters of the free coloreds who previously were thought to rival the white ladies in desirability, because they could marry whites, now became obligated to prostitute themselves to the whites, with whom they lived in concubinage. . . .

The prejudice raised against them is of very recent origin, not dating back more than thirty years.

This prejudice is due entirely to white women's jealousy, and to the impolitic and tyrannical ordinances by which one has, since 1768, attempted to debase the men of color. . . .

People assure me that the Colonial Committee, ceding partially to truth and partially to prejudice, must, to conciliate all parties, propose this middle ground, to not accord voting rights to those possessing a certain degree of white blood that confuses them with blacks by the color of their skin.[2] But for this to occur, they must one more time violate the principle of equality. It is pointless to demonstrate how this prejudicial transaction will augment divisions instead of diminishing them. It would be the source of a crowd of injustices, of hates and jealousies, that would depress the colonies' prosperity. . . .

The white colonists have always shown they are the free men of color's enemies, and now solicit the National Assembly to decree, as a constitutional article, that only they can make laws for free, property-owning men of color.

Can the National Assembly transmit the right of legislation—that it gains from the nation—to a part of the population of a province, to use against the other part, without this first part being held to the laws it makes for the second? . . .

Does the National Assembly have the right to decree the status of free persons of color, property-owners, tax-payers, differently than that of whites, to assign to the first a line of demarcation, that they can never cross, and thereby deprive them of society's advantages? . . .

If the white colonists are authorized to make by themselves the laws for the free men of color, if these laws are only obligatory and only weigh on them, could one then stop the free men of color from emigrating with their fortunes, to go search elsewhere for more equal and just laws? . . .

Unjust laws are those made against the rights of nature, and with the iron fist by which one forces those against whom they are made to obey them, though they are not consulted, and though their interests are injured. . . .

Can the National Assembly, without injustice and without reversing all the Declaration of the Rights of Man, decree that a French citizen, who goes to live in the French colonies, could have their rights degraded there, along with his children's, by legally marrying a person born free, under the pretext that this free person came from a woman who previously lived in slavery? . . .

Louis XIV, in his edict of 1685, granted to freed slaves their proper rights as citizens. Moreover, he obliged those Frenchmen who abused their slaves to marry them and to legitimize their children, if they had not married; and the wife, freed by the act of marriage, was elevated to her husband's condition, as were her children.[3]

Can the National Assembly be less just than a despot?

Club Massiac, Letter to the Chambers of Commerce of Maritime Cities, August 27, 1789 (with ensuing Nantes petition)

Merchant interests mobilized during the early French Revolution to prevent major changes to France's colonial system. Fearful of the abolitionist Society of the Friends of the Blacks' influence, interested parties in Paris formed the Corresponding Society of French Colonists, better known as the Club Massiac (named after the mansion on Paris' Place des Victoires where its central branch met), seeking to develop a national alliance of maritime and commercial merchants to demonstrate the importance of France's Caribbean trading. By late 1789, powerful Chambers of Commerce petitioned and lobbied the National Assembly, trying to stop the new principles of liberty from being applied in the colonial realm. Attempting to prevent the contagion of ideas, they enforced a travel ban against free blacks returning to the colonies on their ships. In trying to block all significant changes not favoring planter interests, however, the Massiac network further destabilized colonial politics: prophesizing quick changes would lead to colonial revolts—believing the National Assembly much more ready than it actually was to decree major changes—the rumors they spread helped make revolt a colonial reality.

The Corresponding Society of French Colonists assembled in Paris, on a member's motion to unite us with all the maritime cities' Chambers of Commerce, in this most frightening crisis . . . inform you that this assembly has unanimously adopted a proposal for a coalition that could have the salutary effect of enlightening the nation about colonial commerce's almost incalculable importance, and the necessity of outlawing forever the system of the Friends of the Blacks that seeks to annihilate it. In consequence, the Society of French Colonists, well-persuaded of the effectiveness of your enlightened aid and patriotism, to give you unequivocal proof of their desire make common cause and unite their wishes and sentiments, invites you to honor them by assisting with their assemblies whose goal is the conservation of our common interests.

We seek intelligence and amicable correspondence on these common interests. We need to take measures for the Colonies' security; the first is to prevent the return of Negroes and Free Men of Color in France to the heart of the Colonies, and you alone, Messieurs, can deter them by refusing, without any distinction or consideration, passage on your vessels: that is the first thing we have to do. We think you will adhere to such precautions for everyone's good. We plead that you give us your ideas and opinions on everything concerning us.

Nantes Petition Against Abolition, Addressed to the National Assembly. [late 1789]

Filled with the most profound respect for your august assembly, the united Chamber of Commerce of Nantes confidently depose in your body their worries and alarms. If the reports they have received are accurate, are you not preparing, sirs, to decree the Negroes' liberty, or at least soon forbid such commerce to the French?

This type of commerce, one must realize, can appear in certain respects contrary to the equality nature has established between all men, but in Europe's present state it is quite necessary to France. Its prohibition must lead to her ruin. It would be criminal to forbid it.

We have no trouble saying that there is no one . . . who does not believe the consequence of prohibiting the Black Trade would be the loss of our Colonies, the annihilation of our maritime commerce, the destruction of our manufactures, the ruin of those it employs, the fall of the industries and arts it supports, the discouragement of agriculture, the devaluing of all types of property, the reversal of the population's fortunes, the despair and the death of the most beautiful country in the universe.

Maximillien Robespierre, Interventions in Colonial Debates, May 12–13, 1791

Robespierre's May 12, 1791 address to the National Assembly intervened in favor of granting equal political rights to free blacks in the colonies. As a universalist, Robespierre passionately defended equal rights for all free French persons, regardless of race. This still required compromising his own principles: Robespierre (like most French revolutionaries) believed the colonial system necessary for France's future prosperity, and explicitly supported continuing the atrocity-laden slave system. Nevertheless, in context, decreeing equal political rights for "free men of color" was a major step towards racial equality in an American slave society—a measure unachieved for another hundred fifty years in the United States. The following day, amidst contentious debates, Robespierre—like many other commentators—prophesized potential race war if the island's propertied class became divided (as slaves outnumbered free persons ten to one). The colonies could perish if timely reforms were not made—and ought to, if they menaced the principles of French Revolutionary freedom. Indeed, colonial whites overwhelmingly refused to follow the Assembly's subsequent decree of racial equality for free men, exacerbating political cleavages that slaves capitalized upon to begin the Haitian Revolution. As in France, revolutionaries had little success compromising with Saint Domingue's entrenched elites.

May 12 intervention:

I declare, Messieurs, that the free men of color possess the rights that whites today claim exclusively for themselves: civil rights, the only ones all citizens enjoyed before the Revolution. The Revolution has also rendered all citizens political rights: free men of color now possess equal rights with white men. . . .

Have your preceding decrees removed these? No, because as you well remember, you granted them to all active citizens, who possess property in the colonies and pay a contribution of three days' work; and as color means nothing, all men of color paying three days' work are included in this decree and recognized as active citizens. . . .

Your subsequent decrees cannot abrogate whatsoever the preceding ones.

Let us see what the reasons are that you could force and violate at the same time your laws and decrees, and the principles of justice and humanity. You will lose your colonies, you say, if you do not deprive the free citizens of color of their rights . . . .

Why would you lose your colonies? It would be because a party of citizens, those called the whites, want exclusive political rights. . . . Here thus is a factious party threatening to burn your colonies and dissolve the bonds uniting them to the metropolis, if you do not confirm their pretentions! . . .

Alongside the victorious reasons given against this objection, I add that the conservation of political rights you pronounce in the property-owning free men of color's favor will only fortify masters' power over their slaves. Since you are giving all the property-owning free men of color and masters the same interests, if you only make a single party with the same interest in maintaining blacks in subordination, it is evident that subornation will be cemented even more firmly in the colonies. If, on the contrary, you deprive men of color of their rights, you will create a schism between them and the whites, you will naturally reproach all other powerful men, who lack the same rights and interests in defending the whites. You will bring them closer to the negro class. If there is an uprising to fear on the slaves' part against their masters, it is evident which will be more formidable: the one supported by free men of color not having the same interest in repression, since their cause would be almost the same.

May 13 intervention:

If I can suspect that, among the men of color's adversaries, many secret enemies of liberty and the Constitution can be found, I will believe that they have sought to attack your decrees to weaken your principles, so they can tell you one day they control the direct interests of France itself: they ceaselessly assail us over the Declaration of the Rights of Man, the principles of liberty, and how you have so little yourselves believed that slavery is constitutionally decreed. The supreme interest of the nation and the colonies is that you will remain free and not reverse with your own hands the bases of liberty.

Let the colonies perish, if they would cost you your happiness, your glory, your liberty. I repeat it: perish the colonies, and the colonists if they want, by threats, to force us to decree what most suits their interests.

I declare in the Assembly's name, in the name of those assemblymen not wanting to overturn the Constitution, in the name of the entire nation wanting to be free, that we will not sacrifice the deputies of the colonies, nor of the nation, nor the colonies themselves, nor humanity itself.[4]

Antoine Métral, Account of the Bois Caiman Ceremony (August 1791), *History of the Insurrection of Slaves in the North of Saint-Domingue*, 1818

A serious problem for historians studying the Haitian Revolution is the lack of documents written from the slave insurgents' own perspective. Antoine Métral, publishing in 1818, within living memory of the events, claimed to have gained through personal conversations accounts of the ceremonies and speeches preceding the insurrection. Attempting to understand the Haitian Revolution stretches historians' methodologies: recent studies have argued that the oral accounts and myths, often passed by illiterate slaves and semi-literate sailors, more than the piecemeal written historical source-record, gave the Haitian Revolution much of its global impact. Though potentially embellished or fabricated, Metral's work is likely the closest account available of what occurred on the Northern Plain of Saint-Domingue as the insurrectionary planning developed. It presents the insurgents as drawing strength from Voodoo ceremonies synthesizing African and Christian beliefs, and enunciating deep-seated grievances against their human masters. Though on multiple occasions during the ensuing slave insurrection their leaders would attempt to negotiate a truce in exchange for limited emancipations and concessions, here the rhetoric calls for a complete inversion of colonial society—in which the slaves planned to annihilate the white ruling class and subjugate any survivors. The product of a horrifically brutal colonial slave society, insurgent rhetoric called for vengeance.

The conspiracy became increasingly certain. According to the deposition of an old slave arrested the night of August 20, on the fourteenth there had been at the Lenormand plantation, on Red Mountain, an assembly composed of two deputies from each workshop, from the parishes of Port-Margot, Limbé, Acul, Petite-Anse, Limonade, Plaine du Nord, Quartier-Morin and several other places. The conspirators there fixed the day of the insurrection planned for some time. It was reported that before executing the plan, they made a sacrifice on virgin terrain covered with trees, called Lecaiman; that the victim was a black pig they fetishized, and lade with offerings of different kinds. A young priestess, dressed in a white robe, herself plunged the sacred knife into its entrails following the accustomed ceremony. They drank its blood eagerly and took its bristle as a sort of prize to render themselves invincible in combat.

After this sacrifice, they went to the Lenormand plantation, heading to its safest secret spot, taking care to closely guard the avenues. One of the conspirators (they said) expressed himself in this manner: "This is the first time, my dear comrades, that liberty unites us, since the barbarities that pulled us from our fatherland, distanced us from our temples, and the tombs of our fathers, to send us across the ocean into the most inhuman slavery. Each year the sea and the land are watered with our tears and blood.

"We pass the days and nights in excessive work without tasting the soft pleasures of repose, to enrich our masters who live in abundance and laziness, while we lack all the necessities of life. There are not any among us who are not sullied with tyranny's imprint. We grow old before our time and we die in our youth. The rocks, the caves, the woods, are useless for our liberty. We have little rest, which we would be happy to share with the beasts.

"Miscarriages are frequent with our women, whose teats are arid or only have milk for our masters' children. They defile our daughters barely out of childhood, profane our unions by adulteries filled with disgusting pleasures, and do not worry at all about blemishing and disinheriting the children of their blood when it mixes with ours. Such is the miserable destiny oppressing us; the irons, the torments, the tortures make our life hell.

"To what side should we turn our regards? The past only presents us with unexampled crimes towards our race; the future will perpetuate them, with our offspring only born to serve.

"Children of the Sun, what is there in common between us and these masters? Separated by the sea, distinguished by skin-color, but equal by nature, now our face searches the sky, have we been pulled from the countries that created us to remain in servitude across another ocean? The difference between them and us is unimportant: if they were half-naked, covered in our rags, lodged in our huts, if we were wearing fine hats, if young slaves washed our feet, if we threw splendid parties, if we slept softly on delicate beds servants warmed by a fire, they would be our slaves and we would be their masters.

"Oppression has weighed too long over our heads. It could be time for them to serve and us to reign. But do not weigh down the indigenous masters with the yoke of servitude: to cease such service, make no more slaves. Ignite a more noble vengeance! What need have we of ruses and speeches, of somber and black plots, familiar arms of cowardice!

"Agitate with open force. Our population is innumerable, compared to that of our terrible enemies. Our women, our children, our elderly are warriors. Under this climate that kills them, contagion will infect their battalions and leave their weapons in our hands.

"What are we waiting for to carry incendiary torches into these opulent and superb areas, so often washed with our sweat and our tears? May these workshops, eternal instruments of our slavery, become no more than ashes and ruins! That our masters, and their wives, with their children that we will reclaim one day as slaves if they manage to survive, fall together under mortal blows as victims immolated by their personal cruelty. The fire, the terrible fire cannot purify too soon or sufficiently these infected lands, to the end that that there will remain no monument to servitude, nor man, nor generation. Only then, dear comrades, will we experience liberty.

"But if several among us are filled with terror by this mélange of fire and blood, with burning buildings falling, the ruin of such wealth, and so many men's death, when they reexamine all our past calamities, they will turn their attention to the future. Destruction and carnage are inevitable passageways from servitude to liberty. To cease servitude, one must kill and destroy everything to remake it. Often crimes are virtues for those who embrace the future. It will be beautiful to see in recompense on their earth which we will cover in flames, ruins, and cadavers, new monuments, new towns, and a new people who will fly their flags upon the seas, contract alliances, receive ambassadors, make peace and war."

This speech made the most profound impression on the conspirators' spirit. Fury was on their faces . . . .

The flames that would devour so much wealth, and those edifices resembling palaces where the master reigned over a multitude of slaves, rose around midnight on August 22, first on the Noé plantation in the parish of Acul.

Jean-Philippe Garran de Coulon, selections from *An Inquiry into the Causes of the Insurrection of the Negroes in the Island of Santo Domingo*, 1792

The start of the Haitian Revolution hardened the positions of those both for and against colonial reforms. In a report to the National Assembly in February 1792, deputy Jean-Philippe Garran de Coulon attributed the August 1791 uprising primarily to the unsupportable position of the planters, who refused to make concessions in the era of the rights of man. A partisan of the Friends of the Blacks, he believed that major changes—including the abolition of the Atlantic slave trade and humanitarian reform of colonial slavery—were necessary for the colonial order's survival. The Legislative Assembly, however, avoided major measures, hoping military repression would succeed in place of social reforms. The planters' lobby made major changes to the colonial order appear politically impossible. The rebellion in Saint-Domingue worsened.

After a contest of five years between the friends of justice and the African slave-dealers, the moral, physical and political evils of that disgraceful traffic have been fully developed and ascertained by the kingdom at large. The conviction of truth has been followed by the glow of honest indignation, and the voice of the people has called their legislators to wash away the national stain. Contradicted in their bold assertions, and refuted in their arguments, this trade's abettors had almost withdrawn themselves from the struggle, in which their own weapons recoiled on them: for it may be justly remarked, that the most expeditious method of learning to abhor the slave trade is to read the pieces written in its defense.

At this juncture, when nothing remained but for the people's representatives to comply with their constituents' wishes in pronouncing the trade's abolition, another, hopefully last, attempt is made by its advocates to influence the public mind. A negro insurrection has taken place on the island of Saint-Domingue and some consider this circumstance a proof of the dangerous consequences that could arise from the proposed measure. "Beware," say the trade's partisans, "of how you interfere with the concerns of your West India Islands—let French examples deter you from proceeding a step further in so dangerous a path." But let us be allowed to ask: how far the events that have taken place in Saint-Domingue apply to the question now before the British House of Commons?[5] Were these disturbances in consequence of the trade's abolition by the French? No! . . .

Before we proceed to examine the causes of such enormities, permit us a few reflections on the awful scenes the island of Saint-Domingue has lately exhibited: the picture of these outrages forms the most striking part of the narrative in question. The destruction of flourishing plantations; the burning of houses; the slaughter of whites by secret treachery, or open revolt; the gross violations of female chastity, the destruction of all bonds of subordination, and all the attachments of society, contribute to the dreadful sketch.

Are these enormities to be lamented? They surely are. Can they excite our wonder? By no means. What is the state of the laboring negro? Is he not a being shackled by force? Laboring under constant compulsion? Driven to complete his task by the immediate discipline of the whip? Are affection, lenity and forbearance the result of oppression and abuse? When the native ferocity of Africa is sharpened by the keen sense of long continued injury, who shall set the boundaries of revenge?

Again, how have the fierce dispositions of savage life been counteracted or improved by their white superiors' example? Resistance is always justifiable where force is substituted for right . . . How often have these unfortunate beings beheld their fellows beaten, kept in famine and distraction, behind the bars of an iron cage, in which they were doomed to pass in inconceivable misery their last days of existence? Do we not know that in these wretched islands a human being must resign himself to passing his life in the torments of a slow-consuming fire? Such awfully atrocious acts remaining un-avenged marks out for perdition the country suffering them. When the oppressor thus enforces his authority, what are its effects on the sufferers' resentment?

The Society [of the Friends of the Blacks], say the [National Assembly] deputies, "seize upon the Declaration of the Rights of Man: this immortal work beneficial to enlightened man but inapplicable, and therefore dangerous, to our regulations. They diffuse it in our own colonies. The newspapers in their pay, or under their influence, publicize the declaration amidst our gangs. The Friends of the Blacks' writings openly announce that negro freedom is proclaimed by the Declaration of Rights."

What miserable effects of injustice, rapacity, and oppression! As evidence of their own freedom, Saint-Domingue's colonists read their condemnation. The assertion of the universal Rights of Man, which if true at all ought to be as general as daylight, in the wretched islands of America has emitted only a candle-like light in the Planter's residence, whilst the poor and destitute negro still sits in a dark hut. . . . If all men are born equally free, let the Colonists prove the negroes are not men, and the dispute will be settled. Is the voice of nature and truth to be forever silent, because the Colonies choose to hold in subjection some unfortunate natives of Africa?

Such, however, are the proofs, and such their authenticity, upon which the accusations against the society are founded. This defect is attempted to be remedied, by advertising to some expressions, which in the many and violent debates that have agitated the National Assembly on this subject, have marked the virtuous indignation of its members: "Perish the Colonies sooner than betray our principles," said one of the Representatives. "Perish the Colonies" became indeed "the signal of blood and conflagration," but not amongst the negroes—it was the planters who severed these words from their context, and made them the apology for their own enormities. "Be just and eat grass," said the Abbé Grégoire. "We choose instead to be unjust and live in luxury," the Colonists reply.

National Convention, selections from Debates on the Abolition of Slavery, 16 Pluviôse Year II (February 4, 1794)

The French became the first Atlantic empire to abolish slavery in February 1794—confirming human servitude violated the core principles of the Rights of Man. Yet, French legislators almost certainly would not have done this on their own: indeed, the Club Massiac had effectively neutralized French abolitionists over the Revolution's early years. Yet the ongoing civil war that became the Haitian Revolution—featuring not just French and slave factions, but Spanish and British forces trying to seize France's richest colony—led French commissioner Léger-Félicité Santhonax to free the North Province's slaves in August 1793, hoping to galvanize support for the French forces. With the conflict's outcome still uncertain, the French Convention's measure universalized the decree, also freeing slaves in non-rebel colonies, including Martinique and Guadeloupe. Winning strongman Toussaint Louverture to their side, the French reestablished order in much of Saint-Domingue. Yet, most former slaves remained forced into subordinate relationships with land-owning planters, and Napoleon re-implemented colonial slavery in non-rebel areas in 1802.

One of the three deputies newly arrived from Saint-Domingue made a summary report of the events there. He returned to the cause of the troubles it has fallen prey to, emphasizing the odious politics and intrigues of England and Spain, wanting to cost the republic this valuable colony by organizing civil war. Yet, the negroes armed for the cause of France foiled their perfidious plots with their courage and demanded, as the price of their services, their liberty, which was accorded to them.

The Orator asked the Convention to confirm this promise and allow the colonies liberty and equality's full benefits. . . . .

"Citizen legislators, you can . . . honor humanity through a great act of justice for which she beseeches you.

"Create a new world for the second time, or certainly let it be renewed by you; be its benefactors. Your names will be praised like protecting divinities. You could bring this land a different fate."

Levasseur: "I ask that the Convention, not ceding to a momentary enthusiasm but instead to the principles of justice, loyal to the Declaration of the Rights of Man, decrees from this moment that slavery is abolished over all the republic's territory. Saint-Domingue is part of these territories and we have had slaves in Saint-Domingue. I thus ask that all men be free, without distinction of color."

Lacroix: "In working on the constitution of the French people, we have not paid attention to the unfortunate men of color. Posterity will reproach us greatly for not doing so, but we need to make amends. Have we uselessly decreed that no feudal rights can remain in the French Republic? You have heard one of our colleagues say that there are still slaves in our colonies. It is time to elevate ourselves to the height of liberty and equality's principles. One ought to say we do not recognize slaves in France, but is it not true that men of color are slaves in our colony? Let us proclaim the liberty of men of color. In carrying out this act of justice, you will give a great example to the men of color kept as slaves in English and Spanish colonies. The men of color want, like us, to break their chains: we have broken our own, we have not wanted to submit to any master's yoke; let us accord them the same good deed."

Levasseur: "If it was possible to set before the Convention's eyes the heartbreaking picture of slavery's evils, I would make them shudder at the aristocracy a few whites in the colonies exercise."

Lacroix: "Mr. President, do not suffer the Convention to dishonor itself by further discussion."

The entire assembly rose in acclamation.

The President pronounced the abolition of slavery, amidst applause and cries a thousand times repeated of "Long live the republic! Long live the Convention! Long live the Mountain!"

Two deputies of color were at the tribunal; they embraced (widespread applause).

Lacroix brought them to the President, who gave them a fraternal kiss.

They were subsequently embraced by all deputies.

Saint-Domingue Constitution of 1801

While we lack many expressive documents from the slave insurgents themselves, much of the new order's possibilities and limitations can be seen in Saint-Domingue's Constitution of 1801, passed by a mixed-race representative assembly. Slavery remained abolished and (unlike elsewhere around the Atlantic basin) all positions were opened to everyone regardless of race. Yet, the constitution otherwise appears dystopian. Although most freed slaves preferred subsistence farming, the new constitution bound them to plantation work. While the constitution established a regime of checks-and-balances for the future, General Toussaint Louverture became the new world's first Governor for Life. His powers included introducing legislation, overseeing censorship, and naming his own successor. Catholicism gained a public religious monopoly, censorship of impious publications was strengthened and divorce prohibited. Though in some respects part of a wider "Atlantic Thermidor" that curtailed freedoms across France, the United States, Britain and elsewhere, Louverture's openly despotic rule grew unpopular in the colony. Amidst the French re-invasion of the colony the following year, he would be deposed, arrested, and sent to France, where he died in an Alpine prison in April 1803. Freed slaves were unwilling to submit to a new plantation regime, even if led by African descendants.

On the Territory

The entire extent of Saint-Domingue . . . and other adjacent islands, constitute one colony's territory, part of the French Empire but subject to its own laws. . . .

On its Inhabitants

Slaves cannot exist in this territory; servitude has been abolished forever. All men are born, live, and die free and French there.

All men, whatever their color, are eligible for all work.

No other distinctions exist except those of virtues and talents. No superiority exists except that granted by law to exercise a public charge. The law is the same for all, whether it punishes or protects.

On Religion

The Catholic religion, Roman and Apostolic, is the only one publicly professed. . . .

On Morals

Since marriage, by its civil and religious natures, tends to purify morals, those spouses practicing the virtues demanded by the state will always be distinguished and specially protected by the government.

Divorce will not occur in the colony.

The status and rights of children born through marriage will be defined by laws tending to spread and maintain social virtues, to encourage and solidify family ties.

On Men in Society

The Constitution guarantees individual freedom and safety. No one can be arrested except via a formally expressed order, issued by a functionary legally granted the right to arrest and detain in a publicly designated place.

Property is sacred and inviolable. Every person, either through themselves or their representatives, has the free use and administration of what is recognized as belonging to them. Whoever infringes upon this right renders themselves criminal towards society and responsible as concerns the person affected.

On Cultivation and Commerce

The colony, being essentially agricultural, cannot allow the least interruption of its labor and cultivation.

Every plantation is a factory requiring the unity of cultivators and workers; it is the tranquil asylum of constant familial activity, within which the landowner or his representative is necessarily the father.

Every farmer and worker is a family member and a shareholder in its revenues.

Any change in domicile by the cultivators brings with it the ruin of farming. . . .

On Government

The colony's administrative reins are confided to a Governor, who directly corresponds with the [French] government in all matters relating to the colony.

The Constitution names as governor Citizen Toussaint Louverture, General-in-Chief of Saint Domingue's army. Given the important services the general has rendered the colony during the revolution's most critical circumstances and following the wishes of its grateful inhabitants, control is granted him for the rest of his glorious life.

In the future, each governor will be appointed for five years, and can be renewed every five years for reason of good administration. . . .

The citizen chosen by General Toussaint Louverture to take control of the government upon his death, will swear to the Central Assembly to execute the Constitution of Saint-Domingue and remain attached to the French government. He will be immediately installed in his functions, in the presence of the army generals in active service and the departmental leaders who will all, individually and ceaselessly, swear to the new governor to obey his orders. . . .

He proposes to the Central Assembly the propositions of law as well as those changes in the Constitution that experience may render necessary.

He directs the collection, payment and use of the colony's finances and, to this effect, gives all orders. . . .

He oversees and censors, via commissioners, every word published on the island. He suppresses all those arriving from foreign countries that tend to corrupt morals or trouble the colony. He punishes the authors and vendors, according to the case's seriousness.

If the Governor is informed that there is a conspiracy in progress against the colony's tranquility, he will immediately arrest its presumed authors, executors, or accomplices. After having them submit to extra-judiciary interrogation, he will have them brought before a competent tribunal if appropriate.

Haitian Declaration of Independence, 1804

Haiti did not become an independent country until 1804, after a Napoleonic invasion tried (and failed) to re-implement white planter rule. The final Declaration of Independence, issued by General Jean-Jacques Dessalines, a former slave, describes long years fighting the French as the new nation's formative experience. To prevent further caste warfare, all French citizens were banned from the island and—in a stunning reversal of property arrangements elsewhere in the New World—all whites were soon barred from owning property. The Declaration also addresses their revolution's limits, however, pledging to respect the sovereignty of their white-controlled, slaveholding Caribbean neighbors and pledging instead to develop a new national model from within. Dessalines, however, soon took the title of Governor-General-For-Life and then Emperor Jacques I (in conscious emulation of Napoleon), overseeing a dictatorship that ended with his assassination in 1806. With white-controlled countries hostile to Haiti's very existence, the richest colony of the eighteenth century became the poorest country in the Western hemisphere over the nineteenth, twentieth, and early twenty-first centuries.

Citizens,

It is not enough to have expelled from your country the barbarians who bloodied it for two centuries. It is not enough to have broken the always-renewing factions who dance around the phantom of liberty France exposes to your eyes. There must be a great act of national authority to assure liberty's empire forever in the country whose birth we have seen. It must shock inhuman government, which has long held our spirits in the most humiliating torpor, out of all hope of subjugating us again. In the end, we must live independent or die.

Independence or death . . . May these sacred words rally us and may they be our war-cry and rallying point.

Citizens, my compatriots, I have reassembled for this solemn day those courageous soldiers who, right before taking their last breaths of liberty, let their blood flow to save it. Those generals who guided your efforts against tyranny have not yet done enough for your happiness . . . The name "Frenchman" remains a gloomy one in our lands.

Everything here conjures memories of that barbarous people's cruelties: our laws, our manners, our cities, all still carry the French imprint. What can I say? There exist Frenchmen in our island, while you believe yourself free and independent of this republic that has fought all nations, it's true, but never vanquished those wanting to be free.

And what are we? Victims of fourteen years by our credulity and indulgence. Defeated, not by French armies, but by the piteous eloquence of their agents' proclamations. When should we let ourselves breathe the same air as them? Their cruelty contrasts with our patient moderation, their color to ours, the length of the seas separating us, our avenging climate, tells us enough that they are not our brothers, that they will never become them, and that if they find asylum amongst us, they will still be the conspirators behind our troubles and divisions.

Indigenous citizens, men, women, daughters and sons, look around this island. Look at yourself, your wives, husbands, brothers, sisters. What can I say? Look for your children, those still suckling at the teat! What have they become? . . . I shudder to say it . . . the prey of these vultures. In the place of these dear victims, worried eyes only see their assassins; like a tiger disgusted by blood, their hideous presence reproaches you for your insensibility and slowness to take revenge. . . .

And you, precious men, intrepid generals, who, insensible to your personal injuries have resuscitated liberty by pouring out your blood, know so you have done nothing if you do not offer nations a terrible but just example of the vengeance a proud people ought to enact to recover their liberty, alongside a jealousy for maintaining it. Let us frighten all those still tempted to further ravish us, starting with the French. They should quiver when approaching our coastline, if not by the memory of the cruelties they have exercised, at least by the terrible resolution that we will devote ourselves to putting to death anyone born French who sacrilegiously soils with his foot the territory of liberty.

We have dared to be free, dared to be by ourselves and for ourselves, like a grown child . . . What people has fought for us? What people wants to profit from the fruits of our labor? And what more dishonoring absurdity than to win only to be slaves? Slaves! Leave to the French this epithet . . .

Led us guard ourselves that the spirit of proselytism does not destroy our work. Let our neighbors breathe in peace, that they live freely under the empire of the laws they have made, and let us not, hardened revolutionaries, make ourselves the legislators of the Antilles, winning our glory by troubling the peace of the islands neighboring us.[6] They have not, like our own, been bled of their innocents' blood. They have no vengeance to exercise against those authorities protecting them.

Happy to not have known the scourges destroying us, they can only offer us good wishes for our prosperity. Peace to our neighbors! But anathema to the name "Frenchman"! Eternal hatred to France! That is our cry. . . .

Does there exist amongst you a cold heart who does not tremble to pronounce the oath that must unite us?

We swear to the entire universe, to posterity, to ourselves, to renounce France forever and die sooner than to live under its domination. We will fight to the last drop for the independence of our country!

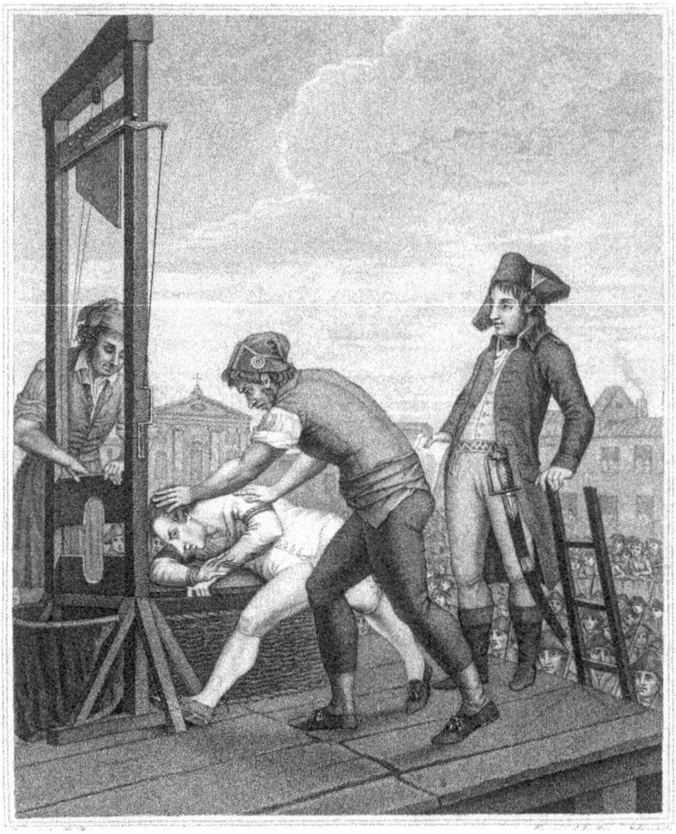

FIGURE 12.1 The Death of Robespierre. © *Christophel Fine Art / Universal Group / Getty Images.*

Seemingly in an instant, Maximillien Robespierre went from being the French Republic's hero to its scapegoat. Rather than submit to a new round of proscriptions, the National Convention rose against his leadership on 9 Thermidor Year II (July 27, 1794), leading to his capture that night and execution the next day. Despite having coldly allowed so many sentences to be carried out previously, many revolutionaries and printmakers took pleasure in seeing Robespierre's submission to the same fate. While actually less gory than the real event—Robespierre had either been shot or attempted suicide the night before, leaving him with a gory facial wound the executioner dramatically revealed to the crowd by ripping off the bandage moments before the final blade fell—the white-clad incorruptible here elicits no sympathy before his indifferent captors. Many of the Year II's great ambitions were soon repudiated or forgotten by the subsequent Thermidorian and Directory regimes. While successful in calumniating Robespierre and his accomplices, they would prove far less able to craft a principled or durable political order themselves.

12

The Thermidorian and Directory Eras

While, in many narratives of the French Revolution, the era's greatest aspirations died with Robespierre, the French Republic nevertheless continued. Some revolutionary principles—especially equality of opportunity—persisted. Yet, democratization was increasingly undermined by elite corruption and cynicism. While the Directory believed themselves to be maintaining a fragile center ground, in practice this meant suppressing political passion on both the counterrevolutionary right and neo-Jacobin left. By 1799, the Directory had become notorious for political manipulation and possessed little deep support from the French people.

The Thermidorians, after having overthrown Robespierre, sought to create a durable political basis for their regime. Quickly, surviving National Convention members distanced themselves from the atrocities they had themselves approved: "terrorist" entered the political lexicon for the first time and the recent atrocities were pinned squarely on Robespierre and his closest (also condemned) henchmen. The regime distanced itself from the populace: Jacobin clubs were closed, price controls repealed, and Parisian protests suppressed. The Constitution of 1793's expansive rights were reduced, while (in staggered voting like that used by the United States Senate today) only one-third of the National Assembly's seats were open for voting in the first election. The Convention repealed price controls on Christmas Eve 1794, re-defining economic freedom as a right of capitalistic exploitation. Principle seemed to pale before pragmatism for the jaded legislators who had survived the terror.

Authorities repelled popular attempts to contest Directory policies. Paris' *sans-culotte* movement was dismantled—with dozens of popular leaders shot or guillotined—after the failed protests of Germinal, Prairial and Vendémiaire in 1795. In spring 1797 elections, 205 of 216 deputies seeking legislative reelection were defeated, mostly by conservative (sometimes covertly royalist) candidates. In the Coup of 18 Fructidor, the elections were annulled, and 130 opposition figures would be exiled to the tropical "dry guillotine" of French Guiana. In 1798 elections, Neo-Jacobin success at the polls led the Directors to expel over two hundred left-wing legislators. Popular apathy and political exhaustion were not as total as some in the Directory would have liked. Having experienced the gamut of political regimes, the populace sensed the government's shortcomings. The Directory's "centrist" claims failed to mask their privileging of business interests over those of both the aristocracy and working people. Ending the pretense of free elections, the Directory effectively lost its popular mandate.

With the military having become the government's most successful appendage, and civilian leadership wanting, many predicted another coup. The revolutionary armies produced numerous charismatic generals who would have happily profited from such opportunity. Napoleon Bonaparte, conqueror of Northern Italy, was among the most fearsome for the corrupt legislators. The Egyptian expedition of 1798 won approval in large part to take him far from domestic intrigue. Even if he had not returned, however, the Directory likely would not have long endured. For all the incredible audacity of the early revolutionary legislatures, the Republican government—despite featuring many of the same officials from the virtue-obsessed Convention—declined into a corrupt, unimaginative, unrepresentative, and repressive regime.

Jean-Lambert Tallien, selections from "System of Terror" speech, 11 Fructidor Year II (August 28, 1794)

After his guillotining, Robespierre became villainized for the Year II's crimes and excesses—with many of the accusations coming from his former collaborators. Jean-Lambert Tallien had served on the Committee of General Security since January 1793, participated on mission in the repression of Vendée revolt in Western France, and likely assisted in engineering the uprising of May 31–June 2 against the Girondins. Having helped lead the revolt against Robespierre on 9 Thermidor, Tallien precisely a month later orated his famed "System of Terror" speech. Terror, he argued, had accelerated under radical Jacobin "terrorists" (a term he made famous), diminishing French liberty in inverse proportion. By identifying the terror with Robespierre more in death than they had in life, legislators—though implausibly claiming themselves to be the victims of a system they constructed and approved—could distance themselves from the tactics that had become common over the preceding year. Though the Thermidorian and Directory governments continued engaging in political repression and censorship, they attempted to renounce the use of terror as a political tactic.

Your committees are now organized. The government resumes its functions: all aspects of public administration, overseen in the most active manner, will set back on course the ship of state battered for so long by all factions.

But we need not, we cannot, hide the long shadow of Robespierre still extending over the republic's soil. Spirits so long divided, so violently agitated by this evil genius, this tyrant of opinion, this declared enemy of his country's liberty, are still not reconciled, as all good citizens desire . . . we must, within these walls where Capet and Robespierre's liberty-killing plots were discovered and punished, foil aristocratic evil-doers' projects. We must, by honestly showing our sentiments, prove to France and all Europe that we are worthy of representing twenty-five million men and assuring their happiness after establishing and consolidating public liberty. . . .

For a government to securely finish the revolution, it cannot itself be a motor for counter-revolution. Even a passing tyranny cannot be among those methods for establishing liberty, since, by exercising it securely and without punishment for a year, a month, a day, they need it to remain, at least during this interval, atop all opposition. . . .

The system of terror requires, as I said before, not only arbitrary and absolute power, but endless power . . .

Although the system of terror did not presuppose endless power for those exercising it, it nevertheless becomes necessary and leads one to usurp it. How, in effect, can anyone return to the crowd, after having made so many enemies? How can one not fear vengeance after committing so many crimes? How, finally, can one not profit from terror, spread by tyranny, to perpetuate tyranny, when there can be no other means of escaping eternal justice?

The system of terror supposes continually new and growing excesses: chopping twenty heads does nothing if today you do not chop thirty, if tomorrow you do not chop sixty; and, however quick the progression may be, they will need to continue from the resentments rising in people's spirit each day.

Thereby, the more life is rendered odious, the more death must be rendered terrible for it to be feared. The prospect of hemlock once sufficed to frighten the imagination; then it became necessary to frighten them with the image of death via the effusion of blood; then it became necessary to surround the victim with other victims, cutting down the ones before the others; then it became necessary to multiply the number, and make a man see the death of fifty others before his own; then to dispense the victims via cruel arts . . .[1]

The system of terror supposes the most concentrated power, the closest possible to unity, and necessarily approaches royalty. There can be unity of action or will in a council or committee, since it acts through a regular and equitable administration, since its actions are traced by law or reason; but in an agency of terror, where there are no fixed rules, where everyone can reproach another for having done or wanting to do too much or too little, unity cannot result except through everyone's blind subjugation before one person . . .

Is this anything except tyranny, and what other interest except tyranny can demand terror? Legitimate authority, the choice of the greatest number, has no need of these tactics to triumph or prevent isolated resistance. Terror can only be useful to a minority wanting to oppress the majority; whether this tyranny is exercised by a king, a triumvirate, a ten-man committee, by thirty, it doesn't matter; this is tyranny in all its abomination . . .

When terrorism has ceased for an instant to cause trembling, it can only tremble for itself. . . .

I come to a second reflection. I assert that, when terror's agents are not reduced to trembling for themselves, they render the people incapable of receiving liberty and enjoying its benefits. Terror, forcibly reducing the soul, makes people lose their spirit. In forcing one to face all perils, it forces them to see everything therein. Its force renders existence uncertain, contradicting liberty and avoiding death by accepting servitude. When terror is made in liberty's name, it does more than create indifference to liberty, it spreads hatred of it and makes this hatred not only an incurable but hereditary malady, which fathers transmit, under the names of prudence, cowardice, and servitude to their children. Terror, when it has become the spirit's habitual state, concentrates man in himself, the smallest part of himself, I mean his physical existence: it breaks all connections, smothers all affections, de-fraternizes, de-socializes, demoralizes. It reduces the soul to the purest egoism. Oh! How often, during recent times, has it broken connections, destroyed friendships, dissolved relationships! For a year, what changes has it particularly brought in the mutual rapports between the two sexes! The experience of a year has shown how the art of making men tremble is an infallible means of corrupting and debasing women! . . .

This system was Robespierre's; he set it in practice with several subordinates' help, many of whom perished with him, while many others are buried alive by public contempt. The Convention was their victim, never their accomplice. The nation and Europe charges Robespierre for these crimes . . .

The Convention must reject the idea of this royal justice, which has no power except at the cost of equality; it is no more suitable for a time of revolution than for ordinary time. This is the justice of cannibals; it cannot be that of the French people.

Eusèbe Salverte, selections from *The First Days of Prairial*, Year III (1795)

After seeing their collective influence diminished through terror during the Year II, Parisian *sans-culottes* re-mobilized amidst the food shortages of the Year III, demanding full implementation of the Constitution of 1793's expansive freedoms. Yet after the Convention repealed price controls on Christmas Eve 1794, making the price of bread an acute concern for the working classes, protesters found legislators hostile to their demands. A large, peaceful demonstration on 12 Germinal secured no concessions, while arrests of popular leaders accelerated thereafter. A major protest mobilized a month and a half later on the first day of Prairial, but failed to show the same restraint as its predecessor. A poet and former employee of the Ministry of Foreign Relations, Eusèbe Salverte offers the most detailed (albeit somewhat hostile) account of the uprising, integrating intelligence on the insurrection's mobilization with a narrative of the events at the Convention. While most of the protesters remained peaceful, the crowd's killing of deputy Jean-Bertrand Féraud discredited the movement. Over 1200 arrests and 36 executions were carried out in Paris' more rebellious sections over the following days, effectively ending the radical *sans-culotte* movement.

The month of Floréal passed in profound inaction. The disarming of the terror's agents, dictated by the law, was gently effectuated in several sections, and in others not enacted at all.[2] Could someone, in effect, hope for the sessions to possess a vigor absent from the National Convention? On 10 Floréal, the Section of Montreuil declared itself in permanence.[3] From the evening of the eleventh, in that of Bonnet of Liberty, a gathering, aided by a copious distribution of *Eau-de-Vie*, menaced public security.[4] Authorities contented themselves with arresting the principal agitators; none of them appeared in court. These light agitations were only the prelude to a terrible shock; like the thickening of clouds that crowned Vesuvius, accompanied by subterranean murmurs, presaged to the unfortunate Calabrians the deluge of fire about to assail them . . .[5]

It was easy to predict that the people's enemies would undertake new efforts. Conjunctures favored it; scarcity did not end. The privations seemed from day to day more unbearable to misled beings, persuaded by the agitators that the lack of foodstuffs came only from the senate's incompetence or malevolence.

The rapidly growing depreciation of *assignats* raised a universal malaise.[6] The suffering majority accused the minority without examination, an inevitable effect from the nature of things; and particularly targeted authorities too weak to punish these imaginary crimes. They would satisfy with blood this somber severity, natural to weak men embittered by long depression. . . .

The plans communicated announced an alarming fermentation that each day grew more widespread. Finally, on 30 Floréal, according to the general noise, one had to expect that day or the next the blooming of a terrible movement. The *décadi* passed tranquilly, the conspirators' interest was to wait for the moment when unemployment rendered the class of manual laborers more susceptible to outside impressions; when the senses, already heated by the debauchery inseparable from days of rest, were enhanced by drunkenness.

The first of Prairial, the call to arms, rung that morning in several sections, alarmed the weak, and invited the seditious to gather without delay, to win over through their speed those whose duty was to contain them. Parisians, fatigued by overly frequent riots, could no longer rise except by the pressing sound of the alarm bell. . . .

Soon, a gathering of women, real *furies*, covered Carrousel Square and National Palace's courtyard. They demanded bread with great cries; but their tired eyes, their ferocious words, expressed the most ardent thirst for human blood.

They sent a numerous attachment into the Convention's bleachers. Their outrageous and menacing vociferations troubled the Senate. The President ordered that the seditious visitor's gallery be emptied; armed men accomplished this. Calm returned for a few moments.

But knocks at the door became louder: the senate's entrance was finally forced by the rebels. Féraud, back for twenty days from the Army of the Moselle, Féraud, who in the north and the south had shown his courage, and guided the republic's standards to victory, the sound and estimable representative Féraud, whom France would soon cry for, ran before the furious, exhorted them, begged them, conjured them on his knees to respect the senate, to not lose the Republic. They did not listen. From his body lain on the ground, he wanted to block their attack; they trampled him with their feet. His colleagues picked him up, half-dead, overcome with sadness.

The seditious spread around the Convention's aisles. The guard, forming a line around the representatives, forced their retreat. . . .

Around the Convention, the gathering became ceaselessly more violent and numerous. One noticed, amongst the women, men with writing on their hats. These words were the rallying cry: "Bread and the Constitution of 1793." . . .

The rebels, more numerous this time and better-led, gained the advantage . . . encumbering the tribunals; their multitude inundated the room; armed men overwhelmed the tribunal, desks, rostrum and legislators' seats. . . .

Féraud, throwing himself before the guns aimed at the President, wanting to defend this unfortunate man, was hit himself. He fell onto the tribunal's steps. They dragged him by his hair into a hallway, where they finished massacring him. His severed head was set on the end of a pike, paraded in the hall, and stopped before the executive desks: for several instants, to the smiles and lengthy applause of a bloody multitude, they raised it before the president's eyes.

Boissy d'Anglas occupied the chair.[7] With a covered head and tranquil eye, with the most intrepid attitude of calm, Boissy saw a thousand assassins around him, while being the subject of their denunciations and fury . . . The Republic seemed annihilated, patriots saw themselves dispersed, compromised, paralyzed, the authorities without force, the government's committees hated and proscribed, the Convention dissolved, bloodied . . .

If the rebels had seized this moment, their triumph was assured; Boissy's courage would have precipitated his death. One of the traitors, Romme, for example, had resumed his functions to voice the planned propositions.[8] The factious had the force in their hands to assure compliance. Thus, before the sun's setting, all would be finished for the Convention, Paris, and France. . . .

Meanwhile, the government committees were assembled; the rebels, by an incalculable fault, had not thought of dissolving them and taking their papers. They unanimously decreed to not recognize any act by the Convention, as it would not be free; but before enacting the measures that would have ended their oppression, hoping to avoid the blood that might flow in this terrible struggle of liberty against anarchy, the committees attempted a last method of pacification. Legendre, in their name, invited the representatives to remain at their posts, and good citizens to retire, so that the Convention could deliberate. Terrible cries rose from the room and the tribunals interrupted Legendre, and despite the efforts of the President who wanted him to continue his speech, he was forced to retire. . . .

But the moment of [the insurgents'] all-powerfulness had passed. The end of the day recalled home all worrying men, and a great number of others not enlightened enough to realize how incomplete their triumph was. . . .

François-Marie Boissy d'Anglas, selections from *Preliminary Discourse on the Constitutional Project*, 5 Messidor Year III (June 23, 1795)

Though claiming to represent the French Revolution's highest principles, in practice the new Directory government presided over the retreat of French democracy. As seen in the *Preliminary Discourse* of François-Marie Boissy d'Anglas, a moderate Convention legislator who had allied with anti-Robespierrist Montagnards to accomplish the Coup of Thermidor Year II, introduced the leadership's plans to revise the radical Constitution of 1793. Considering broad liberties as promoting "anarchy," d'Anglas, speaking for the constitutional Committee of Eleven, called for the return of elitist government and the enforcement of social order. Jacobin radicalism could not be enshrined, he argued, as revolutionary chaos and destabilization would have to cease for the republic to solidify. Instead of freely empowering the full French people, d'Anglas called for propertied persons to reestablish and defend the social order. Democracy, to the constitutional committee, represented violence and irresponsible decision-making. Prosperity, they asserted, would be brought about by those with vested interests in property and commerce. The Directory government established under the revised constitution successfully deterred popular protest and muzzled the press, but limiting popular political engagement left it vulnerable to elite corruption and conspiracy.

The same is true for a great nation as for a great man: the goal of its works, the principle of all its actions, the sum of its most perilous and trying undertakings, is to obtain a state of glorious repose filled with dignity. Thus, a nation that agitates itself, that surrenders to the stormy movements of a revolution, does not aspire, amidst such effervescence, to anything except to enjoy in calm the fruit of its works and the sacrifices it has endured. Today you can realize this hope of the French people, in fixing with a bold hand the end of their overly prolonged agitations; today you can fulfill the friends of liberty's most constant expectation, and end the terrible combats its conquest has cost. Your Commission of Eleven presents to you its work on the constitution.

Representatives of a free people, unite all your spirits' faculties, engage all your souls' energy, impose silence on all other passions except those for the public good. The time has come when you are going to fulfill the most imposing duty of the most august mission. Twenty-five million people's destinies are in your hands; it depends on you to finally bring light from the shadows, order from chaos, happiness from torment, repose from agitation, justice from arbitrariness, liberty from license, public credit from the mistrust of particular interest, and all the truths of the social order from the disastrous chimeras of anarchy. . . .

Finally, the happy era has arrived where, ceasing to be liberty's gladiators, we can be its true founders. I no longer see in this assembly the villains who soiled it; this temple's arches no longer ring with their bloody vociferations, with their perfidious propositions. . . .

The French Revolution, that the ignorant in their deliriums try to call the work of a handful of seditious writers; this revolution they believed destroyed itself by sarcasm, corruption, intrigue, conspiracies, artifices and hidden maneuvers; this revolution has thrown back all its enemies, resisted its own excesses and furors. She was not the production of a few individuals, but the result of enlightenment and civilization. She is the fruit of centuries and philosophy, she is the daughter of the divine art that multiplies with so much rapidity, conserving for future generations all conceptions of genius. Her principles will be placed in all men's hearts. Error, despotism, superstition, ignorance, will be long prevented from developing; but the flame of the sciences, the arts, and reason, coming to dissipate these shadows, will be born in the light, and, gaining invincible force, will soon embrace all spirits by a triple love of justice, liberty, and equality. . . .

It is in this spirit, representatives of the people, that at your orders we have examined the Constitution of 1793, carefully seeking to conserve all that could be useful, while modifying or changing all potentially contrary to your unique goal: the health, liberty, and glory of the French People. But, it is our duty to declare to you that this constitution, composed by the ambitious, written by intriguers, dictated by tyranny, and accepted through terror, would only be the formal conservation of all the elements of disorder, the instrument prepared to serve the eagerness of greedy men, the interest of shifty men, the false pride of the ignorant, and the ambition of usurpers.

We declare to you unanimously, that constitution was nothing other than organized anarchy . . .

For a long time our ideas, in this regard, have been decided and the insurrection of Prairial changed none of our opinions. . . .

Civil equality, in effect, is all a reasonable man can hope for. Absolute equality is a chimera; for it to exist, there must be an entire equality in spirit, virtue, physical force, education, fortune in all men. . . .

We must be governed by the best: the best are the most educated and interested in maintaining the law . . . . A man without property, on the contrary, requires constant virtuous efforts to interest himself in the order that conserves nothing for him, and for him to oppose himself to the movements that give him some hope. . . .

If you give men without property unlimited political rights, and if they ever find themselves in the legislators' seats, they will excite agitations or allow them to be excited without fearing their effect; they will establish or allow to be established taxes harmful to commerce and agriculture, because they will not have felt, nor feared, nor foreseen the deplorable results; and they will finally cast us into violent convulsions we would only escape with difficulty, and of which the sorrows would long be felt over all France's surface.

A country governed by the proprietors is the social order; that of non-proprietors governing is of the state of nature. . . .

We propose thus that you decree that, to be eligible for the legislature, one must possess some sort of real estate.

Declaration of the Rights and Duties of Man and Citizen, Year III (1795)

Whereas 1789 and 1793's Declarations of Rights broadcast each era's grandest ambitions, the reduced 1795 Declaration of Rights represented a reaction against the great promises of its two (more famous) predecessors. The right of resistance to oppression, so prominent in the previous two declarations, was eliminated entirely. While still following the same format as prior declarations, the document was reconceived as a series of duties to the law and state. Liberty, rather than a force for social revolution, became reconceived as an expression of the social order—with a meritocracy of the propertied given most real power. As the Directory proved unwilling to uphold even these limited freedoms, subsequent Napoleonic constitutions neglected to include a Declaration of Rights at all.

The French People proclaim, in the presence of the Supreme Being, the following Declaration of the Rights of Man and Citizen.

1. The rights of man in society are liberty, equality, security, property.
2. Liberty consists of the ability to do that which does not bother the rights of others.
3. Equality consists of the law being the same for all, whether it protects or punishes. Equality admits no distinction of birth, no hereditary powers.
4. Security results from the efforts of all to assure each person's rights.
5. Property is the right to enjoy and dispose of your lands, your revenues, of the fruit of your work and industry.
6. The law is the general will, expressed by the majority of citizens or their representatives.
7. What is not forbidden by the law cannot be prevented. No one can be constrained to do what is not ordered.
8. No one can be called to justice, accused, arrested, or detained, except in the cases determined by law, and according to the forms prescribed.
9. Those who solicit, expedite, sign, execute, or have executed arbitrary acts are guilty and ought to be punished.
10. All rigor unnecessary to secure a suspect must be severely punished by the law.
11. No one can be judged except after being heard or legally called upon.
12. The law ought only to discern the penalties strictly necessary and proportional to the crime.
13. Every act aggravating the penalty determined by the law is a crime.
14. No law, whether criminal or civil, can be applied retroactively.
15. Every man can engage his time and services: but he cannot sell himself or be sold; his person is not an alienable property.
16. Every tax is established for the general utility: they must be split between the taxpayers, proportional to their means.
17. Sovereignty resides in the universality of citizens.
18. No individual, no partial reunion of citizens can claim sovereignty.
19. No one can, without a legal delegation, exercise any authority without fulfilling a public function.
20. Every citizen has an equal right to participate, immediately or eventually, in the law's formation and the nomination of representatives of the people and public functionaries.
21. Public functions cannot become the property of those exercising them.

22. The social guarantee cannot exist if the division of powers is not established, if their limits are not fixed, and if the responsibility of public functionaries is not assured.

Manifesto of the Directors, selections, 14 Brumaire Year IV (November 5, 1795)

Soon after taking power, the Directory issued a proclamation to the French, seeking to galvanize public opinion—but also beseeching patience as they attempted to construct a durable political system. With all five Directors former Convention legislators, they did not repudiate the preceding revolution, but sought to change its trajectory. Their *Manifesto* continued Jacobin emphasis on unity—yet sought to end retributions, reestablish public order, and revivify the economy. Calling for calm and patience, they asserted public happiness could return with social peace and prosperity. The Directory soon became tainted by corruption and political repression, however, and failed to win the enduring confidence of most French people.

The Executive Directory to the French People.

Frenchmen, the Executive Directory is now established.

We are resolved to maintain liberty or perish. Consolidating liberty is our firm desire, alongside applying the constitution in full force.

Republicans, rest assured, its fate will never be separated from your own. Inflexible justice and the strictest observation of laws will be its rule. Actively fighting royalism, revivifying patriotism, punishing all factions vigorously, extinguishing all party spirit, annihilating all desire for vengeance, making concord reign, reestablishing peace, regenerating morals, re-opening sources of reproduction, bringing back industry and commerce, strangling speculation, giving a new life to arts and sciences, reestablishing abundance and public credit, returning to public order instead of the chaos inseparable from revolutions, and finally procuring to the French Republic the happiness and glory it waits for: this is the task of your legislators and the Executive Directory; it will be the object of constant meditation, and the solicitude of one and all.

Sagacious laws, seconded by the most prompt and energetic measures of execution, will soon make us forget our long sufferings.

But the repair of so many problems and the doing of so much good cannot be a single day's work. The French people are just and loyal: they feel that, in the state's present confusion, at the moment when its government is confided to us, we need time, calm, patience, and confidence proportional to the necessary efforts. This confidence cannot be misplaced unless the people are won over to the perfidious suggestions of royalists, who renew their traumas, of delusional fanatics and public leaches always calculating our miseries.

They cannot be misled, if the people avoid attributing to the new authorities disorders accumulated over six years of revolution, which cannot repair themselves except with time . . . these agitations have had no effect except to augment their authors' discredit, while preventing production and abundance, which cannot occur except through the fruits of order and public tranquility.

Frenchmen, you will not hinder a newborn government, you will not require from it, at birth, all it will do when it acquires the vigor it is capable of: but you will second with wisdom the always-active efforts and imperturbable march of the Executive Directory towards promptly establishing public happiness, and soon you will irrevocably, with the glorious title of Republicans, assure national peace and prosperity.

Gracchus Babeuf, *Analysis of the Doctrine*, Year IV (1796)

François-Noel (Gracchus) Babeuf established a key link between French Revolutionary "equality" and that of later Communist and Anarchist movements. Trained as a domestic servant under the Old Regime, Babeuf became a revolutionary journalist, taking a new first name from the ancient Roman senator who had sponsored land reform and the transfer of wealth to the poor.[9] After Robespierre's fall, Babeuf founded the *Tribune of the People* newspaper, advocating for the radical Constitution of 1793's principles and soon criticizing Thermidorian revisions. Many have traced the origins of modern communism back to Babeuf's *Doctrine*, which extended the principle of revolutionary "equality" (either equal opportunity or subsidies to encourage "fair shares for all") into advocating equality of wealth, prophesizing a society with neither rich nor poor. This pamphlet helped Babeuf hatch an underground Conspiracy of Equals, though the movement was successfully infiltrated by government spies. Babeuf was arrested before the conspiracy could be set in motion, tried, convicted, and guillotined in May 1797.

Analysis of the Doctrine of Babeuf, Tribune of the People, Proscribed by the Directory, For Having Told the Truth.

I. Nature has given each man an equal right to enjoy all things.

II. Society's goal is to defend this equality often attacked in the state of nature by the strong and the mean, and to augment common pleasures by everyone's work.

III. Nature has imposed on everyone the obligation to work. No one can escape work without crime.

IV. Work and pleasure ought to be communal activities for everyone.

V. There is oppression when one is exhausted from work and lacks everything, while another swims in abundance without doing anything.
VI. No one can, without crime, appropriate exclusively for themselves the products of the earth or industry.
VII. In a real society there does not need to be rich or poor.
VIII. The rich who refuse to renounce the superfluous are for the indigent poor the enemies of the people.
IX. No one ought, by the accumulation of things, to deprive another of the instruction necessary for their happiness: education ought to be communal.
X. The revolution's goal is to destroy inequality and reestablish the happiness of all.
XI. The revolution has not finished, because the rich absorb all goods and control them exclusively, while the poor work as veritable slaves, languishing in misery while counting for nothing in politics.
XII. The Constitution of 1793 is the true law of the French: because the people have solemnly accepted it, because the convention does not have the right to change it. To supersede it, the Convention shot the people calling for its implementation. It happened because they chased away or guillotined the deputies who made defending it their duty, because the terror against the people and the influence of the Emigrants presides over the writing and pretended acceptance of the Constitution of 1795, which did not win a quarter of the votes 1793's obtained.[10] The Constitution of 1793 consecrated each citizen's inalienable right to consent to the laws, exercise political rights, assemble, claim what is considered useful, learn, and not die of hunger, rights the counterrevolutionary act of 1795 has openly and completely violated.
XIII. Every citizen is held responsible for reestablishing and defending, by the Constitution of 1793, the people's will and happiness.
XIV. All the powers emanating from the pretended Constitution of 1795 are illegal and counterrevolutionary.
XV. Those who helped write the Constitution of 1795 are guilty of treason against the people.

General Jean-Pierre Ramel, *Secret Anecdotes of the Revolution of 18 Fructidor*, published Year VI (1799)

In the retreat of grand principles after Thermidor, Revolutionary elites turned to naked self-interest in attempting to retain political power. The

Directory featured three major coups to eliminate political opponents. General Jean-Pierre Ramel narrates the origin of the Coup of 18 Fructidor Year V (September 4, 1797), in which the conspirators openly fabricated threats to remove newly elected conservative legislators and seize additional power for themselves. Lives and careers were cheaply dispensed with as conspirators attempted to assemble a winning coalition. Ramel came out on the losing side, being arrested and deported to French Guiana—known as the "dry guillotine" due to the high prevalence of deaths there from tropical disease—before escaping to London and returning to France under Napoleon, thereafter serving with distinction in Haiti, Italy, Spain and Portugal. Few fates were certain amidst the intrigues of the late-1790s, as the fragile Directory combatted assaults from many sides.

Several days beforehand, the most important legislators found themselves together. A member of the Commission of Inspectors proposed attacking the Directory, and arresting the three members Barras, Rewbell and Laréveillère-Lépaux.[11] The majority, composed of compromisers, opposed this. "The Constitution suffices to defend us," said one member.

"The constitution can do nothing against cannons," Villot replied, "and some will use cannons to contest your decrees. Soldiers will do nothing for you; they will follow their commanders. You do not want to decide for yourselves; you will be lost." Everyone let the matter rest there. Villot, Pichegru and Delarue, who simply demanded authorization to attack, were treated as hotheads.[12]

The next day, two members of the Commission of 500 went to Carnot's house. This director received them poorly. His friend Lacuée had persuaded him that the royalists only could profit from the agitation they wanted to unleash, and that his three colleagues' downfall could only be a pretext. Carnot thus responded to the commission's members that he would not consent in any manner to the planned arrests, that he saw royalists behind the curtain, and did not want to be hung.

Lacuée, one of the Directoral observers, had arranged things in a manner to have nothing to worry about from one party or the other. The triumvirate owed him a lot, but he had contributed much to his colleagues' troubles. . . .

It was Merlin who presented the plan and main ideas; he did not consider yet, that in his turn he would one day be "Fructidorized." Rewbell approved Merlin's project; Barras conceived some worries and left to the patriarch of Theophilanthropy the glory of deciding for him.[13] Finally, Sottin determined the question, in assuring that on the same night the counsels would attack. This Sottin was not an idiot [*sot*], he knew only fear gives courage; he was intimidating and Barras became brave. Sottin, active, enterprising, proposed to shoot Carnot and 42 legislators, including Thibaudeau and Dupont de Nemours; but Laréveillière and especially Dondeau, thereafter the Minister of Police, found this measure dangerous and doubted its practicability. They postponed deciding their fate until after the victory.

There was also the question of shooting the commander of the Guard of the Two Counsels, ex-Minister of Police Cochon, General Morgan, police agent Dossonville and three or four journalists. . . .

Sottin proposed to the triumvirate, during the night of 17–18 Fructidor, to post public notices of an address announcing the Directory was only repulsing force with force, and that it would be attacked by the troops of the two councils. "This explanation will be easy to unmask," Larévellière said, "the people would not believe it."

"They will believe it for a day," responded Sottin, "that's all that's necessary . . . what they think after tomorrow matters little to us." The ingenious minister finished the proclamation: before five in the morning it was posted across Paris and permitted to spread across the departments.

Before firing the alarm canon, the triumvirate gave the order to arrest Directors Barthélemy and Carnot.[14]

FIGURE 13.1 *Jacques-Louis David,* Napoleon Bonaparte, 1798. © *Imagno / Getty Images.*

In an era of grand ambitions and youthful, charismatic leadership, Napoleon Bonaparte took France by storm. Only 27 years old at the beginning of his Italian campaign of 1797, Napoleon seized the initiative, inflicted great losses on his Austrian and Piedmontese foes, and forced upon them a victor's peace. Jacques-Louis David, once an ardent revolutionary and the painter of the *Death of Marat*, became Napoleon's most able propagandist, in this unfinished 1798 work capturing the ambition of the thin young general with flowing locks—and later, painting the still-more iconic portrait of Napoleon on horseback crossing the Alps. Though claiming to be the product of the French Revolution when it suited him, Napoleon still more represented the Romantic era—embodying the power of singular genius, while seeking sublime victory on the battlefield to overturn the ossified powers of old Europe.

13

The Rise of Napoleon

The Napoleonic Empire was—and was not—a logical outcome of the French Revolution. A history of the revolution in some respects ought to end at Napoleon Bonaparte's seizure of power, yet is incomplete without him. Though an unintended consequence of the revolution—most early revolutionaries were paranoid of a "Julius Caesar" or "Oliver Cromwell" figure seizing power—his dictatorship grew from powerful trends the French Revolution set in motion (or sometimes, the reaction against them).

In continuities, Napoleon rose as a result of the meritocracy French Revolutionaries created. A minor noble from Corsica could never have risen far under the Old Regime—regardless of his talents, the young man named Buonaparte would have remained an obscure officer or perhaps a poet had the revolution not intervened. Without the emigration of 10,000 aristocratic officers, followed by an expansion of the armed forces, together with an intensification of warfare and push for total victory, the Napoleonic era would have been impossible. The Consul and then Emperor reigned atop a vast military-bureaucratic engine: the conquests of the revolutionary armies and then his own empire could not have been achieved without the massive conscription that started in 1793. Once installed, Napoleon's regime solidified legal equality, promotion based on merit, the revolutionary redistribution of lands, and enlightened reforms—all principles inherited from the revolutionaries—while spreading and codifying such principles across much of Europe. Napoleon happened into circumstances that enabled his success.

Yet in many other respects, the Napoleonic regime marked a profound break with the spirit of the revolution. Representative government—already badly weakened under the Directory regime—now lost all effective power. Napoleon tightened censorship, rebuilt secret police forces, and encouraged a cult of personality that distorts views of the era even for historians today. Those elements of popular input remaining—particularly voting referendums, which Napoleon innovated—were heavily managed, giving the populace little alternative but uncertainty and potential political persecution if they dared dissent from the ruling consensus. Despite having risen to power as the product of a meritocracy, Napoleon put his siblings on many European thrones and took Marie-Antoinette's niece as his second wife. Domestically, he made women and children legally subordinate to their husbands and fathers, reversing revolutionary gains in social policy. Napoleon's regimes re-directed French nationalism to serve him, celebrating his charisma and military triumphs—but in the escalating losses on the battlefield, French life was held cheap by a man attempting to dominate Europe. The principles of Napoleonic rule ultimately paled before Napoleon's selfishness, opportunism, and megalomania.

Napoleon continues to fascinate—indeed, more biographies have been written of him than any other individual. An ambitious man with a great capacity for work—especially in his younger years, able to exhaust his rivals and subordinates—he managed help shape virtually all aspects of his administration (not just the army, but public works, social policy, policing, the arts, etc.). An aspiring writer in his youth, his voluminous correspondence has dominated how historians have sought to understand him. Attempting to get past Napoleon's own distortions requires a careful reading of the sources, for silences and compensations alongside the braggadocio of Napoleon and his underlings.

Napoleon's legacies are manifold. He helped bring legal equality to Europe (whereas previously nobles had often been held to a separate legal standard). Romantic writers of the nineteenth-century considered him a great hero, a self-made genius who bent Europe to his will. More ambiguously, both the French example and reaction against French rule helped create modern nationalism in Germany, Italy, Poland, Spain, and elsewhere—with Napoleon's Confederation of the Rhine particularly enabling Germany's path to unification. European integration under the Empire also prefigured the European Union's more recent trans-national governance. Negatively, Napoleon's campaigns (both on the battlefields and in the surrounding areas they ransacked) killed millions—"living off the land" regardless of the suffering induced. In his ruthless seeking of new conquests, Napoleon's warmongering prefigures the darkest attempts at European empire-building in the mid-twentieth century. Though a pivotal era in the creation of European modernity, during the Napoleonic age most French Revolutionary principles and possibilities were ultimately held cheap by an opportunistic leader.

Napoleon Bonaparte, selections from *First Speech as Consul*, November 10, 1799

Napoleon Bonaparte came to power amidst the fourth coup of the Directory period and his likelihood of retaining power appeared little better than that of his predecessors. Only thirty years old, Bonaparte had achieved renown on the battlefields of Northern Italy—but just escaped a French military catastrophe in Egypt, where he had left his army under thin pretense in an untenable situation. Only fake news spread by his political allies made him still appear a successful military leader. Now, the day after the Coup of 18 Brumaire, he needed to awe political brokers with far more experience than himself into supporting his fledgling Consulate government. In a tactic copied by dictators around the world over the two centuries to follow, Napoleon claimed to be above all parties, while claiming his opponents were only motivated by petty interests. Napoleon thereafter rapidly marginalized elected officials, establishing an authoritarian system under his own control in which most subordinate power lay with appointed bureaucrats.

Frenchmen!

Upon returning to Paris, I found division amongst all authorities and agreement on only one truth: that the constitution was half-destroyed and could not save liberty.

All parties came to me, confided their designs in me, unveiled their secrets, and asked for my assistance: I refused to be a man of party.

The Council of Ancients has called me: I have responded to their appeal.[1] A plan of general restoration had been concerted by those men in whom the nation is accustomed to consider the defenders of liberty, equality, and property. This plan demands an examination that is calm, free, exempt from all influence and all concern. In consequence, the Council of Ancients has resolved to transfer the Legislative Body to Saint-Cloud; it has charged me with deploying the force necessary for their independence. I believe it a duty to my citizens, to the soldiers perishing in our armies, to the national glory acquired at the price of their blood, to accept the command.

The councils gather at Saint-Cloud; the republican troops guarantee security outside, but assassins establish terror within: several deputies of the Council of Five Hundred, armed with daggers and firearms, have spread death-threats.[2]

Necessary plans are discarded, the majority disorganized, the most intrepid orators disconcerted, and the inutility of every wise proposition evident. . . .

I present myself to the Council of Five Hundred, alone, without arms, head uncovered, in such manner that the Ancients received me with applause: I come to support the majority of their wills and assure them of their power.

The daggers menacing the deputies are also raised against their liberator. Twenty assassins aimed at my chest: the *grenadiers* guarding the legislature that I left outside ran in and threw themselves between the assassins and me. One of these brave *grenadiers* was struck by a dagger's thrust, cutting his coat. The rest carried me out.

At the same moment, cries of "outlaw" were heard against the laws' defender. This was the fierce cry of assassins against the force destined to suppress them.

They pressed themselves around the President, menaced him with their mouths: with arms in their hands, they ordered him to pronounce me "an outlaw." I was warned of this: I ordered him removed from their fury, and six *grenadiers* of legislature's guard took him out of there. Soon after, the *grenadiers* entered at a charging pace into the room and evacuated it.[3]

The factious, frightened, dispersed and ran away. The majority, no longer intimidated, returned freely and peaceably to their session-room, to hear the necessary propositions for public safety, deliberate, and prepare the beneficial resolution that needs to become the new and provisional law of the Republic.

Frenchmen! You doubtlessly recognize the zeal of a soldier of liberty in such conduct, that of a citizen devoted to the Republic. Conservative, protecting, liberal laws are secured by the dispersion of the factious oppressing the Councils and who, for becoming the most odious of men, have not ceased to be the most contemptible.

Concordat. Year IX, 1801

After eight tumultuous—largely unsuccessful—years of Dechristianization, Catholicism officially returned to France with the Concordat of 1801 between the French state and Catholic Church. Napoleon, though a religious freethinker himself (who considered conversion to Islam while in Egypt), now re-committed to Catholicism. Yet, the Concordat saw the Church's standing only partially restored in France: rather than the state religion it was now only the "religion of the majority of the French." The Church had to renounce all claim to lands sold by revolutionaries, bishoprics and parishes were redistricted and reduced in number, and priests had to swear an oath to the French government, who paid their salaries. Though the agreement was somewhat coerced, as the French army then occupied Rome, the Church gained back the remaining revenues of Europe's richest country, and France's faithful no longer had to worship illicitly. Non-believers and those of other faiths, meanwhile, were not forced to return to outward religious conformity or pay Catholic tithes. The Concordat remained in effect until France enacted a formal separation of church and state in 1905.

Convention between His Holiness Pius VII, and the French Government.

The Government of the Republic recognizes that the Roman and Apostolic Catholic religion is the religion of the great majority of French citizens.

His holiness equally recognizes that this same religion has received and now once more awaits the greatest benefit and greatest luster from the establishment of the Catholic faith in France, and the personal profession made to it by the Consuls of the Republic.

In consequence, after this mutual recognition, equally for the good of religion as for the maintenance of interior tranquility, they have agreed upon the following:

I. The Roman and Apostolic Catholic religion will be freely exercised in France. The faith will be public, while conforming to the police regulations the government judges necessary for public tranquility.

II. The Holy See, in concert with the government, will redistrict France's dioceses.

III. His Holiness will declare to the titleholders of French bishoprics that he expects from them, with firm confidence for the good of peace and unity, every sort of sacrifice, even of their seats.

After this exhortation, if they refuse this sacrifice commanded for the good of the church (a refusal His Holiness nevertheless does not expect), provision will be made by the new titleholders to the government of their new redistricted bishoprics, in the following manner:

IV. The First Consul of the Republic will nominate, in the three months following the publication of His Holiness' bull, the archbishops and bishops affected by redistricting. His Holiness will confer the canonical institution according to the forms established in consultation with French authorities, before making the governing changes.

V. The nominations to bishoprics thereafter vacated will also be made by the First Consul, and the investiture will be given by the Holy See, in conformity with the preceding article.

VI. The bishops, before commencing their functions, will directly swear, before the First Consul, the oath of fidelity in usage before the change in government, expressed in the following terms:

"I swear and promise to God, on the Holy Scriptures, to remain obedient and loyal to the government established by the Constitution of the French Republic. I also promise to receive no intelligence, nor assist in any council, nor enter any league, either domestically or abroad, contrary to public tranquility; and if, in my diocese or outside it, I learn that something is being plotted against the state, I will inform the government."

VII. Ecclesiastics of the second order will take the same oath to civil authorities designated by the government.

VIII. A prayer in this form will be recited at the end of mass, in all the Catholic churches of France:

"*Domine, salvam fac Rempublicam*; [God save the Republic]
Domine, salvos fac Consules. [God save the Consuls]"

IX. Bishops will redistrict their diocese's parishes, which will not take effect until the government consents.

X. The bishops will nominate parish priests.

Their choice will be limited to persons the government agrees to.

XI. Bishops will have a chapter in their cathedral and a seminary for their diocese, without the government being obligated to endow them.

XII. All the metropolitan, cathedral, parish, and other non-alienated churches necessary for the faith, will be placed at the bishops' disposition.

XIII. His Holiness, for the good of peace and the Catholic religion's happy reestablishment, declares that neither he, nor his successors, will trouble in any manner the buyers of alienated ecclesiastical lands, and that in consequence the ownership of these lands, along with the rights and revenues attached to them, are inalienable in their hands or those of their inheritors.

XIV. The government will ensure suitable treatment to the bishops and priests whose dioceses and parishes will be eliminated via redistricting.

XV. The government will equally take measures so French Catholics can, if they wish, contribute to churches and foundations.

XVI. His Holiness recognizes that the First Consul of the French Republic possesses the same rights and prerogatives that the old government enjoyed.

XVII. It is suitable between contracting parties, that, in the case where one of the current First Consul's successors is not Catholic, the rights and prerogatives mentioned in the article above, and the nominations to bishoprics, will be regulated, as relates to him, by a new convention.

Ratifications will be exchanged at Paris within four days.

Madame de Stael, *Considerations on the Principal Events of the Revolution and Empire*, published 1818

Madame de Stael remained one of Napoleon's fiercest critics. Daughter of Jacques Necker, making her reputation as a novelist and intellectual salon-holder, Stael spent much of the Napoleonic era (1803–1814) in semi-voluntary exile after she and her lover, liberal thinker Benjamin Constant, spoke out against the regime's growing dictatorial tendencies. Published posthumously the year after her 1817 death, Stael uses the second half of her *Considerations on the Principal Events* to present a damning portrait of Napoleonic dictatorship. Bonaparte's "tyranny" to her rested on brutal opportunism, undermining liberty, setting factions against one another, and using the press to disseminate favorable propaganda. Rather than representing an enlightened triumph, Bonaparte's reign to Stael seemed the epitome of Machiavellian division and cynicism.

On the Progress of Bonaparte's Absolute Power.

One must try to find tyranny's first symptoms; for, when they grow to a certain point, there is no more time to stop them. A single man enchains the will of a multitude, of whom most individually wish to be free, but whom nevertheless submit themselves because each dreads the others, and do not want to share their thoughts freely. Often a small minority is sufficient to turn those amongst the majority who ignore such things.

Despite differences of time and place, there are points of resemblance between the history of all nations fallen under the yoke. It is always after long civil troubles that tyranny establishes itself, because it offers to all exhausted and worried parties hope of shelter. Bonaparte said himself, with good reason, that he knew how to play the instrument of power marvelously. In effect, as tyranny does not hold itself to any idea, nor is it stopped by any obstacle, it advances through circumstances—athletic, supple and vigorous—at a glance making itself familiar with what, in each person, or each association of men, can serve personal designs. Their plan for dominating France had three principal bases: contenting the interests of men at the cost of their virtues, depraving public opinion by sophisms, and giving the nation the goal of war-making in place of liberty. We will see these diverse routes followed with a rare ability. The French, alas, followed only too well. Nevertheless, it is because of a disastrous genius that this route was taken. Because arbitrary governments have always profited from this nation never having fixed ideas on any subject, Bonaparte has always followed his passions without struggling against his principles. He could have honored France, and supported himself with respectable institutions, but contempt of the human race has dried out his spirit, as he believes profundity only exists in the realm of evil.

We have already seen that General Bonaparte decreed a constitution with no guarantees. What's more, he carefully left in place laws passed during the revolution, to take at his pleasure those weapons appealing to him in this detestable arsenal. Extraordinary commissions, deportations, exiles, enslavement of the press (a measure unhappily taken in the name of liberty) were quite useful to tyranny. He equally emphasized, in adopting them, reason of state, momentary necessity, his adversaries' activities, and the need to maintain calm. Such is the artillery of phrases that founded absolute power, because the threats never ceased. The more one wants to take illegal measures, the more one finds malcontents to motivate new injustices. One always postpones reestablishing the law until tomorrow; this is an inescapably vicious circle because the public spirit one waits for to attain liberty can only result from this liberty itself. . . .

The First Consul's political army was composed of defectors from two parties. The royalists sacrificed their fidelity towards the Bourbons to follow him and the patriots sacrificed their attachment to liberty. Thus, no sort of independent thinking could arise under his reign, because he pardoned egotistical calculations more freely than disinterested opinions. It was by the dark side of the human heart that he believed himself capable of seizing power. . . .

Those among the French who sought to resist the first consul's continually rising authority needed to invoke liberty to combat him successfully. But, at this word, the aristocrats and revolution's enemies cried "Jacobinism," and thus seconded tyranny, although they have subsequently wanted to blame their adversaries. . . .

He soon submitted France's many newspapers to the most rigorous censorship, because he could not command silence from a nation needing conversation, in whatever form it might take, as the Roman people needed circus games. Bonaparte from that point forward established the boasting tyranny from which he acquired such a great advantage. Periodicals repeated the same things each day, without ever being permitted to contradict themselves. The liberty of newspapers differed in several respects from that of books. The newspapers announced the news all classes of people awaited, and the rise of printing, far from being, as some say, liberty's safeguard, can be the most terrible arm of despotism, if the papers, which are the only source for three-fourths of the nation, are subordinated to authority. This is because, like paid troops are more dangerous than militias for the independence of peoples, bribed writers deprave opinion much more than it could be depraved via only oral communication, or when one forms a judgment after the facts. When the curiosity for news can only be satisfied by receiving a pile of lies, since no event can be recounted without being accompanied by a deceiving argument, since each person's reputation dangles on a calumny spread by the gazettes everywhere without giving the person the chance to refute it; since the opinions on each circumstance, on each work, on each individual, are submitted to the orders given journalists, like soldiers following their commanders; then the art of printing becomes what one calls that of the cannon, "the last argument of kings." . . .

These negative powers were insufficient for success, without the impetus of military victories. Order in administration and finances, embellishments for the towns, building canals and great highways, all this that one could extend in the affairs of the interior, was uniquely financed via the money obtained by contributions levied on foreigners. There could be no drop in continental revenues to continue procuring France such advantages. Far from founding durable institutions, the apparent grandeur of this colossus rested only on feet of clay.

Napoleonic Code, Marriage Laws, Year XI 1804 and 1810

The Napoleonic Code, first promulgated in 1804, has traditionally been celebrated as one of the regime's great accomplishments, preserving the legal equality between men many believed to be the Revolution's greatest accomplishment. Under the guise of Enlightened rationality, it carefully codified a single legal system for a country that previously possessed a dizzying array of jurisdictions and unequal penalties under the Old Regime. Still, it provides the basis of the legal system not just in France but also Italy, Belgium, the Netherlands, Spain, Portugal, Poland and much of Germany. Yet, in recent decades, the Code has been harshly criticized for solidifying marital despotism. Napoleon's legal system granted husbands full control over their wife's assets, while giving men preferential access to divorce and lesser penalties for adultery. Under the revised code of 1810, husbands could legally kill a spouse caught *en flagrante* with a lover—while women retained no legal recourse to divorce unless their husband brought a mistress to live with them. Women could be sent to reformatories after a divorce for infidelity, while abortion (traditionally tolerated in European societies) became punishable by hard labor. Whereas the French Revolution had seen unprecedented strides in women's rights, many Napoleonic regulations sought to keep them in a formally subordinate role.

229. The husband may demand a divorce on the grounds of his wife's adultery.

230. The wife may demand divorce on the grounds of her husband's adultery, when he has brought his concubine into their common residence.

231. The married parties may reciprocally demand divorce for outrageous conduct, ill-usage, or grievous injuries, exercised by one of them towards the other. . . .

267. The provisional management of children shall rest with the husband, petitioner or defendant in divorce suits, unless it be otherwise ordered by the court for the child's greater advantage, on the petition of the mother, family, or government commissioner. . . .

275. [On No-Fault Divorce] The mutual consent of married persons shall not be admitted if the husband is not twenty-five years old, or the wife under twenty-one.

276. Mutual consent shall not be received until two years from the marriage.

277. It shall no longer be admissible after twenty years of marriage, nor once the wife has attained the age of forty-five. . . .

298. In the case of divorce caused by adultery, the guilty party shall never be permitted to marry their accomplice. The wife-adulteress shall be punished in this judgment, on the public minister's request, to confinement in a house of correction for a determined period, which shall not be less than three months, nor exceed two years . . . .

1388. Married persons cannot derogate from the rights resulting from the husband's power over his wife and children, nor those belonging to the husband as family head . . . nor from the present code's prohibitory regulations.

1389. They are not allowed to make any agreement or renunciation that would change the legal order of succession for their children or descendants . . .

1390. The married parties can no longer generally stipulate that their union shall be regulated by the customs, laws, or local ordinances heretofore governing different French regions, which are repealed by the present code. . . .

1394. All matrimonial agreements shall be written and notarized before the marriage.

1395. They cannot receive any alteration after the marriage. . . .

1428. The husband manages all his wife's personal property. . . .

[revised 1810 Penal Code]

317. Whoever, by reason of swallowed substances (solid or liquid), by medicine, violence, or any other means, shall cause a pregnant woman's miscarriage, whether she consented or not, shall be punished with solitary imprisonment.

The woman who procures her own miscarriage or consented to the prescription given her shall receive the same penalty, if the miscarriage occurred.

The physicians, surgeons, and other health officers, who prescribe or administer such means, shall be condemned to hard labor, if the miscarriage took place.

324. Murder, committed by the husband upon his wife, or by the wife upon her husband, is inexcusable . . .

Nevertheless, in cases of adultery, provided for by article 336, murder committed upon the wife and her accomplice, at the moment when the husband catches them in the act, in the house where the husband and wife dwell, is permissible.

Pierre-Louis Roederer, *Speech Proposing the Creation of a Legion of Honor*, Year X (1802)

The early Napoleonic regime sought to create a new hierarchy in France, centered on merit instead of birth. This involved creating new awards, the most prestigious of which was the Legion of Honor, rewarding great services to the French nation. Whereas the Old Regime had dispensed diverse "honors," now the Consulate would revivify classical "honor" for exemplary individuals. The award could serve a teaching function, rewarding those services the state found most valuable, but making it a general honor to which all French people could strive. Not surprisingly, however, in practice the Napoleonic regime overwhelmingly awarded the Legion to military men, with 97% of those honored connected to the armed forces. Napoleon realized the pragmatic value of awards, arguing, "It is with such baubles that men are led." Today, while most awardees are civilians, the Legion of Honor remains France's greatest citation. Pierre-Louis Roederer had been a member of the first National Assembly, played an integral role in the insurrection of August 10, 1792, and helped organize Napoleon's coup of 18 Brumaire. Serving diverse diplomatic and administrative roles under the Consulate and Empire, Roederer was awarded the Legion of Honor in 1803.

Really, citizen legislators, what is the power of civil and political laws without the help of moral institutions?

The nature of laws is to contain by interest, that of institutions to guide by enlightenment, passions, and habits. The moral institutions connect men to those things aiding the social machine's movement. They bring into harmony all the passions, all opinions, all habits with all interests, happily connecting each other through wisdom. . . .

The government this year has embraced a system followed by institutions, and that proposed to you is the third submitted to your wisdom.

Public teaching will be reestablished in most favorable manner for promulgating enlightenment: here is the spirited part of reason. Religion has regained access to consciences, for teaching and the inculcation of duties. There remains waiting to be satisfied, in citizens' hearts, that national passion of honor, the other conscience of the French, that sets itself well above duty, and determines what conscience sometimes contents itself with counseling: this is the object and the goal of the Legion of Honor.

Honor has always played a distinctive part in the French character, but when there was no French nation, it was smothered by feudalism. Honors even the elements of honor, were the privilege of a few. Instead of national honor, there were courtly honors, caste honors, corps honors, and finally the honor of the plebian, that false pride which had been reduced to nothing but still worried about dishonor. In all this, without a doubt, French honor developed, but in how limiting and basely mixed a fashion!

The revolution made these nuances and varieties disappear. In opposing the honor of all to the honor of some, in directing the honor of all for the general good, instead of only attaching it to isolated interests; in immersing itself in all spirits, in raising them up, it has prepared the accomplishment of this view or of this prediction that I recall at every hour; we now have a national honor that, after being signaled, demands recognition and recompense. It wants to be recognized, proclaimed, rightly engaged in the public interest. It asks for noble connections to the fatherland, and the legislator has heard it. . . .

Four thousand brave soldiers have already been decorated with arms of honor. But more deserve honorific titles; all desire to see consecrated, by the national view, the distinction they have obtained; but the military men have not only had the glory of courage, and the glory of courage is not the only one to brighten this revolution we are bringing to term: the civil services also wait for their recompense and encouragement. The legion of honor satisfies all these rights, all these interests; it pays the national debt.

Denis Parquin, *Recitations of War*, published 1892

Captain Denis-Charles Parquin, son of a spice merchant on Paris' rue Saint-Martin, at age sixteen joined a cavalry unit in 1803. By the Battle of Wagram in July 1809, he had worked his way up to Second Lieutenant. The battle was a French success, driving the Austrians from the field and forcing them to again sue for peace, re-subduing central Europe and helping Napoleon gain the Austrian princess Marie-Louise for a bride. Yet, in Parquin's account we see little concern for grand strategy or imperial ambitions: instead, Parquin focuses on the lived experiences of those who find themselves in battle, during which the French took 30,000 casualties to the Austrian 23,000. While Parquin proudly relates French units' courage under fire, he also conveys, through the figure of Lieutenant Raux, the fear and trepidation of men risking their lives. While, regrettably, we have only limited source material written by common Napoleonic soldiers (particularly during their campaigns), Parquin's posthumously published memoirs allow us insights into the lived experience of the era's soldiers.

July 5, we bivouacked in a village three leagues from the bridge of the Wagram plain. That evening, sleeping on straw, pell-mell amongst my comrades, in an uninhabited peasant cottage, I awoke at midnight and saw Lieutenant Raux still engrossed in writing.

"What are you doing that at this hour, my dear friend?" I asked him.

"I am writing to my family, and also to a young one I love greatly, who loves me, and is my fiancée. I am writing to them that, tomorrow, in the battle that must take place, I will be killed."

"That's a nightmare you're telling," I told him, "you must believe the contrary."

After that, I went back to sleep until five a.m. I woke up as the trumpet sounded in the village. An instant afterwards, I was on my horse.

As the morning of July 6 dawned, a forest of bayonets glistened along the plain, reflecting the sun's rays in a thousand different directions. Drums could be heard from afar. Everything to us presaged a warm and beautiful day. Our brigade took its position as the avant-garde of *grenadiers* in the Oudinot division. We maneuvered under the enemy's cannonballs since eight a.m.; it was noon before our Colbert brigade, thirty-three squadrons strong, moved at a trot, in squadron column, to occupy the army's center, behind a hundred pieces of artillery commanded by General Lauriston. . . .

We held this tough but honorable position for an hour—we supported the hundred pieces of Guard artillery to prevent an enemy cavalry charge—until finally our fire forced the Austrian artillery to cease theirs. Then the brigade began marching, taking the same trail and keeping the same order it came in. Further away, cannonballs passed into our ranks and fell near the Emperor, before whom we deployed. Prior to arriving at our place on the battlefield, before the re-gathered Grenadiers, we traversed a strong river that snaked across the Wagram plain and, at two p.m., formed a battle line. Three enemy squares in six ranks, supported by the artillery of Prince Hohenzollern, occupied the plain before us. Lauriston rejoined us in great haste, mounting a horse of his father's, and without taking time to substitute a standard saddle for the gold-covered harness of his new mount.[4] . . .

Essentially at the same moment, brave General Colbert raised his brigade, composed of the Fighting 7th and 20th and the 9th cavalry, who courageously charged the enemy squares facing them on the plain. The 7th charged vigorously, the general at their head. But, at a hundred paces, a terrible fire from the square brought great disorder into the regiment's ranks. General Colbert was hit by a ball to the head, several officers were killed or injured, and fifty to sixty infantrymen became casualties.[5] The seventh made a half-tour; Colonel Castex, instead of charging the square he faced, as was his order, preferred to lead his regiment, at a trot, on the square that opened fire on the Fighting 7th.[6]

He thus commanded: "Squadron, pick up your pace to a run, and charge!"

The square could not resist this new charge: it was driven in. . . .

My horse received, in the square we forced in, a bayonet to its left shoulder; and as I retired backwards with my injured steed, I reencountered Lieutenant Raux on my way, who had prognosticated his death the night before. He was going to an ambulance, with a light thigh wound.

"Well!" I told him. "You see that you shouldn't let yourself believe in premonitions."

"It's true," he told me. "I've gotten off lightly. But I had reason to spend last night writing."

These words were no sooner pronounced, than an enemy artillery salvo hit him above the collar, violently striking his head and killing him.

Napoleon Bonaparte, selections from *Memoirs from St. Helena*, published 1821

From his British-guarded rock in the South Atlantic, St. Helena, Napoleon composed memoirs to burnish his legend. Alongside accounts of his greatest battles and military campaigns, Napoleon spent much of the text describing and promoting his government's merits. Countering popular perceptions of despotism, he described the regime as a meritocracy that allowed Frenchmen to rise as high as their talents allowed, and reap the benefits of the revolutionary destruction of privilege. Though his police restrained political liberty, Napoleon asserted he ensured the exercise of equality for the French people. While this account does not fully elucidate the real politics of the Empire, which also created a new nobility, it nevertheless plausibly reflects why Napoleon's regime met so little internal French opposition until its last days. Though few today promote Napoleonic rule as a governing ideal, his regime prefigured the military dictatorships that today control much of the world. Published soon after the exiled Emperor's death, Napoleon's *Memorial* became one of the era's greatest bestsellers and raised the memoir genre to unprecedented popularity. Few political leaders in retirement since have not written their own.

My life has been so shocking, that the admirers of my power have thought that even my childhood must have been extraordinary. They kid themselves. My first years were nothing special. I was only a stubborn and curious child. My primary education was pitiful, like everyone's in Corsica. I learned French relatively easily, via the soldiers of the garrison, with whom I spent time.

I succeeded in what I tried because I wanted it: my will was strong, and my character decided. I never hesitated—this gave me an advantage over all the world. Will depends, above all, on individual temperament. Not everyone can be his own master.

My spirit led me to detest illusions. I always discerned the truth immediately; I always sensed better than others the real state of things. The world has always been for me about the deed, not about rights. Also, I never much resembled any other person. I have been, by my nature, always isolated. . . .

My birth destined me for the service: thus, I was placed in military schools. I obtained a lieutenancy at the revolution's beginning. I never received a title with so much pleasure as this one. The height of my ambition then only was to one day have an epaulette on each shoulder: being an artillery colonel seemed to me the height of human greatness. . . .

[In 1799] The government's weakness set it two steps from death: I found anarchy there. Everyone wanted to save the homeland, and proposed plans to do so. People came to have confidence in me—I was the pivot of conspiracies, but there was not a man leading any of these projects capable of carrying them out. They all counted on me, because they needed a sword. I did not count on anyone and was able to choose the plan best suiting me. . . .

I was only, according to the constitution, the republic's first magistrate, but I had a sword for a commander's baton. There was an incompatibility between my constitutional rights and the ascendency resulting from my character and actions. The public felt it like I did; things could not thus continue, and everyone consequently made their choices. . . .

The revolution's central principle was the extinction of castes: this is to say, equality. I respected that. Legislation needed to regulate such principles. I made laws in this spirit. Excesses arose through the existence of factions. I did not allow them and they ceased. They arose with the destruction of religion, I reestablished it. Faced with the existence of *émigrés*, I allowed their return. Faced with general administrative disorder, I regulated it. Faced with the ruin of finances, I restored them. Faced with the absence of an authority capable of ruling France, I took this role, seizing the reins of state.

Few men have done as many things as I then did, in so little time. History will one day tell of what France was at my accession, and then what it became when it gave laws to Europe.

I had no need to employ arbitrary power to accomplish these immense works. Perhaps no one could have refused me their exercise, but I did not want to force them, because I always detested arbitrariness in everything. I love order and laws. I made many of them: I made them severe and precise, but just, because a law knowing no exception is always just. I made them rigorously observed, because that is the throne's duty, but I respected them. They survive me: this is my work's recompense. . . .

Such was my desire to turn the revolution into a stable establishment, I saw clearly I could not get there except after vanquishing great resistance: there was a necessary antipathy between the old and new regimes. They formed two masses of which the interests were precisely the inverse. . . .

This struggle needed to be finally decided by renewing Europe's social order. I was at the head of the great faction wanting to annihilate the system around which the world turned since the fall of the Romans. . . .

The republican form could not endure, because one cannot make a republic from old monarchies. What France wanted was grandeur. To consolidate the edifice, it was necessary to annihilate the factions, consolidate the revolution's work, and permanently fix the state's limits. Only I could promise France the fulfillment of these conditions. France wanted me to reign over her.

I could not become king. That was an exhausted title. It represented outdated ideas. My title needed to be new, like the nature of my power. I was not the Bourbons' heir. It needed to be something greater than to sit on their throne. I took the name of emperor, because it was greater and less defined.

Never was a revolution so sweet as that which reversed this republic for which so much blood was spilt. We maintained its content; only the word changed. This is why republicans did not dread the Empire.

Indeed, revolutions that do not displace established interests are always gentle.

The Revolution was finally over. It became unbreakable under a permanent dynasty. The Republic only satisfied opinions; the Empire guaranteed interests along with opinions.

These interests were those of the immense majority, because before all else the Empire's institutions guaranteed equality. Democracy existed there in practice and in right. Only liberty was restrained, being worth nothing in times of crisis. But liberty was only being used by the nation's enlightened class: equality mattered to all the world. This is why my power remained popular, even amidst the reversals that flattened France.

My authority did not lie, like in the old monarchies, on a scaffolding of castes and intermediary bodies. It was immediate, with no support except itself, because there was nothing in the empire except the nation and myself. But in this nation all were equally called to public functions. The point of departure was not an obstacle for anyone. Upward mobility was universal in the state. This movement gave me my force.

I did not invent this system: it emerged from the Bastille's ruins. It was the result of civilization and manners that time gave to Europe. One tries in vain to destroy them; they maintain themselves by the order of things . . .

The fall of prejudices had left the source of power naked. We discovered its weakness. It effectively fell with the first attack.

It was thus necessary to remake authority according to another plan. They needed to break habits and prejudices; they needed to escape from the blindness called faith. They were not inherited from any line; they need to be entirely derived from actions, which is to say from force.

I did not thus mount the throne as an inheritor of ancient dynasties, to sit there weakly under the prestige of habit and illusion, but rather to affirm the institutions the people wanted, to bring the laws in accordance with social standards and render France formidable, to thereby maintain its independence. . . .

There was really nothing in the state except a vast democracy, conducted by a dictatorship. This type of government is useful for executing orders, but it is of a temporary nature, because it is only lives in the head of the dictator. I needed to render it perpetual, in making enduring institutions and vibrant corporations, to place them between the throne and democracy. I could not make anything work by the lever of habits and illusions. I was obliged to create everything by its reality. . . .

The spirit of the empire was ascendant movement. It agitated the entire nation. She rose to elevate herself. I placed great rewards at the summit. They were only given through public recognition. These high dignities confirmed more to the spirit of equality, which the lowest soldier could obtain by actions of brilliance.

APPENDIX: MAPS

MAP 1 *France Under the Old Regime. © Encyclopaedia Britannica / Getty Images.*

The largest kingdom in western Europe, France expanded through the efforts of ambitious monarchs over the course of many centuries, integrating autonomous and independent provinces as it grew from a small area surrounding Paris (the Ile de France region) to a major power stretching from the English Channel to the Mediterranean, Rhine, and the rocky Breton coast. Each province, integrated into France through separate charters and treaties, held different rights and privileges, jealously defended by regional supreme courts known as Parlements that could rule new measures unconstitutional. While Cardinal Richelieu, Louis XIV, and their royal administrative successors claimed to be "absolute rulers" of France, in practice they led a diverse kingdom in which they had to arbitrate—sometimes unsuccessfully—vast webs of interests, prerogatives, and jealousies.

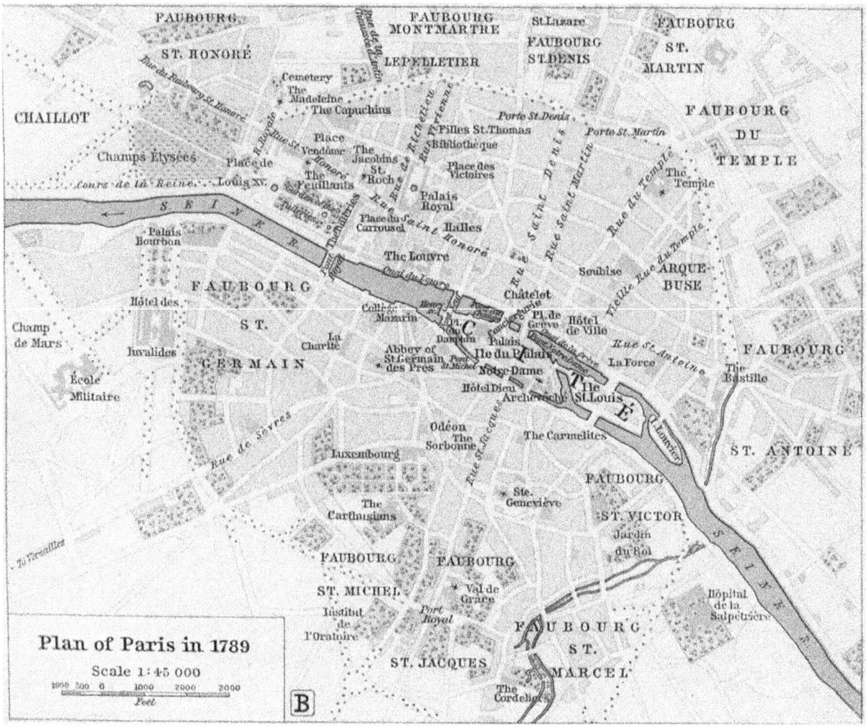

MAP 2 *Paris in 1789. © Wikimedia Commons (public domain).*

With a population of approximately 700,000 people, Paris in 1789 was the second-largest city in Western Europe. Seven times the size of any other French city, Paris had long taken an outsized role in French cultural, intellectual, and political life. Many of France's prominent aristocratic families lived in the western suburbs (*faubourgs*) of Saint-Germain and Saint-Honoré, merchants clustered along the narrow streets of the Right Bank north of the river Seine, while the working-class suburbs of Saint-Antoine and Saint-Marcel in the east teemed with artisans and laborers drawn from across France and beyond. With great size, however, came great vulnerability to both economic crises and food shortages—the massive supplies needed to provision the growing metropolis (its population having barely topped 500,000 in 1700) could not confidently be guaranteed by a stagnant agricultural system and struggling distribution network. As Paris politicized in the late 1780s, the city's insecurities goaded its residents into revolutionary action.

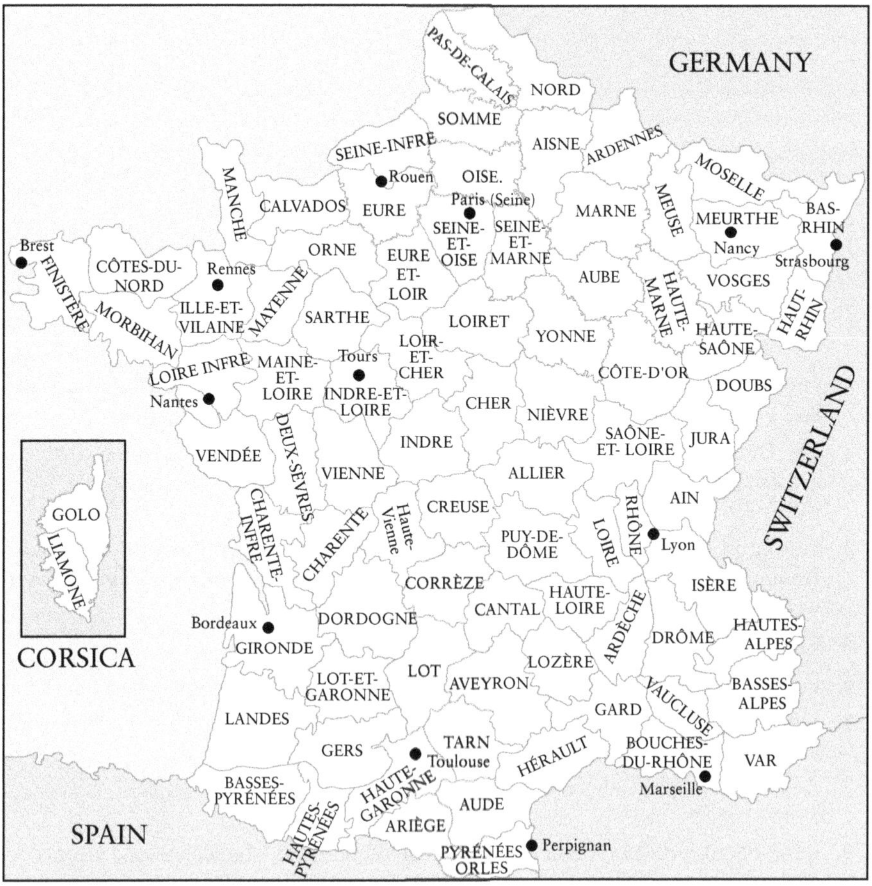

MAP 3 *France in 1790.*

In establishing a new regime, French Revolutionaries sought to eliminate the inequalities of the past—many of which had been tied to province-level tax exemptions and varying regulatory systems. As a result, National Assembly legislators redistricted France into 83 Departments, with each name taken from natural features of the region (usually rivers and mountains). Even where it would have been possible to keep former provincial boundaries, such lines were abolished on purpose to create new affiliations. With the exception of Paris (greater in population though lesser in land, which received its own Department of the Seine), administrators attempted to establish equitable populations and territories for each.

NOTES

Chapter 1

1 Giovanni Vincenzo Gravina (1664–1718), Italian professor of civil and canon law.

2 The Diamond Necklace Affair of 1784–5, an elaborate scam in which con artists convinced the Cardinal de Rohan to buy a large diamond necklace for the queen as a way to curry favor.

3 Pluto and Prosperine were the God and Goddess of the Underworld in Greco-Roman mythology. The Versailles palace gardens have numerous clearings that were periodically used for summer gatherings.

4 Roman author (ca. 125–180 CE), author of *Attic Nights*.

5 Francis Bacon (1561–1626), developer of the scientific method.

6 Lutetian Limestone lies beneath the capital and provided much of its building material.

7 A series of noble, judicial and popular uprisings against central authority, ca. 1648–1653.

8 René-Nicolas de Maupeou (1714–1792), while Lord Chancellor and Keeper of the Seals, attempted to destroy the Parlements' power to register decrees, exiling the noncompliant and instituting replacements with reduced powers between 1770–4. The old system was re-instituted following his dismissal.

9 Lord George Gordon (1751–1793) sparked the "Gordon Riots" of 1780 by stoking Anglican anger against a Catholic Relief Act, leading to several days of rioting in the capital.

10 The Antilles islands in the Caribbean Sea, including the French colonies of Saint-Domingue [modern-day Haiti], Martinique and Guadeloupe.

11 "Well-powdered."

Chapter 2

1 The Constitutional Convention of 1787.

2 Lafayette gave speeches denouncing courtiers profiting from inside information to speculate in lands under consideration for public works projects.

3 The Edict of Tolerance, granting Protestants the right to openly practice their religion in France, was signed by the King on November 7, 1787.

4 The Count of Artois (1757–1836) was sent by the King to force the Paris Parlement to register new tax edicts.

5 Several French provinces possessed their own legislative bodies featuring all three estates.

6 The Brittany region of northwestern France had also seen prolonged contestations over their traditional privileges and ability to strike down "unconstitutional" legislation.

7 The Comte de Clermont-Tonnerre (1747–1792, the letter-writer gets his title wrong) commanded French forces in the Grenoble area. A liberal noble deputy to the Estates General, he would die amidst the insurrection of August 10, 1792.

8 Nuns and property-owning widows were allowed to express their views in Estates General elections through male delegates in all three orders.

9 Tithes traditionally owed by Catholics to the church.

10 Monks are considered "regular clergy," while parish priests are considered "secular clergy" (as they administer to the secular population).

11 Dating from the middle ages, nobles had the right to extract protection payments from their peasantry, though they had long ceded military sovereignty to the central state.

12 The Gabelle was hated salt tax, which required residents in many provinces to pay (varying) inflated prices for required quantities of salt.

13 France's smallest province, in the area surrounding La Rochelle.

14 This request would never be granted.

15 Certain regions (Pays d'état) possessed regional assemblies, with deputies from all three orders, under the Old Regime.

16 The *octroi* was a local tax levied on goods, usually as they entered a walled city.

17 The Salic Law, dating to the first French king Clovis I (ca. 466–511), formally excludes women from succession to the French throne. France has still never had a female head of state.

18 Arbitrary arrest warrants issued by the king under the Old Regime, dating back to the thirteenth century.

Chapter 3

1 A town in the Champagne region of eastern France.

2 France helped suppress the Genevan Revolution, which had tried to broaden voting rights in the Swiss city-state, in 1782.

3 "Bourgeois" started as a medieval term for propertied city residents, but in the revolutions of the 1780s came to refer to propertied middle-class commoners.

The Comte de Vergennes (1717–1787), Minister of France 1781–1787, had sent the troops.

4 A parish church used for electoral meetings in the Saint-German-des-Près neighborhood of Paris.

5 On July 12, 1789, Prince Charles-Eugène de Lambesc ordered his cavalry regiment to charge a mostly unarmed and peaceful demonstration near the Champs-Elysées. The event touched off a riot, leading to rumors of lower-class Parisians attacking the middle and upper-class residents.

6 A district in the Saint-Germain neighborhood of the Left Bank.

7 The Invalides, a large military hospital and retirement home on the Eastern edge of Paris.

8 The Hôtel de Ville, a mile and a half west of the Invalides.

9 The Bastille was a fortress and prison at the medieval eastern edge of Paris, eight-tenths of a mile from the Hôtel de Ville and built in the fourteenth century.

10 Soldiers of Vintimiglia: a mercenary regiment from northern Italy.

11 Swiss Guards: an elite mercenary force charged with guarding the King and important royal possessions.

12 A religious hospital about 600 yards from the Bastille.

13 An indirect route towards central Paris along the Left Bank of the Seine.

14 Traditionally sung on occasions for thanksgiving.

15 In the Burgundy provinces of eastern France.

16 Royal and aristocratic hunting domains in the Ile-de-France and Picardy provinces.

17 In the Franche Comté province of eastern France.

18 In the Flanders province of northern France.

19 Capital of the Berry province of central France.

20 Capital of the Orléanais province of central France.

21 In the Forez province of eastern France. The red flag was then a symbol of insurrection, but over the following decades would become the international symbol for socialism and communism.

22 "*Main-morte*": the right of lords to inherit the property of their vassals.

23 Previously, peasants had to allow game to eat their ripening crops.

Chapter 4

1 The night of October 2, the Flanders Regiment held a banquet attended by the King and Queen, in which they removed the tricolor symbols from their hats and replaced them with black cockades, representing loyalty to the House of Habsburg. This incensed many patriots when news of the incident arrived in Paris.

2 The Point-du-jour is an entryway to Paris near its southwestern extremity; Sèvres is the closest place nearby to cross the Seine and continue along the road to Versailles.

3 Joseph Priestley (1733–1804), liberal political thinker, theologian and scientist.

4 Charles Stanhope (1753–1816), political reformer and former Member of Parliament; François-Alexandre, duc de la Rochefoucauld (1747–1827), a *Monarchien* noble who had recently served as President of the National Assembly.

5 Richard Price (1723–1791), moral philosopher, dissenting minister, political reformer and mentor to Mary Wollstonecraft.

Chapter 5

1 Louis-Marie Stanislas Fréron (1754–1802), editor of *L'Orateur du Peuple*, a revolutionary newspaper known for denouncing suspected counterrevolutionaries.

2 The Marquis de Lafayette (1757–1834) was then Commander of the Paris National Guard.

3 Parish church just north of Tuileries Palace on the right bank of Paris.

4 Claude Fauchet (1742–1793) was a former Saint-Roch priest and Paris Commune official, who that may became the Constitutional Bishop of Calvados and would be elected to the National Convention in 1792 (before being deposed and guillotined as a Girondin).

5 French Revolutionary orators often began speeches with an appeal to Greco-Roman antiquity to prove their point. The precise origin of Robespierre's allusion, however, appears uncertain.

6 Under the Second-Century B.C. Porcian Laws, Roman citizens could commute death sentences to voluntary exile, unless convicted of treason.

Chapter 6

1 Funds specifically for maintaining the king's retinue.

2 Cornelius Jansen (1585–1638), leader of the Jansenist movement that the Catholic Church came to consider heretical, and Luis de Molina (1535–1600), their chief theological opponent. "*Ultramontaine*" means "over the mountains": looking beyond the Alps from France to the Pope's leadership in Rome.

3 The National Assembly passed the Civil Constitution of the Clergy on July 12, 1790, requiring priests to swear their fidelity to the French State, even above to the Pope.

4 In calling the French legislature the "Estates General" instead of "National Assembly," Louis refuses to recognize its legitimacy.

5 Armand-Marc, Comte de Montmorin (1745–1792), Minister of Foreign Affairs from 1789–1791.

6 The Count of Mercy-Argenteau (1727–1794) had been Austrian ambassador to France from 1766–1790.

7 The Declaration of Pillnitz, issued near Dresden on August 27, 1791, affirmed the support of Holy Roman Emperor Leopold II and Prussian King Frederick William II, warning revolutionaries they would take military action if French Revolutionaries continued infringing on the rights of the French king.

8 Jean-Antoine d'Averhoult (1756–1792), a Dutch Patriot military officer turned Feuillant member of the National Assembly, an ally of the Marquis de Lafayette.

9 Swedish King Gustav III (1746–1792) faced an aristocratic revolt after restricting their privileges, and was assassinated on March 29, 1792. The Brabant Revolution (October 1789–December 1790) was a Belgian revolt against Austrian rule that created the United Belgian States, only to be crushed by Habsburg authorities.

10 In the "diplomatic revolution" of 1756, France and Austria had become allies.

11 Though part of France, princes of the Holy Roman Empire had long retained feudal rights in the border territory, that France's National Assembly unilaterally abolished.

12 Summary punishment here means immediate execution on the field of battle.

13 The Marquis de Bouillé (1739–1800), a French General in the Seven Years War and War of American Independence who had joined the Prussian forces.

14 On June 20, 1792, approximately 30,000 Parisians had marched across the city and through the Tuileries Palace, confronting the king and asking in vain for him to withdraw his vetoes on war-funding measures.

15 A massacre in which thousands of Protestants were slaughtered by their Catholic neighbors in 1572.

16 In late-June 1792, General Lafayette left his command without permission to appear before the National Assembly, delivering an address denouncing the Jacobin Clubs and demanding their closure. He was allowed to return to his forces without penalty. Treason charges against him were brought to a vote in the National Assembly August 8, but defeated 406–224.

17 Jérôme Pétion (1756–1794) had been removed as mayor following the June 20, 1792 protest.

Chapter 7

1 See Chapter 8.

2 The Swiss Guards had attempted to massacre Parisian *sans-culottes* three weeks earlier at the Tuileries on August 10, 1792.

3 Jaques Cazotte (1719–1792) a monarchist writer and mystic who survived the massacres only to be guillotined on September 25.

4 The last King of Rome, the tyrannical Lucius Tarquinius Superbus (reigned 535–509 BCE, died 495 BCE) was overthrown by a popular uprising in 509 BCE.

5 Proposal made by the Committee of Legislation.

6 Refers to the insurrection of August 10, which overthrew the monarchy.

7 Lucius Sergius Catilina (108–62 BCE), who attempted to overthrow the Roman Republic.

8 At the Bastille on July 14, 1789, of mutinous soldiers at Nancy on August 31, 1790, of republican protesters at the Champ de Mars on July 17, 1791, in the French defeat near Tournai in the Battle of Marquain on April 29, 1792, and with the royal treachery during the insurrection of August 10, 1792.

9 Lawyer from Toulouse (1750–1834) who sat with the moderate deputies.

10 Military officer from Toulouse (1751–ca. 1798) who sat with the radical Jacobins and served on the Committee of Public Safety between April and July 1793.

11 Nobleman from Languedoc (1752–1833), who sat with the moderates.

12 Protestant Minister from Toulouse (1750–1828), who sat with the Jacobins and became a member of the Committee of General Security.

13 Physician from Cessales in Languedoc (1757–1834), who sat with the radical Jacobins.

14 Former postmaster in Languedoc (1742–1814), who sat with the Girondin faction.

15 Former lawyer at the Toulouse Parlement (1750–1823), who sat with the Girondin faction.

16 Former royal Musketeer from Montréal, near Condom (1757–1842), who sat with the Jacobin faction and served on the Committee of General Security from October 1792–April 1793.

17 Lawyer from the Gers department (1760–1842), his political affiliations are uncertain.

18 Author, playwright, bureaucrat and lawyer from Limoges (1753–1793), he was amongst the leaders of the Girondin faction.

19 Cotton merchant from Montpellier (1756–1820), he sat with the Jacobins and served on the Committee of Public Safety from April to July 1793.

20 Former mayor of the Mediterranean town of Sète (1746–1804): alliances uncertain.

21 Former professor of ecclesiastical law in Rennes (1752–1827), arrested with the Girondins in June 1793.

22 Lawyer from Rennes (1750–1829), he sat with the radical Jacobins.

23 Doctor from Montargis (1762–1823), he sat with the moderates.

24 Lawyer from Thionville (1749–1801), he sat with the radical Jacobins.

25 Former bureaucrat, actor and monk from Montreuil (1753–1826), he allied with the radical Jacobin faction.

26 Lawyer from Arras (1758–1794), he was among the most powerful Jacobin leaders.

27 Lawyer from Aucis-sur-Aube (1759–1794), he helped lead the Jacobin faction.

28 Gabriel Guyot de Folleville (1764–1794) served as a parish priest in Dol-de Bregagne and co-founded the local branch of the Jacobin Club there. After 1791's Oath of the Clergy, however, he went underground and took to referring to himself as the "Bishop of Agra" (no such diocese existed in France).

Chapter 8

1 The Academy of Linxes was founded in seventeenth-century Rome, included Galileo amongst its members, and focused on biologically understanding and classifying the natural world.

2 Louis XVI was known to consume large quantities of alcohol.

3 Marie Antoinette possessed the Petit Trianon at Versailles as her personal refuge away from the main palace. The Comte d'Artois, her rumored lover, possessed the Château de Bagatelle in what is now Paris' Bois de Boulogne.

4 The Feuillants were a moderate breakaway faction from the Jacobins in mid-1791 endorsing reconciliation with the monarchy after the Flight to Varennes. They gained the affiliation of a third of the Legislative Assembly elected that fall. Overtaken by events, they had vanished as a faction by the election of the National Convention.

5 In an era before elevators, the humbler inhabitants of an urban building took the upper floors.

6 Local governing district, where residents could deliberate on local and sometimes national affairs.

Chapter 9

1 Lucius Sergius Catilina (108–62 BCE), Roman senator who conspired to overthrow the Roman Republic; Gaius Julius Caesar (100–44 BCE), general who began turning Rome from a republic into an empire before his assassination.

2 The National Convention did not abolish slavery in the French colonies until February 4, 1794.

3 Refers to domestic servants.

4 Several French army mutinies occurred that year, with enlisted soldiers revolting against their aristocratic officers.

5 Nicolas Boileau-Despréaux (1636–1711), French poet and critic.

6 On August 12, 1793, the Convention had broadly decreed "all suspects are to be arrested," but charged the Committee of Legislation with developing the best enforcement method.

7 Tacitus (ca. 56–120 CE) was a Roman Senator mostly remembered for his *History of the Roman Empire*; Niccolò Machiavelli (1469–1527) was a Florentine diplomat mostly remembered for *The Prince*, his manual on power politics.

8 William Pitt the Younger (1759–1806) was British Prime Minister from 1783–1801 and 1804–1806. Though a reformer in his youth, he became the implacable foe of French militaristic expansionism.

9 Lafayette had betrayed the Revolution to cross enemy lines to the Austrian army in fall 1792, only to be imprisoned.

10 The Duke of Orléans (1747–93), despite re-naming himself Philippe Egalité and casting a decisive vote for Louis XVI's death, was arrested as a member of the Bourbon royal family and executed for unproven conspiracies in October 1793; General Charles-François Dumouriez (1739–1823) defected to the enemy Austrians in March 1793, with Orléans' son, the future French King Louis-Philippe (1773–1850, r. 1830–1848).

11 Léopold Renaudin, Jacobin Club member and former Paris Commune representative.

12 François Chabot (1756–1794) had attempted to poison himself shortly before his arrest on bribery and corruption charges related to France's East India Company.

13 The "Decadi" was a ten-day week, implemented by revolutionaries to disrupt the Christian calendar and increase productivity.

14 A decree further simplifying the legal process to allow for the swift conviction of alleged conspirators.

15 Oliver Cromwell (1599–1658) undermined the English Commonwealth to become its Lord Protector.

16 The Revolutionary Calendar instituted in fall 1793 made weeks ten days long.

Chapter 10

1 In June 1789, Joseph II abolished Council and Estates of Brabant, while refusing to respect the municipal rights and privileges of Brussels, in an attempted absolutist coup.

2 General Charles Gray led the Baylor Massacre in Old Tappan, New Jersey on September 27, 1778.

3 A medieval legislature similar to the Estates General.

4 Joseph II (1741–1790, r. 1765/80–90), Holy Roman Emperor, had initiated a striking series of centralizing reforms, in what historians would subsequently describe as a form of "Enlightened Despotism."

5 Piedmont-Savoy over the border from Southeastern France, included French-speaking Savoy as well as nearby Italian-speaking lands, had its capital in Turin.

6 Non-Anglican Protestants and Catholics were denied voting and office-holding rights in eighteenth-century Ireland.

7 France was organized into state-level "departments" in 1790, replacing the ancient provinces.

Chapter 11

1 The Treaty of Aix-la-Chappelle, finalized in early 1749, ended the War of the Austrian Succession and was followed by a period of unprecedented prosperity in the Caribbean colonies.

2 Committee established by the National Assembly in 1789 to consider colonial issues and grievances.

3 The Code Noir of 1685 granted slaves rights of fair treatment, but had typically not been enforced in the colonies.

4 Robespierre, a then a legislator without executive powers, had no ability to speak for the Assembly as a whole.

5 The British House of Commons voted to abolish the Atlantic slave trade in 1791, but the House of Lords refused to approve the measure.

6 Referring to the islands of the Caribbean, all of which still possessed slavery under British, French, Spanish, Dutch and Danish sovereignty.

Chapter 12

1 Hemlock is a poison used for executions in Ancient Greece, most famously that of Socrates.

2 Paris administratively remained divided into 48 sections, each possessing significant local autonomy.

3 "In permanence" meant the ability to convoke extraordinary meetings anytime, a measure used in times of crisis.

4 A highly alcoholic fruit brandy.

5 Classical allusion to the eruption of Mount Vesuvius in 79 A.D.

6 Revolutionary paper money that had lost most of its value by 1795.

7 See following document.

8 Gibert Romme (1750–1795) was a leading Jacobin politician who had developed the Republican Calendar. One of six deputies condemned to death for aiding the protesters, he committed suicide in his prison cell.

9 Tiberius Sempronius Gracchus (ca. 169–133 BCE).

10 The Emigrants Babeuf refers to are the counterrevolutionary nobles he fears have infiltrated the government.

11 Directors Paul Barras (1755–1829), Jean-François Rewbell (1747–1807) and Louis-Marie de La Révellière-Lepeaux (1753–1824).

12 Generals Jean-Joseph Villot (1748–ca. 1814) and Jean-Charles Phichegru (1761–1804). Delarue's identity is uncertain.

13 Theophilanthropy, the "Friends of God and Man," was a deistic faith founded during to the revolution that sought to develop a naturalistic alternative to Christianity.

14 François-Marie, Maruis de Barthélemy (1747–1830), Lazare Carnot (1753–1823).

Chapter 13

1 Council of Ancients: upper legislative branch (senate) of the Directory government.

2 Council of Five Hundred: lower legislative branch of the Directory government.

3 Grenadiers were specially trained assault troops.

4 Likely Auguste-Jean de Lauriston (1790–1860), son of General Jacques-Alexandre de Lauriston (1768–1828).

5 General Pierre-David de Colbert-Chabanais (1774–1853) survived the battle despite being thrice shot in the head.

6 Colonel Bertrand-Pierre Castex (1771–1842) rose to general by 1813.

BIBLIOGRAPHY

Alpaugh, Micah. *Non-Violence and the French Revolution: Political Demonstrations in Paris, 1787–1795*. Cambridge: Cambridge University Press, 2015.

Andress, David. *Massacre at the Champ de Mars: Popular Dissent and Political Culture in the French Revolution*. Boydell: Royal Historical Society, 2000.

Andress, David, ed. *The Oxford Handbook of the French Revolution*. Oxford: Oxford University Press, 2015.

Andress, David. *The Terror: The Merciless War for Freedom in Revolutionary France*. New York: Farrar, Straus and Giroux, 2005.

Auriocchio, Laura. *The Marquis: Lafayette Reconsidered*. New York: Knopf, 2014.

Baczko, Bronislaw. *Ending the Terror: The French Revolution After Robespierre*. Cambridge: Cambridge University Press, 1994.

Baker, Keith Michael. *Inventing the French Revolution: Essays on French Political Culture in the Eighteenth Century*. Cambridge: Cambridge University Press, 1990.

Bell, David A. *The First Total War: Napoleon's Europe and the Birth of War as We Know It*. Boston: Houghton Mifflin, 2007.

Bell, David A. *Men on Horseback: Charismatic Power in the Age of Revolution*. New York: Farrar, Straus and Giroux, 2020.

Bell, David A. *Napoleon: A Very Short Introduction*. Oxford: Oxford University Press, 2018.

Benot, Yves. *La Révolution française et la fin des colonies*. Paris: Découverte, 2007.

Blackman, Robert H. *1789: The French Revolution Begins*. Cambridge: Cambridge University Press, 2019.

Blanning, T. C. W. *The French Revolutionary Wars, 1787–1802*. London: Routledge, 1986.

Blanning, T. C. W. *The Origins of the French Revolutionary Wars*. London: Routledge, 1986.

Bourke, Richard. *Empire & Revolution: The Political Life of Edmund Burke*. Princeton: Princeton University Press, 2015.

Brown, Howard G. *Ending the French Revolution: Violence, Justice and Repression from the Terror to Napoleon*. Charlottesville: University of Virginia Press, 2006.

Brown, Howard G. and Judith A. Miller, eds. *Taking Liberties: Problems of a New Order from the French Revolution to Napoleon*. Manchester: Manchester University Press, 2002.

Caiani, Ambrogio A. *Louis XVI and the French Revolution, 1789–1792*. Cambridge: Cambridge University Press, 2012.

Campbell, Peter R., Thomas E. Kaiser and Marisa Linton, eds. *Conspiracy in the French Revolution*. Manchester: Manchester University Press, 2007.

Caron, Pierre. *Les massacres de septembre*. Paris: Maison du livre français, 1935.
Chartier, Roger. *The Cultural Origins of the French Revolution*. Durham, NC: Duke University Press, 1991.
Cheney, Paul. *Cul de Sac: Patrimony, Capitalism and Slavery in French Saint-Domingue*. Chicago: University of Chicago Press, 2017.
Chickering, Roger and Stig Forster, eds. *War in an Age of Revolution, 1775–1815*. Cambridge: Cambridge University Press, 2010.
Clarke, Joseph. *Commemorating the Dead in Revolutionary France: Revolution and Remembrance, 1789–1799*. Cambridge: Cambridge University Press, 2007.
Cunningham, Noble E., Jr. *Jeffersonian Republicans: The Formation of Party Organization, 1789–1801*. Chapel Hill: University of North Carolina Press, 1957.
Darnton, Robert. *The Forbidden Best-Sellers of Pre-Revolutionary France*. London: Fontana Press, 1997.
Desan, Suzanne. *The Family on Trial in Revolutionary France*. Berkeley: University of California Press, 2004.
Desan, Suzanne, Lynn Hunt, and William Max Nelson, eds. *The French Revolution in Global Perspective*. Ithaca, NY: Cornell University Press, 2013.
Doyle, William. *Aristocracy and Its Enemies in the Age of Revolution*. Oxford: Oxford University Press, 2009.
Doyle, William. *Origins of the French Revolution*. Third Ed. Oxford: Oxford University Press, 2001.
Doyle, William, ed. *The Oxford Handbook of the Ancien Régime*. Oxford: Oxford University Press, 2012.
Doyle, William. *The Oxford History of the French Revolution*. Third Ed. Oxford: Oxford University Press, 2018.
Dubois, Laurent. *A Colony of Citizens: Revolution & Slave Emancipation in the French Caribbean, 1787–1804*. Chapel Hill: University of North Carolina Press, 2004.
Dwyer, Philip. *Citizen Emperor: Napoleon in Power*. New Haven: Yale University Press, 2013.
Dwyer, Philip. *Napoleon: The Path to Power*. New Haven: Yale University Press, 2009.
Edelstein, Dan. *On the Sprit of Rights*. Chicago: University of Chicago Press, 2019.
Edelstein, Dan. *The Terror of Natural Right: Republicanism, The Cult of Nature, and the French Revolution*. Chicago: University of Chicago Press, 2010.
Egret, Jean. *The French Pre-Revolution, 1787–1788*, Wesley D. Camp, trans. Chicago: University of Chicago Press, 1977.
Elliot, Marianne. *Wolfe Tone: Prophet of Irish Independence*. New Haven: Yale University Press, 1989.
Englund, Steven. *Napoleon: A Political Biography*. Cambridge, MA: Harvard University Press, 2005.
Fitzsimmons, Michael P. *The Night the Old Regime Ended: August 4, 1789 and the French Revolution*. University Park, PA: Penn State University Press, 2003.
Fitzsimmons, Michael P. *The Remaking of France: The National Assembly and the Constitution of 1791*. Cambridge: Cambridge University Press, 1994.
Forrest, Alan. *Conscripts and Deserters: The Army and French Society during the Revolution and Empire*. Oxford: Oxford University Press, 1989.

Friedland, Paul. *Political Actors: Representative Bodies and Theatricality in the Age of the French Revolution*. Ithaca, NY: Cornell University Press, 2003.
Furet, François. *Interpreting the French Revolution*, Elborg Forster, trans. Cambridge, MA: Harvard University Press, 1981.
Garrigus, John D. *Before Haiti: Race and Citizenship in French Saint-Domingue*. New York: Palgrave Macmillan, 2006.
Garrioch, David. "The Everyday Lives of Parisian Women and the October Days of 1789," *Social History* 24 (1999): 231–49.
Garrioch, David. *The Making of Revolutionary Paris*. Berkeley: University of California Press, 2002.
Garrioch, David. *Neighbourhood and Community in Paris, 1740–1790*. Cambridge: Cambridge University Press, 1986.
Geggus, David Patrick and Norman Fiering, eds. *The World of the Haitian Revolution*. Bloomington, IN: Indiana University Press, 2009.
Gendron, François. *The Gilded Youth of Thermidor*, James Cookson, trans. Montreal: McGill-Queen's University Press, 1993.
Godechot, Jacques. *The Taking of the Bastille: July 14, 1789*, John Hall Stewart, trans. New York: Faber & Faber, 1970.
Godineau, Dominique. *The Women of Paris and their French Revolution*, Katherine Streip, trans. Berkeley: University of California Press, 1998.
Goldstein, Jan. *The Post-Revolutionary Self: Politics and Psyche in France, 1750–1850*. Cambridge: Cambridge University Press, 2005.
Goodman, Dena. *The Republic of Letters: A Cultural History of the French Enlightenment*. Ithaca, NY: Cornell University Press, 1993.
Goodwin, Albert. *The Friends of Liberty: The English Democratic Movement in the Age of the French Revolution*. Cambridge, MA: Harvard University Press, 1979.
Gough, Hugh. *The Terror in the French Revolution*. Second Ed. London: Houndsmills, 2010.
Greer, Donald. *The Incidence of Terror During the French Revolution: A Statistical Interpretation*. Cambridge, MA: Harvard University Press, 1935.
Gruder, Vivian. *The Notables and the Nation: The Political Schooling of the French, 1787–1788*. Cambridge, MA: Harvard University Press, 2007.
Gueniffey, Patrice. *Bonaparte, 1769–1802*, Steven Rendall, trans. Cambridge, MA: Harvard University Press, 2015.
Hardman, John. *The Life of Louis XVI*. New Haven: Yale University Press, 2016.
Hardman, John. *Ouverture to Revolution: The 1787 Assembly of Notables and the Crisis of the Old Regime*. Oxford: Oxford University Press, 2010.
Heuer, Jennifer Ngaire. *The Family and the Nation: Gender and Citizenship in Revolutionary France*. Ithaca, NY: Cornell University Press, 2005.
Higonnet, Patrice. *Goodness Beyond Virtue: Jacobins during the French Revolution*. Cambridge, MA: Harvard University Press, 1998.
Hufton, Olwen. *Women and the Limits of Citizenship in the French Revolution*. Toronto: University of Toronto Press, 1999.
Hunt, Lynn. *Inventing Human Rights: A History*. New York: Norton, 2007.
Hunt, Lynn and Jack Censer. *The French Revolution and Napoleon*. London: Bloomsbury, 2017.
Israel, Jonathan. *Democratic Enlightenment: Philosophy, Revolution and Human Rights, 1750–1790*. Oxford: Oxford University Press, 2011.

Jainchill, Andrew. *Reimagining Politics After the Terror: The Origins of French Liberalism*. Ithaca, NY: Cornell University Press, 2008.

Jarvis, Katie. *Politics in the Marketplace: Work, Gender and Citizenship in Revolutionary France*. New York: Oxford University Press, 2019.

Jones, Colin. *The Great Nation: France from Louis XV to Napoleon*. New York: Columbia University Press, 2003.

Jones, Colin. "The Overthrow of Maximillien Robespierre and the 'Indifference' of the People," *American Historical Review* 119, no. 3 (2014): 689–713.

Jones, P. M. *The Peasantry in the French Revolution*. Cambridge: Cambridge University Press, 1988.

Jordan, David P. *The King's Trial: Louis XVI vs. the French Revolution*. Berkeley: University of California Press, 1979.

Kaiser, Thomas E. and Dale Van Kley, eds. *From Defecit to Deluge: The Origins of the French Revolution*. Stanford, CA: Stanford University Press, 2011.

Kennedy, Michael L. *The Jacobin Clubs in the French Revolution: The First Years*. Princeton: Princeton University Press, 1982.

Lefebvre, Georges. *The Coming of the French Revolution*, R. R. Palmer, trans. New York: Vintage Books, 1947.

Lefebvre, Georges. *The Great Fear of 1789: Rural Panic in Revolutionary France*, Joan White, trans. New York: Vintage, 1973.

Lefebvre, Georges. *The Thermidorians & the Directory: Two Phases of the French Revolution*, Robert Baldick, ed. New York: Random House, 1964.

Legacey, Erin-Marie. *Making Space for the Dead: Catacombs, Cemeteries, and the Reimagining of Paris, 1780–1830*. Ithaca, NY: Cornell University Press, 2019.

Levy, Darline Gay, Harriet Branson Applewhite, and Mary Durham Johnson. *Women in Revolutionary Paris, 1789–1795*. Urbana: University of Illinois Press, 1980.

Lilti, Antoine. *The World of the Salons: Sociability and Worldliness in Eighteenth-Century Paris*, Lydia G. Cochrane, trans. Oxford: Oxford University Press, 2015.

Linton, Marisa. *Choosing Terror: Virtue, Friendship and Authenticity in the French Revolution*. Oxford: Oxford University Press, 2013.

Lyons, Martin. *Napoleon Bonaparte and the Legacy of the French Revolution*. New York: St. Martin's Press, 1994.

Markoff, John. *The Abolition of Feudalism: Peasants, Lords and Legislators in the French Revolution*. University Park, PA: Penn State University Press, 1996.

Mason, Laura. *Singing the French Revolution: Popular Culture and Politics, 1787–1799*. Ithaca, NY: Cornell University Press, 1996.

McManners, John. *The French Revolution and the Church*. New York: Praeger, 1973.

McPhee, Peter. *Liberty or Death: The French Revolution*. New Haven: Yale University Press, 2016.

McPhee, Peter. *Robespierre: A Revolutionary Life*. New Haven: Yale University Press, 2012.

Melzer, Sara E. and Leslie W. Rabine. *Rebel Daughters: Women and the French Revolution*. Oxford: Oxford University Press, 1992.

Michelet, Jules. *History of the French Revolution*, C. Cocks, trans. London: Bohn, 1847.

Mori, Jennifer. *Britain in the Age of the French Revolution, 1785–1820.* Harlow: Longman, 2000.

Ozouf, Mona. *Festivals and the French Revolution*, Alan Sherdian, trans. Cambridge, MA: Harvard University Press, 1988.

Palmer, Jennifer L. *Intimate Bonds: Family and Slavery in the French Atlantic.* Philadelphia: University of Pennsylvania Press, 2016.

Palmer, R. R. *Age of the Democratic Revolution: A Political History of England and America, 1765–1800*, 2 vols. Princeton: Princeton University Press, 1959–64.

Palmer, R. R. *Twelve Who Ruled: The Year of Terror in the French Revolution.* Princeton: Princeton University Press, 1941.

Parker, Lindsay A. H. *Writing the Revolution: A French Woman's History in Letters.* Oxford: Oxford University Press, 2013.

Pichichero, Christy. *The Military Enlightenment: War and Culture in the French Empire from Louis XIV to Napoleon.* Ithaca, NY: Cornell University Press, 2017.

Polasky, Janet. *Revolution in Brussels, 1787–1793.* Hanover, NH: University Press of New England, 1987.

Polasky, Janet. *Revolutions Without Borders: The Call to Liberty in the Atlantic World.* New Haven: Yale University Press, 2015.

Popkin, Jeremy D. *A Concise History of the Haitian Revolution.* Maiden, MA: Wiley-Blackwell, 2012.

Popkin, Jeremy D. *A New World Begins: The History of the French Revolution.* New York: Basic Books, 2019.

Popkin, Jeremy D. *News and Politics in the Age of Revolution: Jean Luzac's "Gazette de Leyde."* Ithaca, NY: Cornell University Press, 1989.

Popkin, Jeremy D. *Revolutionary News: The Press in France, 1789–1799.* Durham, NC: Duke University Press, 1990.

Popkin, Jeremy D.. *A Short History of the French Revolution.* Sixth Ed. New York: Routledge, 2014.

Popkin, Jeremy D. *You Are All Free: The Haitian Revolution and the Abolition of Slavery.* Cambridge: Cambridge University Press, 2010.

Porter, Lindsay. *Popular Rumour in Revolutionary Paris, 1792-1794.* New York: Palgrave, 2017.

Rose, R. B. *Gracchus Babeuf: The First Revolutionary Communist.* Stanford, CA: Stanford University Press, 1978.

Rose, R. B. *The Making of the Sans-Culottes: Democratic Ideas and Institutions in Paris, 1789–92.* Manchester: Manchester University Press, 1983.

Rudé, George. *The Crowd and the French Revolution.* Oxford: Clarendon Press, 1959.

Schama, Simon. *Citizens: A Chronicle of the French Revolution.* New York: Vintage, 1989.

Schechter, Ronald. *A Genealogy of Terror in Eighteenth-Century France.* Chicago: University of Chicago Press, 2018.

Sewell, William H., Jr. *A Rhetoric of Bourgeois Revolution: The Abbé Sieyès and What is the Third Estate?* Durham, NC: Duke University Press, 1994.

Shapiro, Barry. *Traumatic Politics: The Deputies and the King in the Early French Revolution.* University Park, PA: Penn State University Press, 2009.

Shapiro, Gilbert and John Markoff. *Revolutionary Demands: A Content Analysis of the Cahiers de Doléances of 1789*. Stanford, CA: Stanford University Press, 1998.
Shusterman, Noah. *The French Revolution: Faith, Desire and Politics*. New York: Routledge, 2014.
Smyth, Jonathan. *Robespierre and the Festival of the Supreme Being: The Search for a Republican Morality*. Manchester: Manchester University Press, 2016.
Soboul, Albert. *The Parisian Sans-Culottes and the French Revolution, 1793–4*, Gwynne Lewis, trans. Oxford: Oxford University Press, 1964.
Sonenscher, Michael. *Before the Deluge: Public Debt, Inequality, and the Intellectual Origins of the French Revolution*. Princeton: Princeton University Press, 2009.
Sonenscher, Michael. *Sans-Culottes: An Eighteenth-Century Emblem in the French Revolution*. Princeton: Princeton University Press, 2008.
Spang, Rebecca. *Stuff and Money in the Time of the French Revolution*. Cambridge, MA: Harvard University Press, 2015.
Steinberg, Ronen. *The Afterlives of the Terror: Facing the Legacies of Mass Violence in Postrevolutionary France*. Ithaca, NY: Cornell University Press, 2019.
Sutherland, D. M. G. *The French Revolution and Empire: The Quest for a New Civic Order*. Malden, MA: Blackwell Press, 2003.
Sutherland, D. M. G. *Murder in Aubagne: Lynching, Law and Justice during the French Revolution*. Cambridge: Cambridge University Press, 2009.
Tackett, Timothy. *Becoming a Revolutionary: The Deputies of the First French National Assembly and the Emergence of a Revolutionary Culture (1789–1790)*. Princeton: Princeton University Press, 1996.
Tackett, Timothy. *The Coming of the Terror in the French Revolution*. Cambridge, MA: Harvard University Press, 2015.
Tackett, Timothy. *Religion, Revolution and Regional Culture in Eighteenth-Century France: The Ecclesiastical Oath of 1791*. Princeton: Princeton University Press, 1986.
Tackett, Timothy. *When the King took Flight*. Cambridge, MA: Harvard University Press, 2003.
Tilly, Charles. *The Vendée: A Sociological Analysis of the Counterrevolution of 1793*. Cambridge, MA: Harvard University Press, 1964.
Wahnich, Sophie. *In Defence of the Terror: Liberty or Death in the French Revolution*. London: Verso, 2012.
Walton, Charles. *Policing Public Opinion in the French Revolution: The Culture of Calumny and the Problem of Free Speech*. Oxford: Oxford University Press, 2009.
Woell, Edward James. *Small-Town Martyrs and Murderers: Religious Revolution and Counterrevolution in Western France, 1774–1914*. Milwaukee: Marquette University Press, 2006.
Woloch, Isser. *Napoleon and His Collaborators: The Making of a Dictatorship*. New York: Norton, 2002.
Woolf, Stuart. *Napoleon's Integration of Europe*. London: Routledge, 1991.

INDEX

Lightning Source UK Ltd.
Milton Keynes UK
UKHW021241170321
380427UK00003B/137

9 781350 065307